WOMEN, PHILOSOPHY AND LITERATURE

Jane Duran's stimulating book uniquely brings together five women authors simultaneously through the lenses of philosophy, feminism and literature. Her book problematizes the ancient struggle between philosophy and literature through a contemporary, feminist philosophical reading of these authors. Duran's book thus reads against the grain of both contemporary literary theory and philosophical accounts of literature. In addition to these provocations, Duran brings together two women of color, Toni Cade Bambara and Elena Piniatowski, along with feminist standbys Woolf and Beauvoir, and the less often philosophically read author, Margaret Drabble. In doing so, she provides a productive interrogation of standard feminist readings of literary philosophers. The result will be of interest to philosophers, feminists, and literary theorists.

Ann E. Cudd, Director of Women's Studies,
Professor of Philosophy, University of Kansas, USA.

*For the members of the Society for the Study of
Women Philosophers*

Women, Philosophy and Literature

JANE DURAN
University of California – Santa Barbara, USA

LONDON AND NEW YORK

First published 2007 by Ashgate Publishing

2 Park Square, Milton Park, Abingdon, Oxon OX14 4RN
711 Third Avenue, New York, NY 10017, USA

Routledge is an imprint of the Taylor & Francis Group, an informa business

First issued in paperback 2017

Copyright © Jane Duran 2007

Jane Duran has asserted her moral right under the Copyright, Designs and Patents Act, 1988, to be identified as the author of this work.

All rights reserved. No part of this book may be reprinted or reproduced or utilised in any form or by any electronic, mechanical, or other means, now known or hereafter invented, including photocopying and recording, or in any information storage or retrieval system, without permission in writing from the publishers.

Notice:
Product or corporate names may be trademarks or registered trademarks, and are used only for identification and explanation without intent to infringe.

British Library Cataloguing in Publication Data
Duran, Jane
　Women, philosophy and literature
　1. Women authors - 20th century 2. English fiction - Women
　authors - History and criticism 3. English fiction - 20th
　century - History and criticism 4. Philosophy in literature
　5. Feminism in literature
　I. Title
　809.3'9384'082

Library of Congress Cataloging-in-Publication Data
Duran, Jane.
　Women, philosophy, and literature / Jane Duran.
　　p. cm.
　ISBN 978-0-7546-5785-9 (hardcover) 1. Literature--Women authors--History and criticism. 2. Women and literature--History--20th century. 3. Women and literature--History--19th century. 4. Literature, Modern--20th century--History and criticism. 5. Literature, Modern--19th century--History and criticism. 6. Philosophy in literature.
　I. Title.

PN471.D87 2007
809.3'9384082--dc22

2006034416

ISBN 978-0-7546-5785-9 (hbk)
ISBN 978-1-138-27251-4 (pbk)

Contents

Preface vii
Acknowledgements xi

Part 1   The View 1

    Chapter One   Introduction 3

Part II   The Europeans 21

    Chapter Two   Margaret Drabble and Philosophy 23
    Chapter Three   The Feminist Drabble 41
    Chapter Four   Woolf, Metaphysics and Life 59
    Chapter Five   The Body *à la* Woolf 77
    Chapter Six   Beauvoir's Philosophy and Literature 95
    Chapter Seven   *Écriture* and the Other 113

Part III   The New World 131

    Chapter Eight   Toni Cade Bambara and the Black Vision 133
    Chapter Nine   Afrocentric Womanism 151
    Chapter Ten   *El Mundo de Poniatowska* 169
    Chapter Eleven   *Las Mujeres de Mexico* 187

Part IV   Closings 205

    Chapter Twelve   Wrapping it Up 207

Index *219*

Preface

Work on novelists, literary genres and the like might be thought to be the province of a department of literature, or of an academic program dealing in those issues; work in feminist theory has been done by philosophers and a number of thinkers from a number of disciplines, but there is little work available at the moment that addresses the intersection of such issues. This work aims to fill this particular gap—if an argument can be made that the work of women writers merits discussion in the vein of feminist thinking, and if another sort of claim can be made that some literature is philosophical (and this claim has, indeed, been successfully made), then it ought to be an intriguing exercise to try to discern the philosophical and feminist elements in women's writing.

Another set of questions asks us what literature is worth pursuing, who the authors in question might be, and what tacks toward the literature might be taken. In this work, I have taken for granted the now somewhat disputed notion that a good deal of the literature of European origin—or written originally in European languages, including, of course, English as such a language—might be worthy of investigation, and hence, using the novel as an exemplary genre, my first three women writers are from Great Britain or the Continent. The work of Margaret Drabble has always received attention, and although it might be argued that she is not currently as well known as her sister A.S. Byatt, Drabble's carefully-constructed novels not only repay close reading, but lead the reader on a number of conceptual pursuits. That the work of Virginia Woolf might be worthy of investigation in a philosophical context seems indisputable—works such as *To the Lighthouse* and *The Waves* seem drenched in unusual notions of time and the construction of the real. There is, of course, no dearth of commentary on the work of Virginia Woolf. Finally, to round out a somewhat traditionally-oriented triad, the work of Simone de Beauvoir cannot be ignored, clearly, if the project is a philosophical investigation of the work of women novelists.

But what of work of women of color? Although the Black American novelist Toni Cade Bambara wrote in English, her work is filled with allusions to the West African cultures, and a novel such as *The Salt Eaters* cannot genuinely be understood without knowing something about the African continent. Elena Poniatowska's work is in Spanish, and not all of it is currently available in translation. Nevertheless, she continues to draw attention for her stellar writing about the Mexican Revolution, the difficulties of the *mestizaje*, and so forth. Perhaps more important, writing that is partially of non-European origin or inspiration helps us to ask important questions about matters postcolonial, and about canon formation. Not so very long ago, it would have been difficult if not impossible to write a work with the investigatory aims of this project inclusive of women of color. The questions raised by Bambara and Poniatowska are not only urgent—they are philosophical.

This work is constructed in such a way that the enterprising reader can probably skip to her or his favorite author without too much difficulty. The opening chapter, recapitulating lines of argument made by the many now working in the area of philosophy and literature, asks both conceptual and historical questions about this area, and about the time-honored dispute between the poets and the philosophers. But many with extensive training in either literature or philosophy will already be familiar with these sorts of problems, and the chapters on the individual authors are placed in such a way that the opening material can be omitted. For each author, two separate chapters raise the questions that a philosophical and philosophical/feminist project demands. The first chapter for the given author addresses the writing in question from the standpoint of traditional categorizing in philosophy; one might, for example, expect metaphysical or ontological concerns (however metaphorically expressed) to be prominent, and so each section of the first chapter in the relevant pair covers an area of either philosophical thought, literary criticism, or some combination of the two. Both Continental and more standardly analytical lines are employed and, where possible, criticism that might already have a similar flavor (if such criticism exists) is alluded to. The second chapter of the two on a given writer is the chapter specifically concerned with feminist theory; here the idea is to explore the feminist themes—the presence of which, of course, varies from author to author—with an eye to such contemporary issues as *écriture* and possible intersections with feminist epistemology.

The volume closes with a concluding chapter designed not only to summarize the issues but to reinvestigate such questions as putative essentialism with respect to the status of work done by women, and so forth. If literature can indeed be philosophical (and a spate of recent journal articles in several publications seems to attest to the fact that it can be so thought of, even in current philosophical conceptual schemes), then one might well wonder why it is that the area seems to be so problematized, and why so little work has been done in this particular intersection, that of feminism, philosophy and literature. Perhaps one answer to this question is that trying to come up with categories that allow us to do work on this topic is more difficult than might at first be thought—there is a great deal that hinders feminism as a philosophical category, according to some, let alone feminism, or philosophy, as expressed in a novel with a female author. In any case, a great deal of analysis is needed, and at least some of that analysis has been done here.

One of the foci of the current wave of feminist theory has been global, and still another focus is probably best characterized as historical. A work in global feminist epistemologies, for example, might want to help us fill in the blanks on why it is that the temptation to employ first-world categorization schemes is so great when dealing with other cultures, even though we, as investigators, may strongly suspect that such conceptualization patterns are off the mark. Another work—one written primarily from a historical point of view—may encounter similar difficulties with conceptual schemes, even if it addresses almost entirely work done in European cultures. The present work, dealing with material that is not overtly intended to be philosophical, runs up against not only the problems of the first and second sorts of works (particularly since Woolf's writing, for example, is no longer contemporary), but a whole new host of problems. It proves virtually impossible to avoid a certain tendentiousness in analysis—the point, after all, is to try to pull philosophical themes out of the various novels and the other literary works. But all of these projects would seem to be worthy ones. If we can find recent publications addressing the philosophical significance of work by Melville or Walt Whitman, it would seem to be a valuable effort to examine writing by Drabble—or Poniatowska—not only for the same sorts of issues, but for that very difficult issue, the existence of a feminist pattern or aim in the work itself.

The resurgence of feminist theory demands that we use every possible method of investigation in our desire to come to grips with women's thought and feminist concerns. Since it is clear that philosophy and literature as a whole, although burgeoning, still remains an underinvestigated area, this somewhat rarely-addressed intersection asks for more analysis. There have always been women writers in the various literary traditions, just as there have always been women philosophers. Anne Conway and Mary Astell speak to us in one way; the new work done by feminists in Tamil Nadu or Nepal in another. An exciting approach for feminist theory would seem to be to scrutinize the work of well-known women writers, at least some of which has already been the topic of extended criticism. We serve feminism—and philosophy—poorly if we fail to make as many investigations as we might, especially given the richness of the material. The present work has as its goal the opening of new territory, and the establishment of new lines of argument about the work of women writers, and women's thought in general.

Acknowledgements

A number of feminist projects in philosophy have seen the light of day in recent years, but any project that tries to find the intersection between philosophy and literature will always be a difficult one. This particular work draws together strands from my last two books, one on global feminist epistemologies and one on women philosophers seen through a historical lens. As usual, I thank a number of groups and meetings of seminars at the University of California at Santa Barbara for inspiration; for this particular effort, meetings of the Political Theory Reading Group have been especially helpful, and so have some seminars and get-togethers sponsored by the Gevirtz Graduate School of Education.

My teaching at Santa Barbara has also been extremely fruitful, and once again I have to cite more than one department. Especially pertinent were meetings of classes for Black Studies, particularly Black Women Writers and Black Philosophy and Social Thought. The former, taught with a number of different syllabi, yielded exciting outcomes on more than one occasion. Bambara was always an unusual challenge, but also always more than worth the effort. In addition, classes for Women's Studies and the Gevirtz Graduate School of Education helped this work enormously; the seminar on Philosophies of Education for the latter proved more than useful, as I found that, in teaching Simone Weil, I had to once gain address more than one Simone.

More so than any other particular endeavor, writing for *Philosophy and Literature*, where I published an article on Virginia Woolf and the philosophical view of time in *To the Lighthouse* in 2004, proved to be the catalyst for much of this work. Thanks once again to Denis Dutton and Garry Hagberg for their comments, and also for valuable opportunities to review for this exciting and innovative journal. The material on Simone de Beauvoir is not only related to my examination of her in my more historically-oriented work, but is also an offshoot of work originally done for the Society for the Study of Women Philosophers, some of it dating back more than a decade. A paper on Simone and Stendhal was read to that group during one of their first meetings with the Eastern Division of the American Philosophical Association. In addition, various meetings of the American Society for Aesthetics have been of great assistance, both the national meetings in autumn and regional meetings in Monterey, California in the spring. Papers on decadence and related topics were read to both the national and regional gatherings.

For conversation, insight and assistance of all kinds, I thank Kourtney Bristow, Debra Jones, Cecile Tougas, Sara Ebenreck, Teri Dykeman, Elliott Butler-Evans, Sylvia Curtis, Kim Goto, Pam Yeagley, Lorena Bunuelos, Lorraine Gaines, Roberto Strongman, Cedric Robinson, Earl Stewart and Paul Coulam. Audience members were particularly helpful when papers were read aloud, and my work on aesthetics, the body and themes taken from the *Symposium* received helpful comments at the meeting of the American Society for Aesthetics held in Monterey in April 1997. In addition, I thank the editors of the *Newsletter on Philosophy and Feminism of the APA*, and Fergus Kerr of *New Blackfriars*, where work on Mechthild of Magdeburg was published in 2005. Finally, for assistance above and beyond the call of duty, I thank Donna Ryczek, who helped me pull the manuscript together. Viewing literature through a philosophical lens remains a valuable and exciting effort.

PART 1
The View

Chapter One

Introduction

The strength of the old contest between philosophy and literature is such that it recurs in a variety of guises, even in contemporary work. New work being done on rhetoric and philosophy or philosophy of literature; lines of Continental theory; the current mania for deconstruction—all of these areas signal to us that the demarcations between "philosophy" and "literature," never strong in the first place, are now more blurred than ever.

The battle not only recurs, but seems to grow in force. If it seems important to some in philosophy to try to make the boundaries clearer, it has also seemed important to some trained in literature to try to create murkier edges. But the existence of the debate and its force tell us something important; literature can inform, can apprise us of the existence of issues, and can shape our attitudes in areas such as morality and aesthetics. Philosophy—especially any sort of philosophy not in the analytic tradition—can itself be analyzed in terms of its rhetorical content and style, and can, at least in some instances, be analyzed along the same lines as literature. These points push us in the direction of acknowledging changes in the general area of disciplinary boundaries, and of the disciplines as a whole.[1]

This dispute would not be so crucial were it not for the long history of philosophy's having attempted to cast itself in a mold that might best be termed "arbiter of all things," and of its having, strenuously, attempted to divorce itself from other areas of endeavor. But the rise in historical theory, and all of the other contemporary movements—feminism, postcolonial theory and so on—has left its mark on philosophical thinking, for better or worse, and it is no longer possible for philosophy to have the same level of pretension that it did of old. The fact that, (as is usually trotted out in such arguments), the debate goes back to Plato and Aristotle does nothing to lessen its ferocity.

Philosophy, then, can be thought of as a kind of writing, and since we already think of literature in such terms, it is much easier to begin an analysis of their intersection. Some authors seem to lend themselves to such an overview: the work of Henry James, Tolstoy, Melville and others has long been deemed to be philosophical, and thinkers such as Nietzsche and Kierkegaard are clearly already literary. What is needed is a much more precise focus on what the boundaries are, and how they are transgressed. It is perhaps not surprising that in the canon of those authors whose work has already been labeled as conceptual, there are surprisingly few women writers. Virginia Woolf, perhaps; Simone de Beauvoir certainly—but then we acknowledge that she is a philosopher. The task, then, is to try to be precise

---

1 Cherwitz, Richard A. (ed.) (1990), *Rhetoric and Philosophy*, Hillsdale, NJ: Lawrence Erlbaum Associates, Inc.

about the women authors whose work has been left out of the list of those who have enlightened us conceptually and to try to make more use of what they have done. If it is the case that a number of women writers have been omitted, why is their omission glaring? What, if anything, is noteworthy about their work?

An investigation into the contribution of women novelists, particularly from the standpoint of the intersection of literature and philosophy, begs the question of women's general intellectual contribution, and in what ways it may be different from that of men. This is a question that we will revisit throughout this work. But if it is clear that we can at least minimally make the case that women have their own tack, so to speak, it is obvious that it requires articulation. The general conundrum over philosophy and literature, whatever the gender of the author, was addressed years ago in an essay by J. Hillis Miller. The piece is titled "Literature and Religion," but its general point is more than relevant:

> Exactly what does it mean to say that religious meanings are present in a poem or a play? It may mean the following: The poet belonged to a certain culture. Among the elements of that culture were religious beliefs. These were part of the worldview of his age, and naturally they enter into his poems, since all men are subject to the spirit of their times.[2]

Although Miller will go on to reject this rather flat historicism, this line of argument has such obvious appeal that it does a great deal to render the debate moot in an immediate sense. Of course, the reader is tempted to say, every writer does participate in the spirit of her culture, and in that sense every work is inherently religious (or philosophical). The task, then, is to try to be a great deal more precise about what it is in which the worldview consists, insofar as it is manifested in the literature in question.

If, as we have seen, rhetoric, literary theory and, certainly, common sense, propel us in the direction of recognizing a great deal of literature as having philosophical import, one might inquire why this line has been so controversial. In part it has to do with the ancient battle between philosophy and literature, which we will examine shortly. But in part it also has to do with the difficulty of saying what it is that is philosophical about a given work. The general tone of a work (as Miller implies) may be philosophical: its content, in some rare instances, may be overtly laden with philosophical theory. (We need only to think of twentieth-century French novelists here.) But the range of literature is such that the vast majority of works will fall somewhere in between these two extremes: Without being as blatant in their construction as *Nausea* or *The Stranger*, many works will be driven by a philosophical sense that is perhaps larger than a mere *zeitgeist*. One thinks for example, of various of the novels of Virginia Woolf—the use of time in *To the Lighthouse* is nothing short of phenomenal as a construct, and it impels the reader to accept that a certain sort of phenomenological view of time is at work. More recently, A.S. Byatt has written of the decline of something like the traditional historical novel, and its replacement by another sort of historical work. Although Byatt scarcely mentions her sister, the work of Margaret Drabble would seem to be a fine exemplar of Byatt's general

---

2   Miller, J. Hillis (1991), "Literature and Religion," *Theory Now and Then*, 73.

thesis: works such as *The Ice Age* or *The Peppered Moth* play with our notions of time, including the present, past and future.

In general, then, we want to be able to say that there is a philosophical component to a work that is clear enough that we can set it out, without necessarily having to make the claim that it is the driving force of the novel in question. Our efforts in this regard are probably assisted by the fact that, currently, a great deal of what passes for literary theory is derived from positions that are indisputably philosophical. Terry Eagleton's classic *Literary Theory* makes this clear, and as he indicates in the Afterword to the most recent edition the drive to the philosophical was moved by postmodern considerations:

> What was perhaps most in question [in the late 1960s] was the assumption that literature embodied universal value, and this intellectual crisis was closely linked to changes in the social composition of universities themselves. Students had traditionally been expected, when encountering a literary text, to put their own particular histories temporarily on ice, and judge it from the vantage-point of some classless, genderless, non-ethnic, disinterested universal subject.[3]

The push away from this view-from-nowhere sort of conceptualization pattern helped drive all of the moves in theory that themselves are now widely regarded as philosophical. Thus readings now became at least somewhat more theory-laden, and in a relevant way, simply because of the new push of category. What this meant, of course, is that it was now possible to see strands in works that had remained hitherto unexamined or undiscovered. The "madwoman in the attic" was always there; she had been there in the first edition, so to speak. Her presence was simply unremarked upon until a combination of feminist theory and what would emerge as postcolonial readings gave a new impetus to the categorization of nineteenth-century classics.

If the new theory gave greater weight to the notion that it was possible to see literature philosophically and, indeed, to see philosophy as literature, it is fair to say that that notion had always been present, at least to some extent. Readers of Dickens a hundred and a hundred and fifty years ago responded to his social concerns intuitively, even if they were not always aware of what they were doing. Woolf's work was clearly seen as having philosophical import from the beginning; it was recognized that the startling takes she provided for the reader themselves relied upon new concepts of time and the self. It is simply the case that the infusion of theory in the past twenty or so years has sped along the process of reading and re-reading with a philosophical eye, and has assisted in the articulation of relevant views. In a brief editorial marking the twenty-fifth anniversary of the journal *Philosophy and Literature*, Denis Dutton and Garry Hagberg write: "[the journal] has provided a home for anyone convinced by the initially counterintuitive notion that a close study of fiction can play an irreplaceable role in epistemology, ethics, philosophy of

---

3 Eagleton, Terry (1996), *Literary Theory*, Minneapolis: University of Minnesota Press, 191.

language and even metaphysics. Philosophy is about life from the broadest possible perceptive, and so is literature."[4]

So, one might suppose, the difficulties in drawing lines and stepping over boundaries are not as great as might first be imagined. Such a sanguine view is somewhat out of place, however, because the battles between philosophy and literature are ancient and complex. It is not possible to begin to think across the boundaries—or even along the boundaries—without recapitulating some of the original skirmishes. The ancients were afraid of the arts (and rightly so, in some instances) because of their potential to evoke the emotions and do damage to the quest for rational inquiry. But the new ways of categorizing that have been bequeathed to us in recent times may be of assistance here.

The blurring of boundaries that characterizes contemporary theory also assists us in articulating new views of the arts and of the role of the emotions in general, views that may make it easier to see either literature as philosophical or philosophy as a form of literature. If everything is a "text," then surely we have no difficulty in assimilating actual hard-copy, real world, non-metaphorical texts under one large rubric. If philosophy is something more than the discipline of philosophy as practiced in American colleges and universities—and almost everyone agrees that it is—then surely we can characterize *Middlemarch* as philosophical. On the other hand, if George Eliot's work may be thought of as a form of philosophy, then philosophy itself, especially Continental work, is clearly part and parcel of literature.[5]

The ancients recognized the place of the emotions and emotional responses in our lives—they simply did not want those responses to rule over our more rational selves. If we can think of an emotional response as simply one part of a network of responses to a situation, or even a claim, we are well on the way to being able to articulate a place for literature and literary works. The poet's divine madness, after all, may simply be one way of approaching the eternal—the point is that it is not the only way. But presumably those with even minimal philosophical training already knew that. Our task is to tease out the philosophical in literature, and then see how those moves, within the framework of pieces authored by women, might assist us in developing views about the world and the world's objects that will ultimately be of value to us.

The Ancient Battle

Discussions about philosophy and the arts almost always take Plato and Plato's caveats about the arts as a point of departure. The chief discussion occurs in the *Republic*, of course, but the worth of the arts is mentioned in many Platonic dialogues. Plato's attack on the arts, and some forms of literature in particular, is so much a part of this debate that it is regularly referred to even in other debates. Martha Nussbaum,

---

4 Dutton, Denis and Garry Hagberg (2002), "War of the Worldviews," *Philosophy and Literature*, **25** (1), April.

5 Villanueva Gardner, Catherine (1999), has, in fact, made such an argument about George Eliot in her *Rediscovering Women Philosophers*, Boulder, CO: Westview.

for example, mentions the topic in *The Therapy of Desire* in connection with the thought of Epicurus:

> Epicurus did not write poetry. Indeed, there is evidence that he was hostile both to poetry and to forms of education that nourish a desire for it.... And since it is obvious that most conventional poetic genres are deeply committed in their very structure to the very desires and emotions that Epicurus denounces as empty—to fear, love, pity and anger—Epicurus has a strong additional reason...for avoiding poetic language in particular. Even popular and non-elite poetry would fall under this critique—a point already seen by Plato in his attack on epic and tragedy....[6]

Here Plato's strong attack is the barometer by which to measure Epicurus', and the assumption made by both parties—that poetic literature is in some sense harmful—is clearly articulated by Nussbaum. We already know that the argument was fairly simple: the arts (here a certain form of literary art) tend to arouse the emotions in ways that are difficult to control, and hence encourage behavior that is irrational and that, even when forcefully fought against, may be hard to govern. But there is a corollary to this argument, when thought through, that ought to put us on guard: if the arts function by mimesis, what is it that they mimic?

The short answer, cast in Platonic terms, is that they may very well mimic the worst in human behavior. But it is human behavior that they do imitate—and from this imitation we can learn. Jowett's version of the old dispute, as rendered in Book X of the *Republic* contains the following lines:

> There is an ancient quarrel between philosophy and poetry; of which there are many proofs.... Notwithstanding this, let us assure our sweet friend and the sister arts of imitation that if she will only prove her title to exist in a well-ordered state, we shall be delighted to receive her...[7]

The best chance, perhaps, for the arts to make their case along this line of thought is that they may furnish us with the opportunity to overcome our desire to give way to our emotion. Plato does not, of course, spend much time on this possibility—he appears to think it highly unlikely. But as Nussbaum contends, "Plato's dialogues do, however, represent such a figure [a 'wise and serene character' who wards off unhealthy emotion]: a Socrates who cares little for the prospect of his own death, and who pursues his philosophical search regardless of his external circumstances."[8] It is not so much that we can use models of such individuals taken from the arts themselves, although that might also take place at a given time, but that we can form some aspects of ourselves on the basis of what we learn from the arts, even if, in many cases, the learning is negative rather than purely imitative.

Thus the ancient quarrel seems to be predicated largely on the notion that most of us will not be able to withstand the temptation toward irrational behavior that is placed in front of us by the arts. But some, of course, will. And there is nothing in

---

6 Nussbaum, Martha (1994), *The Therapy of Desire*, Princeton: Princeton University Press, 154–155.
7 Plato, trans. Jowett (1991), *The Republic*, New York: Vintage, 378–379.
8 Nussbaum, Desire, 93.

the ancient quarrel, as it is commonly articulated, to suggest that we might simply benefit, as functioning human beings, from seeing a wide range of human behavior. Perhaps we are simply better off for having been exposed to a number of possibilities taken from a number of circumstances—that this might very well be the case does not seem to have been part of the ancient quarrel.

That the ancient quarrel has been an ongoing battle is something of which we are reminded when reading a number of contemporary critics. Not only do the editors of *Philosophy and Literature* feel the need to state that they are interested in "the healthy entertainment of battle,"; similar statements recur throughout much recent theory and criticism.[9] Eagleton, for one, recasts the rise of English as a discipline in schools and universities (as opposed, say, to classics) as part of a general wave of interest in inculcating the finer virtues. But on this go-round literature seemed to have the upper-hand, as he notes. This somewhat unusual circumstance was dictated not so much by any absence of philosophical thought against which the literary arts might oppose themselves, but by the very nature of the regnant philosophy of the time. In the early part of the twentieth century a powerful group of critics pushed for the rise of English; part of their argument was that "attention to 'words on the page'…[was valuable] not simply for aesthetic of technical reasons, but because it had the closest relevance to the spiritual crisis of modern civilization."[10] At a slightly earlier point in England, literature had been opposed to the thought of the utilitarians, that "drably discursive pursuit."[11]

Even contemporary philosophers whose thought has largely been deemed to fall outside the areas of interest of analytic philosophy have themselves taken positions on the ancient debate. The battle between philosophy and poetry, as it is often titled, is so well-known that it seems to need no introduction. In "Approaching Abjection," a selection from *Powers of Horror*, Kristeva notes:

> Purification is something only the Logos is capable of. But is that to be done in the manner of the Phaedo, stoically separating oneself from a body whose substance and passions are sources of impurity? Or rather, as in the Sophist, after having sorted out the worst from the best; or after the fashion of the Philebus by leaving the doors wide open to impurity, provided the eyes of the mind remain focused on truth?[12]

As Kristeva goes on to claim, "Catharsis seems to be a concern that is intrinsic to philosophy …[even though] Plato has kept only…the very uncertain role of poets whose frenzy would be useful…after having been…purified in its turn by wise men."[13]

But what is this "purification"? The implication of the somewhat odd conjunction of Eagleton and Kristeva is that the purification is a refinement or stepping back from the emotional content of literature once it has been conceded that literature is, after

---

9 Dutton and Hagberg, in *op.cit.*
10 Eagleton, *Literary*, 27.
11 *Ibid.*, 22.
12 Kristeva, Julia (2000), "Approaching Abjection," in Cazeaux, Clive (ed.) *The Continental Aesthetics Reader*, New York: Routledge, 542–562.
13 *Ibid., ibid.*

all, about life, and that it is, already, in that sense philosophical. After all, it was Plato who referred to the frenzy of the poets as a "divine madness"; he demarcates it in that way because it is obvious that at least some of the impetus that drives the arts pushes toward the realm of the Forms in the same way that dialectic might. It is simply the case that dialectic pursues its path more straightforwardly, and without unnecessary permutations and epicycles. Once all of the foregoing is taken into account, it does not seem that the lines are so clearly drawn in the ancient battle after all.

But there is, of course, a reason for the historically pronounced tendency to place literature, and the arts in general, at odds with poetry. It has to do with the very notion of the possibility of stepping back, as it were. Cultivating the ability to distance oneself from the emotions is not at all an easy task: it is something that requires great effort, and a sort of self-training. (This is why, in *Therapy of Desire*, Nussbaum spends so much time on the work of those whose thought is a tonic to the passions, such as Lucretius.) Thus the lack of consonance mentioned earlier between the English philosophy of the nineteenth century and its literary counterparts: one had gone in a direction completely divorced from an emotional response to analysis—the sort of thing frequently parodied in Dickens—and the other, at least insofar as Romanticism was concerned, had moved in a diametrically opposed direction.

The Czech thinker Jan Potocka has noted, in his recently-translated *Plato and Europe*, that there is an intrinsic relationship between myth and the origins of Western thought that has not received its due.[14] He reminds us that "In a certain sense, we still live in myth just because we live *in the natural world*, in a world that manifests itself to us.... You also find a protohistory there.... This is a myth, this is the mythical world!"[15] His point, of course, is that the world always consists of what there is (on some barebones account) and our interpretation of it. And what there is is not separable from interpretations—in this sense, philosophy and literature are not nearly as divorced as some have thought.

Even some of the more cherished critics on the notion of the ancient battle admit that Plato finds a place for the artist in the ideal city or state—it's simply that that place may not have much in common with what we today would think of as the role of the artist. Plato's concept of the artist who can function as a citizen instills in us the idea that an artist ought to inculcate virtue. Rupert Lodge notes:

> Only if you encourage them [artists] to follow their own ideas and use their own trained taste in their own ways, will they be able, as well as willing, to do their artistic best for the community.
> All this is for Plato, himself a writer, and a highly original writer, elementary and obvious....
> He is himself busied in the creation of a new art: the art of philosophical dialogue.[16]

Lodge sees Plato as an artist; more importantly, whether we are willing to assign that status to Plato or not, it is clear that Plato sees that art is part of life and that they are inextricably intertwined. He simply wishes that the artist would not engage in

---

14 Potocka, Jan (2002), *Plato and Europe*, Stanford: Stanford University Press.
15 *Ibid.*, 43–44.
16 Lodge, Rupert C. (1953), *Plato's Theory of Art*, New York: Humanities Press, Inc., 276.

mimesis of that part of life that he feels panders to the less worthy parts of the soul. The artist has a choice, and if he chooses aright, then we can use him in our attempts to fulfill the mission of the city.

Is it possible to resolve the ancient quarrel in a way of which Plato might at least have minimally approved? The short answer seems to be something along the lines of a provisional yes, given that the arts will cause us to experience an emotion that we may be instructed in other ways to regard with a certain distance. Those "other ways" may or may not come from the arts; most likely, they will not. But if we develop our capacity to take the vision that the arts have to offer, and then to use our most rational selves to work with the vision, we may find that the dispute between the poets and the philosophers is not quite so serious. Nussbaum herself alludes to this in *Poetic Justice* when she says that the problem with the ancient poets was that they presented heroes who were too deeply flawed. Then, "forming bonds of both sympathy and identification, they cause the reader or spectator to experience pity and fear for the hero's plight. Plato saw correctly that it was no trivial matter to remove those…objectionable elements from tragedy, for they inform the genre itself…."[17] Some genres may be less susceptible of reform than others, and some reformed genres may, in a sense, no longer be what they purport to be. But the crucial element here is not the genre: it is the uncontrollable pity, fear, and so on aroused by it. If we develop a more thoughtful capacity that enables us to stand back somewhat from our experience of the emotions, we will have gone a long way toward mastering ourselves in the way in which Plato would have wanted (and, it need be said, in a way that was seldom exhibited by the protagonists of many ancient dramas).

Contemporary work has been done on the boundary of philosophy and literature precisely because so many philosophers have thought that literature has a great deal to offer on a conceptual level. It speaks to moral and even epistemological concerns: it allows us, by indirection, to try to develop our own notions of what might constitute a way out. But there is no question that literature can be dangerous. Unchecked emotions can do untold damage. It is this sort of problem about which the ancients were concerned, and it is this sort of problem that led to the quarrel in the first place.

Fantasy and Philosophy

If the world of the imagination is that realm that yields literature, and if that endeavor has often been thought to be antithetical to philosophical development, we need to investigate some of the intersections of these two areas that, historically, have borne fruit. Certain philosophical quests, schools and theoretical overviews have been informed, from the outset, by an imaginative overview. It is clear, as has been remarked, that some literature has been noted for its philosophical stance—this much is not in dispute. But it might well be asked what imaginative marks are to be found in philosophy itself.

---

17 Nussbaum (1995), *Poetic Justice*, Boston: Beacon Press, 53–54.

Within what has been termed broadly political philosophy, the notion of the ideal state—or, bluntly, the concept of a utopia—has been the site of a great deal of imaginative, if not fantastic, writing. Imagination, by definition, takes us beyond what can be derived from the realm of the senses. We take information derived from the five senses, and ask how things would be if certain external features—or even internal features—were different. Here the philosophical conceptualization process is aided by imagination, although it might still be argued that rational categorization has the upper hand.

What is most remarkable is that these particular political projects are among those that show to be best advantage the intersection between philosophy and literature. In a recent piece titled "Changing Times in Utopia," Gorman Beauchamp has claimed:

> The goal of utopia is, as William Dean Howells's spokesman for Altruria puts it, "an order so just that it cannot be disturbed." This statement provides the crucial clue for understanding the utopian attitude for stasis and change: if, that is, a truly and wholly just order were once achieved, either in the imagination or in reality, then any change in the structure embodying justice would necessarily represent a falling away, a decline from the idea.[18]

Here Beauchamp delineates the crucial role that imagination plays in this very important aspect of political thought: it is clear that "stasis" and the "wholly just" are not attributes or states to be found in human affairs. They are, rather, imaginative constructs, and their very impossibility in our actual lives lends them their poignancy. Hence, as goals, they are powerful motivators: they call us to a plane of thought and category construction to which we might not be able to ascend without their somewhat fantastic input. Beauchamp goes on to examine the utopian societies of Plato, More, Edward Bellamy and William Morris, but his larger point remains: a utopia by its definition has reached perfection, and is not susceptible of growth.

Aside from the obvious response that it is precisely works such as the *Republic* and *Utopia* that strike us as being among the most literary of traditionally philosophical efforts, the more rigorously inclined philosopher might also be tempted to note that exercises in utopian thought in political philosophy are, in some sense, among the most ridiculous of efforts. But that is the narrow view—it is precisely these sorts of efforts that pave the way for other thinking, and in the twentieth century we can see how enormous portions of political theory derive from the impetus toward these efforts that originally produced "utopian" thought. Even the more instrumentalist theories of the nineteenth century, such as utilitarianism, clearly had the ideal society in mind.

The sort of exercise in fantasy that proves fruitful for political discussion is, of course, a somewhat rare instance of actual literary endeavor. The large question, then, is what we can discern in more standard literary fare that speaks to philosophical concerns. The answer is that there is a great deal more such material than we commonly think. This has been noted by many authors and is, indeed, a staple of

---

18 Beauchamp, Gorman (1998), "Changing Times in Utopia," *Philosophy and Literature*, 22 (1), April, 219–230.

criticism, but seldom obtains the attention that it deserves. Any marked shift in rhetorical devices in literary efforts usually marks a shift in the author's stance, and frequently a shift in worldview. Modernist stream-of-consciousness signals to us much the same sort of implicit claim as early twentieth century phenomenology: consciousness is paramount, and in a sense creates its own worlds. Ironic detachment, long a staple of literature (Bloom, for one, sees it even in the ancients) indicates to us that things may not be as they seem—literally or figuratively.[19] Shifts in the use of these devices create ruptures for us, as readers, and these ruptures, either intentionally or unintentionally, may provide slants that are themselves evocative of philosophical stances.

Wayne Booth, in *The Rhetoric of Fiction*, has written of the difficulties that ironic detachment may create in comprehension for the reader, and his views on this topic are instructive for the larger project of limning the boundaries between philosophy and literature. In one of the chapters on the general topic of impersonal narration, Booth warns of various troubles, from the comparatively straightforward "lack of adequate warning that irony is at work," to more recondite matters.[20] But in one of the most intriguing sections, Booth subjects *Portrait of the Artist as a Young Man* to a similar sort of analysis, and finds that a number of literary effects, of which Joyce is obviously the master, are "capable of blinding us to the possibility of our making judgments not shared by the narrator or reflector himself."[21]

Interestingly enough, at least some of what Booth is concerned about in this section is more or less straightforwardly philosophical. Booth claims that critics have been bemused by Stephen Dedalus' aesthetic theory, set out in the novel as if it were a developed stand. An aesthetic view, we can agree, is perforce a philosophical view: but the difficulty here is, whose view is this? Is it actually Stephen's view, according to Joyce? Or does Joyce intend us to stand back from the text in such a way that we gather that Stephen feels concern himself about what might be his own view? The number of possible moves here is dazzling. As Booth writes:

> Critics have had even more difficulty with Stephen's aesthetic theory, ostensibly developed from Aquinas....[I]s it...an ironic portrait of Stephen's immature aesthetics?... Finally, what of the previous villanelle? Does Joyce intend it to be taken as a serious sign of Stephen's artistry, as a sign of his genuine but amusingly pretentious precocity, or as something else entirely?[22]

The irony here—as one can't resist saying—is that in setting out these possibilities, Booth has provided us with a good deal of ammunition for one side in any debate or disagreement over the relationships between literature and philosophy. Joyce is not overtly philosophical in the way that the utopians are, of course. It is simply the case that a close reading of Joyce forces the reader to consider a number of options

---

19 Bloom, Harold (2002), *Genius: a Mosaic of One Hundred Exemplary Creative Minds*, New York: Warner Books, Inc., 117.

20 Booth, Wayne C. (1983), *The Rhetoric of Fiction*, Chicago: University of Chicago Press.

21 *Ibid.*, 324.

22 *Ibid.*, 328.

which, in this case, have to deal with philosophical theory, and which, even in other parts of the novel, push us in similar directions because of their implicit stance on consciousness itself. One does not often expect to learn about aesthetics from the youthful protagonist of a fictional work.

Finally, even a critic such as Bloom points us in a similar direction in, of all works, his recent *Genius*.[23] It is remarkable how frequently his own analysis of certain passages from a variety of authors imputes to them views that might be deemed to be philosophical. Bloom sees that the importance of epiphanies for Virginia Woolf's characters is implicitly ontological: the epiphanies reveal the underlying structure of things for one brief moment. Woolf signals this to us by her various shifts, such as the famous middle passages of *To the Lighthouse*, but she also sometimes simply has her characters make statements to the effect that an insightful moment is taking place. In a section on Woolf in *Genius*, Bloom focuses on the less-examined *Between the Acts*, and says this about Woolf and her construction of the moment:

> *Between the Acts* is a difficult novel to describe, but beautifully easy to read. The entire community of the English cultural tradition is intimated, but mostly by moments of being, epiphanies or privileged moments until the village audience of the pageant comes to see that they themselves are the conclusion....[24]

Phenomenologically, a certain sort of reality is disclosed for Woolf, and she makes it clear that her novels are to be read as portraying such moments of disclosure for some of her main characters. Lily Briscoe says at the end of *Lighthouse* that she has "had her vision," but so has Woolf, and so have we all if we have done the work on our interiors that being the possessor of such visions requires.

Thus far we have outlined three ways in which things literary might also be deemed to be philosophical: in their depiction of alternate realities, such as is the case with utopian literature; in their use of distancing and difficult or unreliable narrators to signal a shift in what is presented as believable, and in their rhetorical presentation of moments of insight that may indicate the presentation of an ontology. None of these, of course, necessarily excludes the others, and a great many more devices might be enumerated and examined. But the existence of the ancient quarrel, used as a point of departure in the previous section, reminds us once again that the difficulty with all of the foregoing is not so much whether we can plausibly argue that literature can and does make philosophical points: the difficulty is what we are to do with them. The fact that literature seems to leave this decision to us—that we have to decide what our response to a given utopia might be, or whether we approve or disapprove of Stephen's nascent aesthetics—makes the situation very complex and leaves us vulnerable to exactly the sort of all-or-nothing emotional response that had been thought to be damaging in the first place.

Almost all literature that we would traditionally deem worthy of the rubric avoids didactic pronouncements in this regard and is, as we have already said, potentially dangerous. Judith Fetterley's "resisting reader," may not, at a tender age, have built up enough resistance to identification with the male protagonist of *Portrait* and may

---

23 Bloom, *Genius*.
24 *Ibid.*, 329.

naively assume that a number of adventures are available to her, too, with a similar lack of consequences. But these are choices that every adult must make, and there is nothing in philosophy to discourage us—in fact, everything to encourage us—from making our own choices.

Literature introduces us to worlds, worldviews, and interiors—both authorial and fictional—with which we would not otherwise have had contact. What we make of these introductions is, of course, our own affair. But it is important to note that we do not have to be sophisticated readers to become acquainted with new thought patterns. It is not only unnecessary to have read Booth's *The Rhetoric of Fiction*, but in some sense positively superfluous. The thirteen-year-old reading *Jane Eyre* already feels a simultaneous kinship with and distance from the protagonist. In trying to navigate her way through these spaces, the adolescent is forced to confront—at whatever level—questions such as "What do I have in common with Jane?" "How is my life different?" "What would I have done differently, in similar circumstances?" The fact that almost every comprehending reader asks these questions of a text, even if only at the most intuitive level, signals that something important is going on between the reader and the text. We need not demarcate that activity as philosophical, but it is difficult to know what else to call the opening of ethical, metaphysical and epistemic spaces that typically accompanies careful reading of recognized works of literature. We can call it simple life questioning but then, once we have thought further about it, we might very well be tempted to call the activity of life questioning philosophy.

Women

The now familiar questions of what women might have to contribute epistemically or in other ways that differs from so-called standard philosophy—or from a traditional stance in literature—have been so often investigated that one feels a twinge of guilt at reworking them here. Nevertheless, the questions still have some importance, and all the more so since the project in which we are engaged here is one that concerns the intersection of philosophy, literature and the issue of women's viewpoint, or what some have called gynocentricity. Women philosophers have now been the subject of a great deal of retrieval, and the work done in literary circles on literature by women has taken on a life of its own.[25] Some of the first attempts at demarcation of the literary version of this question are now classics in their own right: Elaine Showalter's *A Literature of Their Own* addresses one version of the conundrum in the first two sentences of the work.[26] She sets out the area of investigation when she writes:

> English women writers have never suffered from the lack of a reading audience, nor have they wanted for attention from scholars and critics. Yet we have never been sure what

---

25 With respect to the retrieval of work by women philosophers, I have addressed the question in the form of a project on eight separate thinkers in my *Eight Women Philosophers*, Urbana-Champaign: University of Illinois Press, 2005.

26 Showalter, Elaine (1977), *A Literature of Their Own*, Princeton: Princeton University Press.

unites them as women, or, indeed, whether they share a common heritage connected to their womanhood at all.... [The question has been] whether women, excluded by custom and education from achieving distinction in poetry, history, or drama had, in defining their literary culture in the novel, simply appropriated another masculine genre.[27]

On her way to answering this question, Showalter raises a number of points about essentialism, style, the interactions between males and females (both social and intellectual), and so on that now constitute familiar territory. But to try to examine the work of five women writers from the standpoint of philosophical content, and then from the other vantage point of feminist critique, seems to beg the question. Why address this intersection at all? Why not—pushing on with still another version of the vexations with which Showalter began—simply assume that there are writers, that much of literature is at least to some extent philosophical (a disputed area in and of itself, as we have seen), and that, perforce, at least some women writers will have produced work that may be interpreted philosophically, regardless of gender?

The difficulty is that the very arguments we have been addressing with respect to the "ancient quarrel" have another version here. Part of our contention with respect to the classic dispute was a simple one of raising borders: it seems to be agreed by almost all comers that the lines between philosophy and literature are weak and possibly not delineable. But if we can make the comparatively easy slide into a literary philosophical excursion, all of the work that has been done on women's voices virtually demands that the next step—a philosophical investigation of literature by women—be singled out by gender. Indeed, it is a feature of this particular focus that the gender boundaries are probably stronger than the boundaries between "philosophy" *simpliciter* and literature *simpliciter*. Thus any investigation into matters literary from a philosophical standpoint will virtually necessitate the kind of work we are doing here. To fail to make this demarcation would be to ignore an area that has been steadily mapped and re-mapped during the past two or three decades.

Another strong counterargument to the claim that a gender distinction is misplaced in an endeavor limning philosophical and literary intersections involves the notion that women writers themselves, and their critics, have frequently felt called upon to examine gender. This necessity seems to have become more strongly, rather than less strongly felt over a period of time—it is, for example, a more marked feature of twentieth century work by women than work written in the late nineteenth century, although it already was experienced at that time. Showalter begins the last chapter of her *A Literature* in the following way:

> It is easy to see why Virginia Woolf and her generation tried to create a power base in inner space, an aesthetic that championed the feminine consciousness and asserted its superiority to the public, rationalist masculine world.... Today women novelists are continuing a phase of self-discovery and self-scrutiny in forms and vocabularies very different from those employed by Woolf.[28]

---

27 *Ibid.*, 304.
28 *Ibid.*, 298.

A number of critics have felt the need to draw attention—sometimes neglected in the past—to the extent to which women writers have been conscious of their femaleness. Sandra Gilbert and Susan Gubar see some of this as a series of moves by early twentieth-century women novelists who "are either defeated by male intransigence or who overcome their opponents through...indirect strategies and... providential luck...."[29] Like Showalter, they see many of the strategies, tropes and viewpoints employed by women writers as self-conscious ways of moving against male hegemony; that such self-consciousness has been at work in European circles for at least several centuries is obvious from a perusal of literature by, for example, Mary Wollstonecraft or Mary Astell.

If there are, then, strong reasons for making gender a demarcator in a project about literature and philosophy, it is also advisable to repeat the obvious: there are no easy answers, and gender, reliable as a sieve in some circumstances, fails in others. Writers vary enormously in their consciousness of gender, and it is not a dependable marker in many cases. But the fact that its occurrence in ancient philosophy as a method by which separation for educational practices may be made (the *Republic*), its reoccurrence in various parts of the tradition, and its self-conscious use in modern and Victorian literature can all be picked out as leading themes of cultural development pushes us in the direction of creating a place for gender in a work on philosophical literature.

Summing up the facts as she sees them, Showalter reminds us that the "female imagination" is subject to "a network of influences and conventions, including the operations of the marketplace."[30] It is also, of course, subject itself to variations in culture, region and time; the authors whose work we select for investigation will, *a fortiori*, differ in their approaches not only from most male authors but from each other. Nevertheless, one area of commonality for almost all women authors in the contemporary period is their own awareness of the women's movement: because such awareness is now international, Black American women authors, Latin American writers and authors cannot be but affected by the level of awareness of gender differences and the particular difference in writing that that makes. Thus some of what is marked as "philosophical" for women writers may, in some sense, fall under a generalized rubric of the philosophical; other writing with the type of content that frequently receives this label will be more overtly concerned with feminism, race and/or class.

The ancients were concerned not only with the battle between philosophy and the arts, but with the general educability of males and females because they saw these two topics as being interrelated. Socrates asks the young men who start crying at the end of *Phaedo* to leave because they are acting like women; the arts have only the most circumscribed place in the ideal city because they are capable of rousing the same type of unchecked emotional response. The "honeyed muse" makes "pleasure and pain" the rulers of the state where she is unhealthily encouraged—pleasure

---

29 Gilbert, Sandra M. and Susan Gubar (1988), *No Man's Land: the Place of the Woman Writer in the Twentieth Century*, **I**, New Haven: Yale University Press, 80.

30 Showalter, *A Literature*, 12.

and pain and their responses are associated with the female.[31] But women writers from the 1840s or 1850s on—the period that we associate with the growth of the novel as a form—have, in general, taken their own stand on these matters. A utopia might be a society called "Herland"; the presence of men is neither necessary nor desirable.[32] A reasoned moral take on a given matter might involve a fairly high degree of emotionality, rather than the restrained and distanced stance often taken to be characteristic of male thinking. A deeply felt response to male abandonment, violence and injustice might be homicide, or some other act of violence, and these acts might be portrayed in ways to make the reader more sympathetic with the unwed mother, for example, than with her seducer.

There is little question that over the past one hundred fifty years enough gender consciousness has been generated that gender alone becomes a worthy category for literary investigation. More difficult then, particularly when matters philosophical are thrown into the mix, is the investigation of two or three categories simultaneously. A substantial argument can be made that a self-conscious feminism affects much of the work written by women throughout the preceding century, but it is another matter to try to be precise about whether that feminism is itself philosophical, or what other points of view expressive of philosophy might be contained in a given work.

Gilbert and Gubar seem to believe that there is a strong anti-androcentric bias in much of women's writing from about 1920 on. This does, of course, express a nascent worldview—by this time a strain has emerged in literature written by women that appears to articulate the notion that women have a different way of seeing. We might go so far as to say that at least some of this is relevant to ontology construction, particularly when it intersects with race and class issues. Gilbert and Gubar note:

> Ann Petry produces in *The Street*...a...documentary text representing the battle of the sexes not only as a racial but also as a class struggle. In marked contrast to her black female precursor Zora Neale Hurston, who focuses in *Their Eyes Were Watching God* and "Sweat" on the fortuitous triumphs of powerful country women, Petry mourns the helplessness that even the most determined women experience in the city.[33]

It is a short leap from this sort of writing to a number of philosophical points, including the overtly existentialist Black writing of the later Richard Wright (admittedly not a male author). But the challenge in examining a great many novels written by women with an eye toward philosophical points of view and viewpoints that might be deemed to be gynocentric will be to attempt, at least at some point, to disentangle the two.

Fortunately, we have a number of paradigmatic figures with which we can begin. Many commentators have found philosophical themes in the work of Virginia Woolf, independent of any feminist concerns, and of course it is not difficult to make a

---

31 See fn. 7.

32 Gilbert and Gubar specifically link the vision of Perkins' Herland to the political quest of women—they write that "it is a vision of triumphant female community that had inspired the marching and hunger-striking suffragists." (Gilbert and Gubar, *No Man's*, p. 89.)

33 *Ibid.*, 102–103.

similar claim about Simone de Beauvoir. Woolf's concern with time, for example, in *To the Lighthouse*, seems so overtly philosophical that the wonder is that remark has not been made upon it in more Woolf commentary than we actually see in this vein. With Beauvoir the concern long has been that her novels fail to achieve what they might in literary terms because they strive too hard and too overtly to make philosophical points.

Our project here will examine the work of five women writers of the twentieth century taken as exemplary—Margaret Drabble, Virginia Woolf, Simone de Beauvoir, Toni Cade Bambara and Elena Poniatowska. Part of the argument will be, obviously, that we can discern major philosophical strands in the work of these women writers above and beyond their contributions to feminist thought, or their contributions to any sort of written construct that might be analyzed along philosophical lines. Drabble appears, at the moment, to be less well-known than her sister A.S. Byatt; it can easily be argued that she should be a great deal better known than she is. Toni Cade Bambara, author of *The Salt Eaters*, has crafted fantastic prose expressive of a sort of Afrocentric metaphysics. Although Elena Poniatowska is probably best known in the United States for her writings on Mexican activism, she has also written fiction. Each of these women authors has created work that is simultaneously philosophical and, at least in some sense, gynocentric.

Literary Ontologies

In a sense, any novel that is written well enough to hold our attention already offers us another worldview—precisely the world that is demarcated in that fiction. But some novelists (again, notably Woolf and Beauvoir, among others) seem to be presenting us with an actual stance on how our own ontologies are constructed. They are gently instructive, but allow us to consider that the flow of time, for example, may be examined phenomenologically, and when it is so examined we see things completely differently. Such different modes of seeing themselves may give rise to different ontologies.

We must make a crucial distinction, then, between the fictional world that an author creates for us, and philosophical import that appears, at least in some sense, to be part of the novel. In a passage with respect to *Portrait of the Artist as a Young Man* examined here earlier, Booth made the point that authorial distance may leave the reader confused as to what Joyce's actual point with respect to aesthetics is, but Booth has little doubt that Joyce does indeed have some such point. It could be argued, then, that there is a crucial difference between fictions that have no overt philosophical intentions (at least insofar as an alive and sensitive reader can discern them), and those that do. The putative counterargument—that every fiction is philosophical—simply places too much weight on the notion of a created world of fantasy. After all, children's fairy tales, our childhood Golden Books, and many other such sources of fictional views do give us, however truncated, a world of fantasy.

Fiction can give us philosophical views, separate realms, or moral and aesthetic views. In a sense we want to delimit all these views as ontological constructions, because they allow us to see reality in a different way. One of Booth's major concerns in his critical stance toward unreliable narrators is that they may prevent us from developing a moral view toward behavior that we ought to find objectionable. In indicating that the novel can, as a matter of fact, paint a world that is highly objectionable from an ethical standpoint and then refuse to give us the adequate moral tools to deal with such a construction, Booth gives us further evidence about the philosophical import of literature.

The complexity of this area is signaled for us by some of Booth's examples in *The Rhetoric of Fiction*. Although the sophisticated reader might now, for example, know how to read Nabokov, Booth indicates that this has not always been the case. The sort of moral universe that might leap out at us as a result of ambiguous literary efforts, is Booth claims, demonstrated by the early critical reception of *Lolita*:

> We should be very clear that the failures we are talking about do not come from any inherent condition of the novel or from any incompatibility between author and reader. They come from the reader's inability to dissociate himself from a vicious center of consciousness presented to him with all the seductive self-justification of skillful rhetoric. Can we really be surprised that readers have overlooked Nabokov's ironies in Lolita, when Humbert is given full and unlimited control of the rhetorical resources?... We have already seen that Lionel Trilling cannot accept Humbert's—self-castigation as genuine....[34]

Booth is genuinely concerned that it is possible to read this novel as some sort of valorization of adolescent abuse; indeed, his comments about the critics seem to indicate that at least some critical commentary did not see through the layers of irony.

But this, of course, is what makes literature so important, and what allows us to say that it has philosophical import even when the import is unclear, not overtly stated, or possibly not intended. Booth's extensive commentary on impersonal and unreliable narrators is aimed at getting us to see that we may be missing the author's point, but in the cases—and there are many—where the author's main points clearly focus on moral or aesthetic matters, these foci may well be deemed to be philosophical.

Gilbert and Gubar are able to make their points about masculinism, its decline, and the revolt against perceived female dominance precisely because it is obvious from some literature that this is its intended point. Here we have something quite a bit removed from the sort of problem of which Booth was writing, but what these two styles have in common, again, is their philosophical import. Sandra Gilbert and Susan Gubar write of this more self-conscious creation of worlds when they note:

> How did male reactions inflect the engendering of literary history in the twentieth century? To begin with—and most dramatically—writers like James in America and Wilde in England could not help noticing that theirs was among the earliest generations to have female precursors.... Where literary men had traditionally looked for inspiration to the idealized mother or mistress whom convention metaphorized as a muse, turn-of-the-century and twentieth-century men of letters suffered from a disquieting intimation

---

34 Booth, *Rhetoric*, 390.

that the goddesses of literature, like the literary women male readers now encountered in increasing numbers, might reserve creative power for themselves.[35]

What all of this means is that a number of male writers began to consciously battle back against what they thought was an overt female attack in the war between the sexes, and the authors of *No Man's Land* take a tale such as Henry James's "The Death of the Lion" as exemplary.[36]

What we have discussed so far represents, of course, two extremes—literary content bent toward the philosophical, but of unclear intent, and literary content obviously intended to make some sort of statement, and one which might in any case be taken as philosophical. But much of nineteenth century literature, in any case, falls between these two extremes. The narration is characteristically much more reliable, since the modern and postmodern narrators have yet to make their appearance. (There are startling departures, however, such as much of the work of Stendhal, with its detachment.) But this may not make the philosophical content that much easier to decipher: it simply makes it more obvious that the author is trying to make a point, and it is then up to the reader to discern that point.

At an earlier point we recounted the notion that the ancient dispute recurs in philosophical works precisely because philosophy has recognized that it has a dangerous rival. Were it the case that no one had ever been swayed, moved or convinced by a literary work, it is unlikely that philosophers would have thought it necessary to mention the meretriciousness of them. But many, of course, have been swayed—and the fact that this is a generally recognized aspect of culture makes the dispute between philosophy and literature an important one. There can be little that poses a greater danger to reasoned thought that an irrational outburst of emotion encouraged by a well-written, carefully-constructed mimetic device.

Some philosophers have obviously believed that most novels fall into this category. It will be our task in this work to examine a variety of novels and other works of literature by women authors and attempt to gauge to what extent the naysayers have been, or can be, right.

---

35 Gilbert and Gubar, *No Man's*, 129–130.
36 *Ibid.*, 134.

PART II
The Europeans

Chapter Two

Margaret Drabble and Philosophy

The work of Margaret Drabble has impressed many, and she is almost always listed among the top women novelists currently writing in English, particularly insofar as British writers are concerned. Although in the past decade she may have been eclipsed in popularity to some extent by her sister A.S. Byatt, Drabble's reputation goes back to the 1960s. She was already well-enough known at the time of Showalter's *A Literature of Their Own* that she is cited extensively in that text.

What is remarkable about Drabble's renown, however, is not the degree of it, or the extent to which it might in some sense rest on familial comparisons, but the fact that it rests upon what some have believed to be a sort of literary conventionality. In other words, Drabble has most often been categorized as a traditional novelist. Indeed, some have even found her to be the descendant of a number of strong nineteenth century authors; whatever the relevance of these categorizations, few seem to have noticed that Drabble's writing plays a number of tricks on the reader, and that she is one among those who might in some sense be termed "postmodern."

Eleanor Skoller, in her study *The In-Between of Writing*, indicates that Drabble is frequently called "old-fashioned," but Skoller claims that Drabble may best be seen as relinquishing the "authorial stance and interrogat[ing] herself and the world in the process."[1] In a number of novels that are often cited by feminist theorists and others—such as *The Waterfall*, *The Ice Age*, *A Natural Curiosity*, and the recent *The Peppered Moth*—Drabble sets out a narrative only to step back from it at various points, question it (both in her own voice and, frequently, the voice of one of her characters), and, in some cases, abandon it. Drabble's play with a type of historicity might cause us to think that we could characterize her, in a style currently being used by A.S. Byatt, as an "historical" novelist, but there is a great deal going on in Drabble that pushes beyond this.[2]

One of the remarkable strengths of her fiction is a sort of genuine interiority of voice that one seldom finds in contemporary fiction. It would be a mistake to categorize this as stream-of-consciousness: rather, writing in many instances in the third person (and thus still retaining a hint of authorial authority), Drabble seems to be able to give effective vent to her characters' thoughts and concerns in a way that rings uncannily true. Thus Faro, in *The Peppered Moth*, after having attended a conference on genealogy, DNA, and her own family's history starts to wonder where it all began, and where it will end. Alison, in *The Ice Age*, returns to Britain from Wallacia and begins to question—in seeing the oppositions between a first-

---

1 Honig Skoller, Eleanor (ed.) (1993), *The In-Between of Writing: Experience and Experiment in Drabble, Duras and Arendt*, Ann Arbor: University of Michigan Press, 38.

2 Byatt, A.S. (2002), *On Histories and Stories*, Cambridge: Harvard University Press.

world economy, its products, and the economy of "Wallacia," which she had recently left behind—whether she is losing her mind. Jane, in *The Waterfall*, staggers from day to day, hour to hour and minute to minute in her lover's absence by looking at calendars, clocks and time-keeping devices until she begins to experience a sense of depersonalization.If part of what makes literature philosophical, as has been argued in the preceding chapter, is its capacity to provoke thought in general and questions in particular, Drabble succeeds eminently in being a philosophical novelist.

Critics have noted the care with which Drabble is able to evoke entire periods and lifestyles; she is nothing if not a novelist, in some sense, of manners combined with a concern for moral thought. Susanna Roxman claims that "Like George Eliot's novels, those by Margaret Drabble tend to dramatize social problems...."[3] The worlds portrayed by Drabble are frequently evoked through detailed external description combined with, as has been noted, a sophisticated development of the thought train of the protagonist or protagonists. The internal questioning of the main characters—Where will it all end? How did it begin? What does it all mean?—is a staple feature of Drabble's work, and one that stays with the reader, for as she no doubt intends, it reminds him or her of his or her own self-questioning. The bemused contemporary reader, haunted by the newspaper's accounts of current events and disasters far and near, finds in Drabble's created worlds parallel characters with analog concerns. Their personal dilemmas are mirrored in the social paradoxes of British society, and those larger problems loom over the daily lives of her male and female characters as they struggle to cope.

In *The Peppered Moth*, Faro Gaulden calls her mother over the mobile phone after having attended a session on mitochondrial DNA and its trail throughout part of her maternal family, the Cudworths. The sense of the ridiculous hovering over the communications problems is highlighted by the fact that Faro has just met, at the conference, a long-lost cousin, with whom she also (on a personal level) failed to establish meaningful contact. Drabble depicts Faro on the phone:

> Miss Gaulden, by this time, was on her mobile talking to her mother Chrissie in Oxfordshire from a petrol station.... 'You should have come, Mum,' yells Faro over the racket of the garage forecourt. 'It was hilarious! What? Yes, Auntie Dora's fine. And I met this lovely cousin from Iowa. What? I can't *hear* you!'[4]

The general level of miscommunication in Faro's phone call recapitulates miscommunication across the generations, and, in this case, cousinly miscommunication on the preceding evening. For the "lovely" relative had started off his dinnertime conversation with Faro by mentioning that he was married, a sure sign that something altogether beyond an interest in mitochondrial DNA was in the air. As Drabble had written at an earlier point in the novel of some of Faro's forebears, "Sexual attraction and pity do not mix well. They are a dangerous combination, as

---

3 Roxman, Susanna (1984), *Guilt and Glory: Studies in Margaret Drabble's Novels, 1963–80*, Stockholm: Almquist and Wixsell International, 10.

4 Drabble, Margaret (2001), *The Peppered Moth*, New York: Harcourt, Inc., 149.

granddaughter Faro, whose conception begins to seem more and more unavoidable, will one day discover."[5]

The shift in time sequence signaled by "begins to seem more and more unavoidable" is a staple of Drabble's work, and appears in *The Ice Age* and *The Waterfall*, among other novels. The questioning stance with regard to past, present and future not only has a philosophical ring to it insofar as traditional "great questions" are concerned, but more poignantly may well remind the reader of personal travails over similar subject matter. It is this sort of twist at which Drabble excels—a reader's shock of recognition is a familiar feature of criticism, but with Drabble the shock seems to have more impact than with a good many other well-known authors.

Drabble's work has a force and appeal that cuts across many boundaries—she is a favorite of feminist critics, while still being acknowledged as, simply, a masterful author. The fact that her novels are demonstrably British in tone (and that they frequently allude to the British educational system, among other phenomena) does not seem to have made her any less popular with a number of readers around the world. Although she was still comparatively young at the time, and had written only a few works, Drabble is mentioned extensively in Showalter's *A Literature of Their Own*, published in 1977. Part of the reason for the extensiveness of the citations in that work is Showalter's acknowledgement of the fact that Drabble is centrally located in the very tradition under examination, and that a work that delves deeply into the literature produced by the Brontes, Jane Austen, and George Eliot, among others, can do no less than admit Drabble as a true daughter of the tradition.

Showalter signals the importance to us of Drabble's work and her place in the developing pantheon when she writes:

> Like her sister Antonia Byatt...Drabble has been increasingly serious, ambitious and open-minded; her work is the record of a feminist consciousness expanding and maturing. In some respects, she has been clinging to a tradition she has outgrown.[6]

These comments, made two decades ago, point in the direction Drabble was to take. Part of our task will be to see how her work has developed and unfolded, and how that can be related to the perennial issues at the intersection of literature and philosophy.

The Philosophical Drabble

There is a notion of history at work in much of Drabble's oeuvre that, for lack of a better term, is decidedly postmodern. Drabble not only interrogates the historical; she asks what conceptions we ourselves carry with respect to the time in which we are living, and how those beliefs might be related to someone else's view of history, our own budding view of our time, and the general scheme of things. This is a strand that runs throughout Margaret Drabble's work, and that is very much evidenced

---

5   *Ibid.*, 120.
6   Showalter, *A Literature*, 307.

by the decidedly questioning interior monologues in which most of her characters frequently engage.

The Ice Age is a novel that manifests Drabble's talents in the direction of a philosophically-conscious take on history to a high degree. The cold that descends on Britain is, of course, largely metaphorical; it is the cold of depression, post-boom–bust, and a withered empire. At the same time that Britain is drenched in an icy shower, Drabble's four main characters undergo personal trials that cause them to question reality and the historical narrative that they have consistently been taught. The four central characters, Anthony Keating, Alison Murray, Len Wincobank and Maureen Kirby, each seem to feel their own decline, as well as Britain's, in a highly personalized, but somewhat detached, way. In a passage that pulls together their slants, and those of their fellow citizens, Drabble writes:

> Not everybody in Britain on that night in November was alone, incapacitated or in jail. Nevertheless, over the country depression lay like fog, which was just about all that was missing to lower spirits even further, and there was even a little of that in East Anglia. All over the nation, families who had listened to the news looked at one another and said, "Goodness me," or "Whatever next," or "I give up," or "Well, fuck that," before embarking on an evening's viewing of color television, or a large hot meal, or a trip to the pub, or a choral society evening.[7]

We can hazard a guess that the families who said "Well, fuck that" were not the same ones who went to the choral society later. Drabble shows us history from different perspectives, and in drawing the individual view of events and throwing that view up against a more normative take, she begins to undo and unravel that very conception of history and the historical that we take for granted. Byatt claims that "[there is] a refusal of narrative by contemporary historians"; there is also a refusal of history-as-standardized by contemporary novelists.[8] Drabble is among those writers.

Drabble's breakdown of history follows along lines that are often termed postmodern; her fictional eye is attuned to the ways in which historical takes in the past have omitted certain stories or groups. Beatrice Han has noted that "Foucault shows himself to be antimetaphysical in the sense that truth is not for him atemporal, lacking any historicity or a birth within history."[9] In some of her earlier novels shifts in voice and temporal sequence signal to us that this view-of-history move is taking place; in *The Peppered Moth*, one of her most recent works, Drabble deliberately disrupts our notions of history, time, and the inevitable.

To make the point doubly obvious, the protagonists of *The Peppered Moth* are all either present at a convocation in Yorkshire where DNA testing and its effects on genealogical research is the topic of the day, or they are related ancestrally to such characters. Drabble moves swiftly between Faro—present at the conference, and with us today—and her parents Chrissie and Nick Gaulden, and, most poignantly, her maternal grandparents, Bessie and Joe Barron. A significant portion of the novel

---

7 Drabble, Margaret (1977), *The Ice Age*, New York: New American Library, 59.
8 Byatt, in *op. cit.*, 9–10.
9 Han, Beatrice (2002), *Foucault's Critical Project*, Stanford: Stanford University Press, 8.

is taken up with Bessie's doings: she is one of the first young women in Yorkshire to be able to qualify to attend Cambridge, and great things are expected of her. But, alas, she is born too soon, and societal expectations for women, World War II, and various other matters prevent her from living the life that she would have liked to have lived.

All of this is comparatively straightforward, but what is not straightforward is Drabble's use of the authorial voice and timeshifts to disrupt the narrative and force us to ask ourselves the standard ontological questions about ultimate reality, fate and meaning. Drabble is in some cases the usual omniscient narrator, telling us about Bessie's intense study for her exams. In other cases, she becomes the Omniscient Narrator, asking us whether it is possible for Bessie and Joe to escape their fate of wedding each other, thereby bringing Chrissie into the world, and, ultimately, Faro. As the recounting of Bessie and Joe's get-togethers unfolds, Drabble steps back to ask: "Did Joe Barrow suspect, as he walked away, that in that little room he might have embarked on a lifetime of tragic appeasement?"[10] Still more pointedly, Drabble has us visit Faro in her hotel room the night of the conference, after she has met one of her cousins downstairs in the bar.

> She was going mad. For comfort she bashed her head back and forth under the pillow. Was redemption waiting, now, on the horizon, for the human race? ... What of the *already dead*? ... What of those born before the genome? What of those who never had a moment's happiness?[11]

Many individuals might have reflective moments, but it seems to be a hallmark of Drabble's characters that they have such moments at regular intervals. Drabble assumes a certain sort of reader; she assumes someone who, like herself, finds ordinary life fraught with difficulty and problematic enough. What is noteworthy, however, is the extent to which this problematization might be deemed to be historical—Drabble is concerned not only with the personal narratives that we tell ourselves about our own lives (and her characters seem to find these both engrossing and entangling), but about master narratives and their effect on both the individual and on populations.

Since Foucault is usually associated with the current moves to question master narratives of all shapes and forms, various Foucauldian views and pronouncements can prove instructive in an endeavor to read Drabble. Interestingly, one of his most celebrated commentaries on the visual arts seems to shed a great deal of light on what it is that Drabble does in her novels, particularly *The Ice Age* and *The Peppered Moth*. In his commentary on Velásquez's *Las Meñinas*, Foucault asks us to notice how the artist's portrayal of himself at work as part of the painting alters our relationship both to the artist and to his work. Describing the appearance of the artist himself on this well-known canvas, Foucault observes:

> As though the painter could not at the same time be seen on the picture where he is represented and also see that upon which he is representing something. He rules at the

---

10 Drabble, *Moth*, 99.
11 *Ibid.*, 147.

threshold of those two incompatible visibilities.... He is staring at a point...[and] it is we, ourselves, who are that point....[12]

This assertion of a self-consciousness on the part of European culture during the early part of the seventeenth century has been associated not only with the painterly but, at least according to some, it is also manifested in Descartes' *Meditations* and other work of this period. But what is helpful to us about this brief excision from Foucault's lengthy analysis of the painting is that he articulates the oddity of the artist's self-awareness, and his simultaneous awareness of being an object for the observer.

In a way, Drabble accomplishes the same thing in her writing—she is aware of herself both as an author, and aware of our awareness of her. This provides the striking quality so familiar to readers of her work: the sense that she is watching you, that she is watching you watching her, and that you are both involved in the complex creation of her characters, their history, and some greater history. This is more apparent in her work as her work evolves—the sheer chronological proportion of it seems to bear out, in its own way, a great deal of what she means to say.

It remains to be commented upon that Drabble is still, in some circles, considered a "traditional" novelist.[13] But there is little that is traditional about the way in which she pulls back from the text; this is not done in a manner that leaves the reader with a feeling of something familiar, rather the reader feels somewhat stunned. And it is that stunning quality, along with a rare gift for an intellectualized interior monologue, that puts Drabble in the top rank of living writers.

Drabble and Critics

Earlier critics of Drabble's work seem, somewhat surprisingly, to focus on her as a "traditional" author of what one writer termed "women's" novels. This may have been more appropriate at a time when the new energy infused into critical analysis by the women's movement seemed to give everything a feminist turn. More recent critics, however, have appeared to be somewhat more astute in their appraisals—although the term "subversive" is often overworked, it is clear that at least some strands of Drabble's writing are subversive. They subvert our usual notions of chronology and history and they are, in that sense, postmodern.

Both Elaine Tuttle Hansen and Eleanor Honig Skoller are sensitive to the oddities of voice and chronology in Drabble's work, and both of them have something to say about *The Ice Age*, which is generally regarded as a turning point for her. In making their assessments, these writers—particularly Skoller—are alive to the alterations of authorial voice and the distancing from the narrative that make portions of *The Ice Age* a definitive work in Drabble's output.

---

12 Foucault, Michel (2000), "Las Meñinas," in Cazeaux, Clive (ed.), *The Continental Aesthetics Reader*, London: Routledge, 401–411.

13 The back of the Harcourt Brace paperback edition of *Moth* has a blurb from the Washington Post Book World that calls her an author of the "realistic novel."

Skoller has termed Drabble someone who relinquishes the "authorial stance and interrogates herself and the world in the process."[14] Skoller focuses on Drabble's interest in wordplay, and on the shifting accounts of chronology signaled by the moves in the text from focus on the gentlemanly Anthony, for instance, to Len Wincobank and Maureen Kirby. In a similar vein, but writing at a somewhat earlier point, Elaine Tuttle Hansen provides a detailed analysis of some of the strategies that Drabble uses in *Ice Age* to subvert history, chronology, and narration. She claims that:

> In the opening paragraph, then, [where Anthony has noticed an unusual dead pheasant in his pond] the narrative strategy underscores the fact that while the boundary between them is often obscured, there will be at least two different perspectives on the story to follow, the narrator's and the character's. The careful reader is warned from the outset that the distinction will often be a puzzling one but is also obliged to see that the narrator knows more than Anthony and will share that knowledge, in both explicit commentary and more subtle ways (analogy, imagery, etc.) with the reader.[15]

Hansen makes these comments because of the many places in the text where, as we have already seen, Drabble backtracks, flips, or diverts the reader's attention from what appeared to be straightforward narration. In addition to a number of undercuttings of the narrative that appear at key points throughout the text, this more-than-omniscient narrator ends the work with the following lines on Alison, one of her four main characters (and one whose primary relationship had been with Anthony): "Alison there is no leaving. Alison can neither live nor die. Alison has Molly. Her life is beyond imagining. It will not be imagined. Britain will recover, but not Alison Murray."[16] The crucial move here is that from the sentence "Her life is beyond imagining" to "It will not be imagined." The intrusion of the authorial "will" reminds the dazzled reader that this is, after all, simply a novel and that the entire work is a fiction created by the imagination of an inventive human, namely Margaret Drabble. The effect is stunning. There is a Foucaultian distancing here that is worthy of *Las Meñinas*.

Valerie Grosvenor Myer, in an early volume of criticism of Drabble, provides an interesting take on Drabble's particular historicism. Myer sees a clash between a sort of history-through-the-arts approach and what she terms a more Puritan approach; regardless of what this tells us about the later novels, there is no question that history as a chain of culture (however miserable) is part of what Drabble wants to get across.[17] It is as if we are stuck on our planet with a train of circumstances behind us, at least some of which, during odd moments, might provide us with solace. It is clear, of course, that this train is a two-edged sword. It is precisely its existence that perplexes Faro so much in *The Peppered Moth*. But part of Drabble's take on the malleability

---

14 Skoller, *The In-Between of Writing*, 38.
15 Tuttle Hansen, Elaine (1985), "The Uses of Imagination: Margaret Drabble's The Ice Age," *Critical Essays on Margaret Drabble*, Boston: G.K. Hall & Co., Inc., 151–168.
16 *Ibid.*, 166.
17 Grosvenor Myer, Valerie (1974), *Margaret Drabble: Puritanism and Permissiveness*, New York: Barnes and Noble Books.

of history is that we see it differently in different contexts. Our personal slants are the products of the very situations in which we find ourselves as we interpret historical moments. Reflecting on the place of the arts in one of the earlier works, *Jerusalem the Golden*, Myer writes:

> Many of Margaret Drabble's characters share the Puritan suspicion of the arts. An artist herself, she has a very different view as expressed in her books. [T]he arts... represent a whole way of life.... This culture takes centuries to grow, and embodies a set of values, a spiritual generosity, a richness older and more valuable than, completely antithetical to, the narrow penny-pinching utilitarianism in which Clara [protagonist of *Jerusalem*] has been reared.[18]

Pushing Myer's point a bit, one is tempted to say—as later works seem to want to make clear—that it is not simply that the arts represent an "older richness." What is at stake here is another way of seeing; the centuries during which the arts are growing are centuries filled with human lives, many of which represent the most unfortunate of circumstances. Working-class men and women already instinctively know this; the arts (like the classics embodied by Anthony's Oxbridge friend in *Ice Age*) provide a window for a way of seeing the historical in a different mode, as something that had at least moments of light and from which we might be able to catch rays of hope. It is this aspect of Drabble's stance toward the arts that meshes with her concern for multiple histories.

Finally, Lorna Irvine makes similar comments with respect to a sense of time in her essay "No Sense of Ending: Drabble's Continuous Fictions."[19] In still another take on the chronological Drabble, Irvine finds the lack of closure—stated, not simply implied—at the ends of many of the novels extremely important for a variety of reasons. Irvine notes that "Drabble's novels emphasize arbitrary conclusions by their very structures."[20] Irvine is commenting here on the very features for which, so far, we have used passages from *Ice Age* as exemplars. Alison's stated lack of future, and the narrator's simultaneous intrusion into the text, while distancing herself from it, are for Irvine important signals that lack of closure is a feminist mode for Drabble.[21] It is difficult to know how much this particular set of Drabblean twists has to do with issues that might be characterized as feminist—in any case, there is no question that the lack of ending, terse forced ending, or simply implied ending of many of the novels is, as we have seen, a hallmark of her writing. There is also no question that, as Irvine also says, this is a "philosophical" choice.[22] One is not going too far to push this line with respect to Drabble, as the sudden appearance of these markers in the text can do little but send an authorial intent, and also the message that that intent is a crucial one.

---

18 *Ibid.*, 115.
19 Irvine, Lorna, "No Sense of Ending: Drabble's Continuous Fictions," in ed. Ellen Cronan Rose, *Critical Essays on Margaret Drabble*, Boston: G.K. Hall & Co., 73–85.
20 *Ibid.*, 75.
21 *Ibid.*, 74–75. This point is made by Irvine throughout her essay.
22 *Ibid.*, 74.

An intriguing aspect of the body of work that constitutes criticism of Drabble is that, as it proceeds over time, it tends to become more aware of the subtleties of Drabble's writing. Thus earlier criticism seemed to miss or be unaware of Drabble's self-conscious use of history, the notion of a social construction, and the various devices of narration—there is little allusion to any of this material in, for example, Myer's work.[23] Skoller's 1990s compendium of critical views of three women writers, Drabble among them, makes decided use of postmodern terminology; Rose's anthology is somewhere between, with some authors appearing to have a greater awareness of Drabble's irony. As one might expect, a fair assessment of these efforts is simply that they reflect what each decade brought to various readings. Since *A Summer Bird-Cage* was published in 1964, Drabble's early work well precedes the beginnings of the international feminist movement, and is too far back to be expected to exhibit the sort of self-consciousness that came later. The 1970s saw the sort of turn in criticism that made full use of feminist categorization—hence the emphasis on this in Myer's volume. From roughly the mid-1980s on, the rise in the influence of French theory has more or less mandated that, where possible, readings making use of poststructuralist or other "post" categories be given.

It is, of course, a strength of Drabble's work that it lends itself to these various readings. But the one element of commonality here is the emphasis on Drabble's use of interior narration; the effectiveness of this device, especially insofar as it allows the narrator to posit a number of queries, is not in question. Jane, Alison, and Faro (protagonists, respectively, of *The Waterfall*, *The Ice Age*, and *The Peppered Moth*) do not go at life without bewilderment. Their sense of bewilderment, Drabble seems to hope, matches ours.

Feminism

Valerie Grosvenor Myer's work *Margaret Drabble: Puritanism and Permissiveness* has the feminist emphasis that it does because, bluntly, Drabble's early work is overwhelmingly dominated by female protagonists.[24] To say that they have specific concerns is, of course, to say nothing new: so much has often been the case with a number of women authors. But what makes the novels of Margaret Drabble remarkable in this regard is the extent to which their particular concerns mesh with that of the educated or thoughtful person in general—and then spin off from those more generalized questions in various ways that allow for feminist development. Both Jane and Alison have projects, reflect, and are embarked on a range of activities, but their paths are mined with various disasters, many of which are the result of the men in their lives or social male construction in general. Bessie Bawtry, lead female character in the early part of *The Peppered Moth*, is one of the first women from Yorkshire to attend Cambridge. But there is little in England at the time that would make it possible for a woman to benefit from such an education, and the

---

23 Although Myer's book is frequently mentioned in any list of Drabble criticism, it was published in 1974.

24 There seems to be general agreement that few solid male characters are to be found in Drabble's work until *The Ice Age*.

combined social pressures of home, family and the general scheme of things prevent Bessie from making use of the obvious gifts that she possessed. Bessie's plight then becomes the plight of future generations, as her general unease and misery infect those around her, leading her daughter to various forms of rebellion that culminate in Faro's situation.

If we ask ourselves what Drabble intends to accomplish here, it is clear that it is no accident that women are the central characters in so many of the novels.

Early feminist criticism focused on Drabble as part of a wave of British novelists whose work was regarded, at the time, as heralding the new views of women. Before the more decidedly Continental criticism came into vogue, Elaine Showalter had already noticed Drabble's work, and she is featured prominently in *A Literature of Their Own*.[25] In these early attempts to come to grips with Drabble's overall strategies, she is seen, at least by Showalter, as valorizing crucial parts of the female experience. This is particularly remarkable insofar as it betokens a sort of willful ignoring of other aspects of Drabble's writing. Here is Showalter on Drabble and motherhood:

> For Drabble's heroines, at least up to Rose Vassiliou in *The Needle's Eye* (1972), there is a kind of peace in the acknowledgement of, and submission to, female limitation.... Rosamund Stacey [in *The Millstone*]...becomes pregnant in a single encounter with a man she admires but has no claims upon. Rosamund is pretty, self-disciplined, and courageous; but, in bearing a child, she is brought to admit that she has lost control of her own destiny. She is humbled, first by her body, which forces a reluctant admission of femaleness upon her, then by the startling strength of her love for the child.... Children are the compensation for feminine surrender.[26]

It is not so much that Showalter's remarks lack accuracy in their own way; it is simply that questions of "surrender," for Drabble, frequently turn into larger sorts of issues, and, as we have seen, a different sort of reading of Drabble at a later point will emphasize some of these concepts. Surrender to the body is, in fact, a human issue—it is exactly the sort of metaphysical signaling that in *The Peppered Moth* will be taken to its limit as a quest for answers to the great questions of "whyness" and "whatness."

Showalter also writes that "Drabble finds a female resolution to the feminine conflict between biological and artistic creativity."[27] What this resolution is is by no means clear from the later novels: as we have seen, for Alison there is "no ending." The implied resolution asks more questions than it answers. Myer's work, however, puts still another twist on a sort of feminist reading of Drabble: Myer implies that the arts themselves not only provide a richness for cultural continuity (and an implied take on the notions of historicity that seem to be foregrounded in all of Drabble's work), but that fulfillment through the arts is somehow part of a female transcendence. It is probably for these reasons that Myer sees the relationships of the female protagonists in the early novels as being heavily involved in the questions

---

25 Drabble was one of only a few novelists contemporary at that time to be so featured.
26 Showalter, *A Literature*, 305.
27 *Ibid.*, 306.

surrounding the status of arts in human life. Myer sees Jane in *The Waterfall* as someone who attempts to make an artistic pattern from her own life, and she sees Drabble as being self-consciously aware of this—in this case, Drabble is writing about the writer. Myer claims:

> But, Jane writes, "there is no conclusion." She refuses to give us the neat solutions offered us by art, but denied us by life, which continues on its way without end, like the waterfall of the title. *The Waterfall* is a complete and satisfactory statement about the relations between art and life, and the nearest to being a flawless work of art in itself that Drabble has produced.[28]

Newer feminist readings push us in other directions. For the last decade or so, a great deal of emphasis has been placed on "connectedness" as a feminist trope, following along the lines of research of Carol Gilligan and Dorothy Dinnerstein.[29] Although this work was never intended as intersecting straightforwardly with literary criticism, a great deal has been made of such work. It is intriguing that much of what pushes a feminist analysis of Drabble is not so much her portrayal of female characters, but rather her portrayal of changing dynamics for male characters. Showalter compares Drabble to the Brontes because they both have a Yorkshire and moor background; as she says, the Bronte novels have been a "controlling myth" for her writing.[30] But a better comparison might be, blunt though it might seem, between a character such as Mr. Rochester in *Jane Eyre* and some of the characters in Drabble's later novels.

However overworked the notion of connection may be, the alterations in Anthony Keating's character in *The Ice Age* serve perfectly to capture a renascent feminist twist in the post-1980 novels. The original, money-mad Anthony who was responsible for the destruction of a number of old buildings in his quest to build up the "new Britain" is gradually replaced by an oddly-caring, paternal and parental Anthony, who gives up his bad habits, helps to care for Alison's disabled child, and putters around the kitchen cooking. As Lynn Veach Sadler writes, "He believes that he cares more for buildings than people, but his actions belie him."[31] He not only becomes a warmer, less competitive and more fulfilled human being—one more "connected," as it were—but he also begins to question the class assumptions that had driven him in the first place. Originally wanting to break away from the do-nothing, monied group into which he was born, he had set off on a rebellious quest to actually earn large amounts of money. But with Alison gone and in his new role as caretaker of Molly, he notices that he has even less in common with his houseguests (former friends) than he had thought. Of one evening, Drabble writes:

> It grew late, and Giles and Pamela and the chauffeur finished the bottle: Anthony, sober, watched the level drop and began to hope that it would drop so far that his guests would

---

28 Myer, *Puritanism*, 123.
29 Gilligan, Carol (1982), *In a Different Voice*, Cambridge: Harvard University Press; Dinnerstein, Dorothy (1979), *The Mermaid and the Minotaur*, New York: Harper and Row.
30 Showalter, *A Literature*, 304.
31 Veach Sadler, Lynn (1986), *Margaret Drabble*, Boston: Twayne Publishers, 35.

not notice the deficiencies of their accommodation. For, he now realized, he did not think he had any extra sheets.... He himself had not made his bed for weeks.[32]

Anthony has changed in more ways than one. In his new role as housekeeper, he is more concerned about salving Molly's feelings than cleaning—he has completely dropped out of his former life.

Faro's mother and father, in *Peppered Moth*, put a new tack on the dynamic in their own relationship. Chrissie and Nick have a mesmerizing sexual relationship, of the sort that, for a certain generation, defines the 1960s. But Nick is callous, unstable, irresponsible, and a victimizer of women and anyone else who crosses his path. He is also the quintessential male. In her portrayal of Nick, Drabble makes it clear that the lover whose sexual acrobatics caused Chrissie to feel that "She had been freed of the body through the body" is a worthless human being, one of the sort who should be avoided at all costs.[33]

Between the old Anthony and Nick there might have been little to choose. But the later Anthony is that rarest of beings: a biological male who exhibits the caring properties that we associate with women. In this depiction, Drabble indeed achieves something for critics, feminist and nonfeminist alike.

Post-Drabble

Feminist readings of Drabble, taken in conjunction with a sort of large gloss on what might be deemed to be philosophical in her work, push us in the direction of using specific strands of contemporary Continental theory to try to get to the bottom of what Drabble is doing. At an earlier point we had adverted to Foucault: Drabble's repeated twists on the notion of the historical run into her metaphysical preoccupations, and yield an unnerving sense of the contingency of anything thought to be historical.

Lois McNay tells us of how a sense of importance can be attached to Foucault when seen through a feminist lens:

> [O]ne of the central issues is whether it is possible and desirable to formulate and justify strategies of social action and change with reference to universal notions of rationality and morality. In other words, the debate centers around the extent to which Enlightenment metanarratives of rationality and justice are valid in respect to the justification of action in contemporary society.[34]

It is those very "Enlightenment metanarratives" that are interrogated by Drabble in her work. *The Ice Age*, as we have seen, leaves one with a shaky grasp of what is actually constitutive of a history at a given point in time; *The Waterfall* emphasizes the disparity between the views of the female and male protagonists. But it is one of

---

32 Drabble, *Ice Age*, 78.
33 Drabble, *Peppered Moth*, 230.
34 McNay, Lois (1992), *Foucault and Feminism: Power, Gender and the Self*, Boston: Northeastern University Press, 119.

Drabble's most recent works, *The Peppered Moth*, that plays most roughly with our sense of history, destiny, and the human predicament.

Faro's work for a popularized science magazine takes her on a quest involving DNA, Cotterhall Man, and a host of relatives with whom she had originally had little more than a passing acquaintance. Imagining the chain of misery that has brought her to her present life (and, as we have seen, Faro thinks in concrete terms—many couplings are involved), she questions when and where the chain will end. As she and Steve Nieman, inadvertent discoverer of the local skeleton of Cotterhall, tour the site, she is taken in by a collection of artifacts at the site's opening. She looks at a photograph dated 1962:

> To the left of the picture stands a middle-aged man in an overall, with an important wallet in his breast pocket. He is staring intently through his thick serious glasses at a metallic object which he is holding in both hands.... The gentleman's expression of judicious pride is delightful. The caption reads 'This photograph shows the workshop at Peat Handworth Ltd on Common Road, Breaseborough. What this firm used to manufacture is unknown. Does anyone recognize this gentleman or what he is holding?'
> So quickly, says Steve, do we vanish from history.[35]

Faro tries to grapple with the notion that this is her allotment—brief moments, and then a disappearance so abrupt and final that individuals will not recognize something demonstrably hers even after the passage of a mere three or four decades.

But Drabble's point, of course, is that, although such a trajectory might be statistically common, English schoolchildren do recognize the names of, for example, Henry VIII, Catherine of Aragon and Anne Boleyn. The question that the text invites us to ponder is: What arbitrary set of differences yields the completely different result?

Just as Foucault's commentary on *Las Meñinas* tells us about a change in Europe's attitude toward itself, we can position ourselves so as to create differing layers of intelligibility with respect to that which we encounter. This is, in fact, much of Foucault's point, insofar as he is concerned with some conception of history. Clive Cazeaux writes:

> The organization of thought becomes visible, Foucault maintains, through the tension or 'middle ground' which exists between competing epistemes or belief systems, for example, between, on the one hand, the codes and understandings which make us feel at home in a culture—'its languages, its schemes of perception, its exchanges, its techniques, its values'—and, on the other, scientific theories explaining how the world is ordered.[36]

This "tensional middle ground," as Cazeaux has it, is revelatory, and it is precisely this middle ground that constitutes a large part of the thought-provoking apparatus of much of Drabble's work. It is certainly overtly at play in *The Peppered Moth*, since the intersection of science with our everyday lives is one of the points of departure for the text as a whole. Faro is comfortable with a scientific view until that view begins to push her into a realm of discomfiting truths that impinge on her daily

---

35 Drabble, *Peppered Moth*, 273.
36 Cazeaux, *Continental*, 372.

activities. After all, Cotterhall Man once had a life: it is simply that there is no way, now, to get at what that life might possibly have meant. This rather unnerving point of view forces Faro into a new way of seeing.

If Foucauldian views of history are crucial for an understanding of what it is that Drabble sets out to do, her interest in wordplay and similar twists is also a remarkable feature of her novels. Obvious symbolism of the sort that is most likely ironic is also a feature; as more than one critic has noted, birds—at once a symbol of hope and freedom, but oddly detached from hope and freedom in the work in question—abound in *The Ice Age*. The female protagonist of *The Waterfall* is Jane Gray, named, one is tempted to think, for the Queen of Nine Days, except that the spelling is off by one letter. The hypergifted historical Jane of the Tudor period is reported to have taken a dim view of her brief life, and especially her relationship with her parents. Drabble no doubt intends us to see *The Waterfall*'s Jane in the same way.

Each turn in a character's point of view not only provides us with a new lens, but allows us to see through the same lens, as it were, but from a different vantage point. Thus Len and Maureen in *The Ice Age* are both semi-working class, and driven by concern for the material, but Maureen exhibits a level of care for the individual that Len does not. Anthony and Alison come from what was traditionally regarded as a better background in Britain, but it does not avail them in the money-making late 1960s and early 1970s, nor does reverie about their past lives improve their spirit. Bessie Bawtry's Cantabridgian glories are special in her period in *The Peppered Moth*, not nearly so special in her daughter Chrissie's lifetime, and best seen as the result of an accidental DNA sequence during Faro's. The Gauldens, untraceable East Europeans with a past scarred by the Holocaust, are fortunate, according to Faro. If their past really is that unknowable, it is unlikely to be traced.

Just as, on Foucault's analysis, *Las Meñinas* forces on the viewer the unsettling realization that the painter is completely conscious of his work and its effect on the viewer, Drabble's stance in *Moth*, for example, makes the reader extremely aware of her consciousness, as an author, of her effect. The constant use of "see her," with respect to Bessie, particularly in the opening sections of the book, distances the reader from Bessie and her tale in precisely the way that is needed to bring in the later tension of viewing that story as one of accidental matings and mitochondrial pairings. It is difficult to accept that the misery deplored by Faro is more or less an accident of fate, but that is precisely what her work with the Cotterhall Man, and her own writing for science magazines, would suggest. How Faro can make her pain more manageable and more tractable is not something that Drabble can suggest or explain. Perhaps the fact that Bessie later dies on an ocean voyage while watching a television projection of the ship's forward movement in the ocean is as poignant an image as any of what Drabble aims to achieve.[37]

Lynn Veach Sadler remarks, of the ending portions of *The Ice Age*, that "While ambiguity abounds, there are fewer authorial intrusions. The playfulness that remains,

---

[37] Drabble notes that "eternity moves toward her," even while she pretends not to believe in it.

deliberately, provides relief from the gloom that is both reported and conveyed."[38] Drabble's playfulness almost always signals a shift in view, and, as we have seen, that shift in view is crucially important to an understanding of her works. History, grand narratives, our own stories of our lives—all of these are inventions that can be seen from multiple perspectives. Which perspective we choose has a great deal to do with the outcome of the narrative. It is a remarkable feature of Drabble's work that Margaret Drabble, the "traditional" novelist, is a most untraditional chronicler of sequences of events.

Is it Philosophical?

Despite all of our concerns thus far, a number of strands of argument would remind us that a philosophical view is not simply any view. Admiration for Drabble's grasp of literature—indeed, of entire cultures—should not, one could argue, blind us to the fact that her novels have a surface appeal and certainly do not, at least on first reading, seem to carry the weight of either Joyce or Woolf.

Here we reintroduce some material addressed at an earlier point in this chapter, for there is no question that debates surrounding history, or queries with respect to "how we got here" might be regarded as the classic big questions. Rather, we need to ask ourselves if there is anything in an author's style that would prevent our taking her work seriously in this regard, particularly if it appears that she herself does not always take her work seriously.

Drabble is perhaps the best adjudicator of this debate, for the later novels seem deliberately to depart from the measured tone of the earlier ones, and, as many have argued, from the sense felt in some of the earlier works that they were "women's" works. The title of *The Peppered Moth* alone, alluding as it does to Darwinian concerns, evokes the nature of the large issues that Drabble does indeed address. Science occurs not only as an issue, but accurate allusion is made to a number of scientific views, and it is not inaccurate to say that the author does a good job of presenting some of the disputes surrounding the very issues she raises. Again, this self-conscious presentation must strike the reader as having the intention of raising questions of philosophic import.

In our overview of the ancient battle in the preceding chapter, we noticed that part of the concern—at least as articulated by the ancients themselves—was that literature possessed too great a tendency to push the emotions, with too small (or perhaps no) emphasis on training oneself to view things in a detached and deliberate manner. What makes Drabble's novels remarkable is the extent to which she covers both sides of the debate, so to speak. Her protagonists frequently ask themselves philosophical questions, respond emotionally, and then berate themselves for their response. Thus Jane, in *The Waterfall*, is well aware that she is behaving irrationally during the absence of her lover, and her despair is brought on partly by her own inability to control herself. Faro, in *Moth*, realizes that it is fruitless to question science or to become angry because DNA sequencing yielded a certain set of characteristics, yet

---

38 Sadler, *Drabble*, 114.

she notices that she cannot help but respond with anger to the chain of misery, and she is still more angry with herself for having that response. Thus Drabble's work is not only philosophical, but aware of its philosophical pretensions. This makes for much of the distancing that several critics have interpreted as "postmodern," but it also makes for a well thought-out novel, and for much more intriguing reading.

Several critics have wanted to label much of Drabble's metaphysical positioning as a concern for "fate," but it is not at all obvious that the author herself would choose that terminology. Drabble sees herself as an individual who wants to ask life's fundamental questions, and she is literate enough to know that we commonly regard such queries as the province of metaphysics. As Lynn Veach Sadler indicates, Drabble has "moved from the semi-autobiographical to wider and wider canvas." [39] It is not simply fate that interests Drabble—it is how men and women respond to the circumstances in which they are born and reared, and what they make of the hand that they are dealt. If they are thoughtful individuals, then it is inevitable that, along the way and as part of the process, they will begin to question that hand—but Drabble's characters often do this simply as part of a larger questioning. Alison's view of England, its growth, the appearance of its cities, and the general scheme of things after her return to visit her daughter in Wallacia is that it is "monstrous, inhuman, ludicrous." [40]

To do Drabble justice, it is, of course, necessary to widen our scope when considering the philosophical to questions beyond those that fall under the traditional five rubrics of philosophical thought. Contemporary feminist concerns would be deemed by many to be philosophical, and, as we have seen, almost all of Margaret Drabble's critics agree that she does indeed have such concerns. Drabble does not simply naively question woman's place: it is not woman in general, it appears, that really concerns this author. Rather, she is concerned about women intellectuals who have received the sort of education that, in the past, used to be reserved for males. Her concern for Bessie Bawtry in *Peppered Moth* is so great that it nearly overshadows the later characters who clearly are supposed to be important in the work: Bessie is an irritable and unsympathetic woman, but we can see why when we follow her path from a Yorkshire secondary school to Cambridge, and then to a life of drudgery and housewifery, forced on her by a set of circumstances largely beyond her control. That Cambridge was supposed to represent an escape route, and that Bessie was supposed never to have set foot in Yorkshire again, is made clear at several points. But for educated women, in her time and in ours, escapes are often blocked.

The collision of education, social class and gender roles frequently yields explosive results in Drabble's work, and some of the conflict of *The Ice Age* is a result of those flint strikings. We might expect to find more emphasis on Alison, but a number of reviewers have noted that this work is unusual for its strong male characters. Anthony is repelled by his social class, but entranced by Len's financial maneuverings. And yet in the end Anthony does a most unmanly thing—he becomes, somewhat against his will, a househusband. When Alison returns, the woman who should (one would suppose) have applauded her husband's homely attributes is somewhat dumbstruck

---

39 *Ibid.*, 6.
40 Drabble, *Ice Age*, 172.

by his success in this area, and, in an odd role reversal, begins to resent it. The ensuing pages are among the most successful of this particular work.

Taken in Whole

Our view of Drabble's work has thus far pointed in the direction of moving away from her earlier critics, who saw her in "women's writing" categories, and trying to establish a larger view. John Hannay has written of her:

> Art formulates...truths and allows the reader vicariously to confront the irrational. By portraying overpowering emotions in stories with familiar contours, fiction teaches us to recognize inevitable consequences and to appreciate their form. But is recognition and appreciation enough?...
> Drabble speaks frequently in interviews of being in harmony with fate, an acceptance of one's lot that invites grace.[41]

Drabble's peculiar gift seems to be the creation of believable and memorable characters through whom we can see a certain time. It certainly is the case that many of her most sympathetic and remarkable characters are women, but, as we have seen, male characters such as Anthony (or even Chrissie's father, Joe Barron, in *Peppered Moth*) succeed in making a strong impression on the reader. Drabble's attempt to portray the larger picture, along with her sensitivity to the plight of the educated woman, allows the reader to identify strongly with the characters without forgetting that the characters are fictional creations evocative of a time and place. As we have also argued, Margaret Drabble's shifting and kaleidoscopic takes on what might be constitutive of the historical allow her to be characterized, at least to some extent, with a number of authors who usually receive some sort of "post-" rubric when their work is given critical examination.

Drabble is at her best in the evocation of painful interiors and their interplay with the external forces faced by all human beings. Thus Faro's musings about the inevitability of her particular misery, a passage already examined here, become a trope for the misery of every thoughtful person. Jane's anguished longing for her lover in *The Waterfall* has been remarked upon by many as being a particularly poignant portrayal of female love:

> As she sat there waiting for him, waiting for the telephone to ring, waiting for the sound of his car, she thought that it had perhaps been for this that she had emptied her existence, for this dreadful, lovely, insatiable anguish, for these intolerable hopes. She wondered if other people had ever suffered so....[42]

Anthony's difficult passage from resentful caretaker of Molly to fulfilled homeperson examines not only gender roles, but the division that everyone feels between the public and the private life.

---

41   Hannay, John (1986), *The Intertextuality of Fate: a Study of Margaret Drabble*, Columbia: University of Missouri Press, 100–101.

42   Drabble, Margaret (1969), *The Waterfall*, New York: Alfred A. Knopf, 157–158.

Although her focus is on characters who possess enough formal education, or reflectivity, or both, to question a great deal about their lives, it is also the case that Drabble has created a number of characters who are far from thoughtful, and who seem to encounter some of life's larger questions only in bursts or starts. Thus both Len Wincobank and Maureen Kirby of *The Ice Age* are all the more vivid simply because neither of them is particularly intellectually oriented, nor are they given to any sort of tortured response to their everyday lives. When Len and Maureen do finally ask themselves some questions, the reader is stunned—no doubt an intended effect.

Those who see Drabble as a more traditional novelist have probably mistaken her ability to narrate a tale for something more standard than it actually is. Since recognizable character and plot are no longer *de rigeur* in some circles, their appearance in a novel may lead the unsuspecting to a blindness to the work's other attributes. Drabble's work is traditional only in this way: there is indeed a plot, there are characters whose lives can be followed, and there is some sort of denouement to the storyline (although this is, in some cases, in doubt). But Margaret Drabble's repeated twists on chronology, history and place all provide a great deal more food for speculation than some have thought. Those who see her as some sort of heir to George Eliot apparently have missed a great deal of the complexity of her work. Since Showalter was careful to cite Drabble several times in *A Literature of Their Own*, her place in the canon was more or less assured before some of her later works were published. What Showalter actually said is "Margaret Drabble and Doris Lessing are routinely compared by critics to George Eliot and George Sand"; at another point she said "Of all the contemporary English women novelists, Margaret Drabble is the most ardent traditionalist." [43] But Showalter wrote this in the late 1970s, and even then seemed to be basing her judgment on the preponderance of women characters in the works, their names, and so forth. A closer reading of the later novels demands a second look at the entire oeuvre.

---

43 Showalter, *A Literature*, 302, 304.

Chapter Three

The Feminist Drabble

If we experience little or no difficulty in categorizing Drabble as someone whose writing is philosophical in content and tone, it might seem easier, if anything, to characterize Drabble's work as feminist. But this initial take on Drabble—one that, as we have seen, was repeated by almost all of her early critics—is considerably too simplistic if it relies on the usual modes of feminist categorization.

There is no question that Drabble is concerned with women's issues, with the lot of women in general, and of educated women in particular. There is also no question that the female characters in most of her novels tend to be more finely drawn. But there is a great deal more to the assertion that Margaret Drabble's work can be considered feminist than this: there must be, because any such flat characterization, with respect to any category, does not do justice to the complexity of the work of Drabble as an author.

Drabble's novels are filled with female tropes and images that are sometimes easily read, sometimes subtly stated, and sometimes simply stunning in their strength. Images of childbirth, blood, milk, lactation, and female sexuality abound throughout the works; indeed, in some of the novels the passages detailing these images are among the most remarkable and memorable in the novel. Drabble seems to want to push the reader to an acceptance of the female body, and then a movement of transcendence. In this regard, we might think of her overall project as somewhat like that of Simone de Beauvoir. If being female means being enmeshed in the body, then Drabble's women characters are female enough—and in their confrontation with their femininity they frequently move on to a certain strength.

In *The Waterfall*, Jane and James, her cousin's husband, first lie in bed together in the same bed in which Jane has just given birth. This scene occurs within the first few pages of the novel, and there are few passages by Drabble in any other work that are as stunning as this particular sequence for its sheer evocation of the body. Not all of the important images are brought together at once: rather, there is a slow build-up, as Drabble prepares the reader for the near inevitability of James' approach. We are first introduced to the birth bed, with Jane in it:

> Jane lay there, propped up against the pillows, and watched the snow fall beyond the dark shining pane of the window: there was no noise except the woman's heavy breathing, and the small feeble movements of her new daughter, who was trying to suck her emaciated thumb. Everything was soft and still: the whole night and Jane's nature with it, seemed to be subdued in a vast warm lull, an expectancy, a hesitation, a suspension and remission of trial.[1]

---

1   Drabble, *The Waterfall*, 6.

But this is a bed of childbirth, and as James draws closer to it—he is supposed to be sitting with her, watching and trying to help—the fluids of the bedclothes are alluded to and then described on more than one occasion. As Jane needs to get up, James tries to help her:

> And she slid herself out of bed, seeing as she did that she left behind her red blood on the white sheets—pulling the covers quickly over the bleeding—and she started to move, stiffly, to the door.[2]

But Jane suspects, although she perhaps does not want to admit it to herself, that James wants to join her in this bed:

> There was distinctly in him some ominous strain: she wondered whether it was merely the reflection of rumors she had heard, stories reaching her feebly over the years through a thousand alterations, or whether it was the man himself that so affected her. A dangerous man, she said to herself: a dangerous man, sitting mildly there, by the fire, reading, smoking, drinking some tea. She had once thought herself a dangerous woman, and it was in fear of such knowledge that she now lay where she was, in the bed she lay in, lost, harmless, weak, her shadow falling nowhere, occupying no space, blotting out no light.[3]

And then, after several evenings of James' sitting with her, helping her up, making her soft-boiled eggs, and taking diapers out of the room, we are given the following:

> There was a long silence, and then he said, across the whole distance of that large room—and with such intention, as though each foot of that space had been measured and ordained, as though the exact pitch of his voice could reach her only across just such a distance, "I want to be in that bed. The only place in the room is in that bed."[4]

Thus James spends the whole night in her bed, a bed in which she has recently given birth to a child, "profoundly asleep."[5] Drabble pushes the imagery of James, sleep, the bed, blood, sweat and a silent commingling to let us know that this is sexuality and its concomitants seen from a female point of view. Just as the birth of a child is the result of the couplings that preceded it, so the turning toward another—characteristic not only of motherhood, but of any sort of caring—is itself the product of the warmth and tenderness that flow from the body like mother's milk. (In another scene, she nurses the baby with James present.) The ease with which the reader is enticed into this unusual world is matched only, in the text, by the ease with which James enters the bed: after the slow build-up, the expectation, and the quiet watching, his making the decision to sleep with Jane and her acquiescing seem like the most natural of actions. Drabble's mastery of prose signals not only a sure writer, but one who is demonstrably certain of her goals.

---

2   *Ibid.*, 21.
3   *Ibid.*, 29.
4   *Ibid.*, 35.
5   *Ibid.*, 37.

It is passages such as these from *The Waterfall* that make Drabble's writing as overtly feminist and female as it is: the surprised reader is dimly aware of the unusualness of the scene, and perhaps even less aware of the fact that the scene almost certainly could not have been written by a man. A sort of submerged sexuality, shown by James' sleeping the sleep of the innocent (like the baby) is not a male sexual take. Jane is a poet—at one point, she is described as being surprised that someone recognizes her existence outside of her own mind—but the creator of words has here created something else. The fluids of the body have mingled, and the result is the beginning of a long and unusually well-detailed affair, one that alters her conception of her life.

How is Drabble to be characterized as a feminist writer? Only carefully—only if we allow her the depth that is inherent in her work. All of the easy categorizations—the fact that she writes of women's concerns, or the thoughtfulness about the educated woman—have little to do with the parts of her writing that express a sensibility that might be more properly characterized as *écriture feminine*.

Nevertheless, it remains the case that a great deal of what has been written about Drabble expresses feminist concerns in the simpler, more ready-made ways that we have already mentioned. In fact, some critics seem determined to push a line of argument that denigrates Drabble's "feminism" because she does not always delineate her characters in such a way as to give them characteristics that mesh with a politicized feminist view. The emphasis on affairs, on heterosexual relations, and (at least in the cases of Jane Gray and Chrissie Gaulden, to name two characters) on growth fueled by deeply passionate attachment to men has led some writers to try to attribute a variety of motives to Drabble, or to characterize her work in other ways. It is important to try to come to grips with these lines of argument, because they represent a good deal of what is available in terms of published criticism. It is accurate to characterize much of this work as comparatively early—a good deal of it was published before the mid-1980s, and hence inevitably reflects the sorts of feminist views that were available at that time. As Joanne Creighton wrote in 1985, "Margaret Drabble's two most recent novels differ markedly from her earlier fiction.... Drabble here is increasingly preoccupied with the texture of contemporary urban life, including the trends, fads, trappings of mass urban culture.... The environment in which characters live is largely shaped from without."[6] It is also in the middle and later novels that Drabble has a number of male characters, and this facet of her writing cannot be ignored.

One Feminist View

Showalter's take on Drabble as a true daughter of the Brontes and George Eliot reflects the opening lines of argument with respect to the feminist tropes in Drabble's work. As we have seen, there is by no means unanimity on these features. Susan Spitzer, writing in the well-known Rose anthology, has a completely different view, and attempts to problematize the relationship between Drabble and any serious line of

---

6   Creighton, Joanne (1985), *Margaret Drabble*, New York: Methuen, 91.

argument that might be deemed to be feminist. In an interpretation of *The Millstone*, Spitzer takes a tack that can be summarized as one applicable, on Spitzer's terms, to a great many of Drabble's works. Spitzer sees the protagonist, Rosamund, as one who has not really grown by the novel's end. She writes:

> [T]he *Millstone* [is] a novel, [and] a work of realistic fiction. As an agent of mature moral discovery, however, Drabble's novel cannot be counted. The truths Rosamund arrives at a close reading of the text will reveal to be shabby, partial truths that only barely camouflage the more vital current of self-deception flowing through the novel.[7]

Spitzer seems not to be able to accept that the complexity of Drabble's characters is part of Drabble's intent; in fact, at a later point in the text, she specifically indicates that she has difficulty accepting the notion that Drabble intended that the reader see Rosamund as self-deceptive.[8] But it would seem to be a mistake not to allow Drabble this degree of complexity as an author; in fact, a close reading of her texts would seem to demand it.

A similar line of argument might be lodged against Faro (or Chrissie, for that matter) in *The Peppered Moth*. Faro spends a great deal of that novel in a hopeless relationship with Seb, a character who has virtually no redeeming qualities. One of Seb's last maneuvers to attempt to bind Faro to him is to tell her that he has terminal pancreatic cancer, and requires her help. As Faro goes to him—somewhat unwillingly—she admits to herself that it is by no means clear that Seb actually does have cancer, and that it is by no means clear that she believes him. At a later point in the novel, slightly before the end, Faro is able to establish a relationship with the archaeologist Steve Nieman, whose Cotterhall site she had been writing up, and at first she cheerfully tells herself what an improvement Steve is over Seb—he seems honest, and his flat is even clean and decorated.

Faro is in the middle of a long train of thought about the "unimportance" of the lives of those around her when she finally has a small epiphany just before the novel's end. Four pages before the end, in looking over items taken from the deceased members of her family, Faro muses "These are such little people. Unimportant lives in an unimportant place." But the last two paragraphs of the novel show Faro in the middle of a mental search. She has found, among the detritus, a sixpence, and realizes that she can hardly remember the last time that she saw this old-fashioned coin. Then:

> On the way down the stairs, she remembers, with a sense of sudden shock, the last time she had seen a silver sixpence. It had been hidden in the Christmas pudding that Bessie Barron had served up at her last family Christmas at Woodlawn.... Faro stands stock-still on the seventh step, for she can see Grandma's happy face, smiling, as Faro cries out and unwraps the silver treasure. Grandma Barrow had always made a good Christmas pudding.... After Bessie's death, Chrissie Barron had bought all her puddings from a shop.[9]

---

7   Spitzer, Susan, "Fantasy and Femaleness in Margaret Drabble's The Millstone," in ed. Ellen Cronan Rose, *Critical Essays on Margaret Drabble*, 86–105.
8   *Ibid.*, 104.
9   Drabble, *Moth*, 364–365.

It is clear at this novel's end that most of the "growth" that Faro has experienced throughout the work—most of her "insights"—has been a sham. Repelled by her own past and the lives of those who have stayed on in the small towns of the North, Faro has been all too dismissive of the everyday efforts of those who preceded her, efforts without which she might not have existed. The creation of a Christmas pudding with its effort (memorably, also a prominent part of *A Christmas Carol*) is precisely the sort of thing that women have done for centuries and for which they have received little credit. But it is also the sort of thing of which the links of human memory are made, and it is holiday times—again, so largely the product of women's work—that frequently stand out for us as adults. At the end of the novel, Faro is just beginning to see through her own self-deception—but it would indeed be a mistake to believe that Drabble does not intend us to see this.

The line of argument promulgated by Spitzer is noteworthy because it seems to cast Drabble in the ranks of those who, as we have said, are commonly labeled "traditional" novelists. Yet Drabble not only writes the body, so to speak, but she writes the mind, since she gives us female characters whose life courses alter them irrevocably, whether for good or ill. Faro is such a character; so is Jane Gray, and so is Alison Murray. Each experiences a degree of change that causes her to engage in intense self-questioning.

We have been in the process of examining the moral depth of Drabble's work, contra those who would contend that her work lacks this kind of configuration. But it needs to be stated that Drabble's focus on the body constitutes a version of that very writing that has been the crux of so much commentary in the past two decades, *écriture feminine*. It is probably going too far to suggest that Drabble is doing this consciously; there is nothing in her work or the commentary on it that suggests self-conscious employment of French theory (even Eleanor Honig Skoller, who mentions the poststructuralists in connection with Drabble, does not assume that Drabble is consciously aiming in their direction). But it is worth noting that passages similar to those cited earlier from *The Waterfall* evoke much that is in, for example, Cixous, and that there are similar passages throughout all of Drabble's novels.

An anthologized piece by Cixous, perhaps best-known in the English-speaking world for "The Laugh of the Medusa," opens with the following lines:

> I would like to write like a painter. I would like to write like painting.
> The way I would like to live. Maybe the way I manage to live, sometimes. Or rather: the way it is sometimes given to me to live, in the present absolute.
> In the happening of the instant.
> Just at the moment of the instant, in what unfurls it, I touch down then let myself slip into the depth of the instant itself.[10]

The "moment of the instant," the "unfurling," and the "slipping" are all very much a part of Drabble's writing, and particularly in those scenes—memorable in her work—that have to do with sex, childbirth, lactation, or illness. Her often very cerebral characters seem to feel very much more alive when completely engrossed

---

10 Cixous, Helene, "The Last Painting of the Portrait of God," in Cazeaux (ed.), 583–597.

in bodily pleasures, but not just any bodily pleasures. For the characters portrayed in this way are, for the most part, female characters and such bodily pleasures as athletic feats, or the partaking of food and drink do not figure nearly as extensively as sex, specifically female pleasures/sensations having to do with childbirth, or a sort of pleasure-in-illness (the latter is particularly pronounced in the portrait of Bessie Bawtry in *Moth*).

Drabble's prose in these instances captures "the present absolute," and the reader is left with the slightly stunned feeling that the passage in question has somehow perfectly captured a certain sort of moment. There is no distancing, typically, in these passages—and the kinds of ruminations in which male characters might later indulge after sex, or even during sex, do not often appear in Drabble's evocation of these extremely sensual experiences.

Criticism that attempts to assert that Drabble lacks a moral grounding misses the point. Because her work is overlain with a number of conceptual constructs, it may be difficult for the reader to pick them out. They are, as it were, part and parcel of the work. Elizabeth Fox-Genovese, like Spitzer, seems determined to read Drabble as a writer who fails in many ways; in one comment, she tersely characterizes the group of novels preceding *The Ice Age* as "A fictionalized English *Passages*."[11] But this misses the point with Drabble. In her work, the mind and the body are united in new and exciting ways, and the female and feminist tropes of the novels are both close to the surface and hidden in the depths.

Drabblean Ecriture

Although Luce Irigaray is not as closely associated with the notion of *écriture feminine* as some other French theorists, there is no question that what she discusses in, for example, *This Sex Which is Not One*, comes to the same thing.[12] As has been argued in the previous section, it is in this sort of discourse that Drabble's work is seen in its most advantageous setting. The flatter, more standard categories of feminism may not do justice to Drabble's work—indeed, they may lead to remarks such as the one cited by Elizabeth Fox-Genovese.

But Drabble's reliance on the body and her evocation of female sexuality—and other bodily sensations—is itself, in her strongest writing, a sort of an *écriture* of the woman. Here is Irigaray on "The Power of Discourse and the Subordination of the Feminine":

> Strictly speaking, *Speculum* has no beginning or end. The architectonics of the text, or texts, confounds the linearity of an outline, the teleology of discourse, within which there is no possible place for the "feminine," except the traditional place of the repressed, the censured....

---

11 Fox-Genovese, Elizabeth, "The Ambiguits of Female Identity: a Reading of the Novels of Margaret Drabble," *The Partisan Review*, 234–248.

12 Irigaray, Luce (1985), *This Sex Which is Not One*, trans. by Catherine Porter, Ithaca: Cornell University Press.

It is not a matter of toppling that [phallocratic] order so as to replace it—that amounts to the same thing in the end—but of disrupting and modifying it, starting from an "outside" that is exempt, in part, from phallocratic law.[13]

One could, of course, try to argue that there are features of the very structure of Drabble's novels that speak to these issues; one could try to claim that the lack of chronology, switching from first to third person narrative and then back again, or changes in point of view all indicate an attempt at what Irigaray is signaling. That, however, does not really come to grips with the problem. It is rather (however structurally odd or unusual some of the novels are) that there are passages in Drabble's writing where the "linearity" and "teleology" are disrupted because of the very matter about which Drabble writes, and because of her peculiar immersion in it. Thus, as we have seen at the opening of this chapter, there is a great deal in *The Waterfall* that moves along these paths: somewhat fantastic passages about sex and sexuality, and their effect on a woman, written in such a way as to leave the reader astonished. Drabble is gifted at writing about sex from a woman's point of view so that the reader (if not already familiar with it) actually may come to understand it for the first time. Or perhaps the reader, a woman, is too young, or inexperienced, to have any knowledge of what it is about which Drabble is writing. But Drabble's text will push beyond those boundaries. In that sense, which may well be the most important sense, portions of her works will be "outside" the phallocratic law.

We have seen how Drabble handles sex and acts of intercourse; she is no less adept at certain aspects of nursing, lactation and childbirth. These of-the-body experiences have been handled by a number of authors, but Drabble's feeling for them is something new. Thus the very aspects of nursing that most women prefer not to discuss—except, on rare occasions, with other women—are described by Drabble with an intense poignancy.

In writing of *écriture feminine*, Clive Cazeaux says the following:

Julia Kristeva, Luce Irigaray and Helene Cixous are leading figures in contemporary French radical feminism. Within this, however, they work from different and, at times, diametrically opposed viewpoints. Both Irigaray and Cixous entertain the notion of an *écriture feminine* or 'feminine writing' which embodies a new, differential and tactile approach to language. The importance given to the body by psychoanalysis as an object under interpretation is used by Irigaray to turn texts in the history of philosophy against themselves, drawing organic, textured language from arguments which outwardly try to suppress the epistemological significance of the body.[14]

As indicated, it would probably be an overstatement to try to say that Drabble is indulging in straightforward *écriture feminine*, because examples of this are probably best found in, for example, the writing of Cixous. Certainly the standardness of the narration of her novels, such as it is, does not manifest the marked differences that Cazeaux describes above. Nevertheless, the portions of Drabble's work that deal with the bodily topics already presented push in this direction.

---

13 *Ibid.*, 68.
14 Cazeaux, *Continental*, 499.

An "epistemology of the body," as Cazeaux has it, makes use of the connection between the mental and the physical and tends to ask us what it is that we "know" from our bodies that we could not otherwise know. This special, feminine knowledge can only come from certain kinds of experiences—that is why it is no exaggeration to say that a woman who has not, for example, become a mother would not have this sort of knowledge. But she would, presumably, have the knowledge that comes from regular menstruation (except for some very rare cases), and this knowledge, too, can be set out with the appropriate *écriture*.

It is even possible, as we have seen with the example of Anthony Keating in *The Ice Age*, that a male might come much closer to this sort of bodily knowledge than the average, objectifying heterosexual male standardly does. Some of the awareness could come from caretaking—there is an immersion in the physical for the caretaker, such as someone who cares for an elderly person, an Alzheimer's patient, or a small or disabled child (like Molly) that might bring forth a type of thought often associated with females. In any case, Drabble's texts are marked by attention to this kind of awareness, and some of her sharpest and most fluid writing appears to come in these sorts of passages.

Pushing the point a bit further, in a manner that is evocative not only of Anthony's growth, but of the growth of several other characters in the three main novels under consideration, Drabble will also signal an immersion in the realm of the senses simply by a heightened awareness of the detritus of everyday life. Before the passage alluded to earlier, when Faro comes to the realization that Bessie was the one responsible for her childhood plum puddings (into which she used to stick her fingers to find the "lucky sixpence"), there is the passage detailing Faro's exploration of Auntie Dora's leftover belongings:

> Her aunt's old driving licence, and her postwar ration book. A sheet of Polyfotos of a much-replicated fierce-eyed Chrissie Barron, aged about ten, in a panama school hat, and a similar sheet of her Uncle Robert, staring solemnly at the camera and half-strangled by a large knotted school tie. A photograph of the little sisters, Bessie and Dora, in their Sunday best, all frills and embroidery and sweetness. A photo of Grandma Barron's wedding day....[15]

The debris of everyday life is not, as Drabble indicates in another passage, ordinarily the stuff of which history is made, but that is precisely Drabble's point—it is the stuff of which daily lives are made, and daily lives, from the male point of view are frequently overlooked in the course of constructing "history." Thus she promulgates a notion of the lived life that valorizes the feminine, or anything that is not a part of the metanarrative. Cotterhall Man himself is outside of the narrative—he figures in it only because, in his importance as an object of physical remains, he has been discovered by one working in the realm of science, part of the grand narrative. But we all move toward the end that Cotterhall Man has achieved, and in the vast majority of cases we will be forgotten.

The importance of *The Waterfall* and *The Peppered Moth* here in particular is that each of them strongly questions the notion of the master narrative while at the same

---

15 Drabble, *Moth*, 361.

time saving large sections of the text for a sort of *écriture*, as we have seen. Jane's dramatization of the beginning of her affair with James (one that she later criticizes) has an overwhelming emphasis on the bodily, and from a female point of view. This is not the male version of the bodily, with its take on penetration and conquest. James' desire to share female bodily fluids, or to be in the same space in which childbirth has just taken place, is a crucially important evocation of the notion of the feminine. Nick Gaulden is the classic seducer, in *The Peppered Moth*, but Chrissie's anger at him is tempered somewhat by her memory of their extraordinary sex life, a life detailed again, from the point of view of the woman. These sections of these particular novels constitute an exercise in *l'écriture feminine*.

Poststructuralism Again

Lois McNay has recently written in *Foucault and Feminism* of the uses to which Foucault's theoretical stance may be put for feminist analysis.[16] Part of McNay's concern is to get clear on what might be deemed to be unhelpful about spurious attempts to use Foucault, or what she might call misunderstandings of his work. She sees his overall emphasis on the body as the locus of construction for much of Western thought (especially in its opposition to the mind) as extremely helpful for feminist theory, but only if uses of it are able to escape the trap of some sort of "essentialism." As she says:

> It is Foucault's notion of the body as the point where power relations are manifest in their most concrete form which, in the last few years, has made a significant contribution to feminist thinking on the body.... Although a notion of the body is central to a feminist understanding of the oppression of women, it needs to be thought through carefully if what is regarded as patriarchal logic—the definition of the social category of woman in terms of biological functions—is to be subverted and not compounded.[17]

Margaret Drabble intuitively understands these points, and a great deal of what she shows about such characters as Jane, Faro, Alison and Bessie speaks to these very issues. Bessie's becoming a mother, for example, was pivotal in her gradual decline from excited Oxbridge scholar to disgruntled, and nonfunctional, homemaker. In a sense, Bessie was simply the victim of the social forces of her time.

But McNay's reading of Foucault is helpful to us in more than one way. Between the somewhat simplistic reductive essentialism that would elide social factors, and a strict social constructionist view that leaves out the plain reality of the body, McNay postulates for Foucault what she refers to as a "libidinal" view. As she has it, "The libidinal body is used to install a theory of desire and ambivalence into an understanding of how identity is constructed."[18] Her point is that it is at the

---

16 McNay, Lois (1993), *Foucault and Feminism: Power, Gender and the Self*, Boston: Northeastern University Press.
17 *Ibid.*, 16–18.
18 *Ibid.*, 24.

interstices, the intersections of the material body and the social inscriptions upon it that the female body, in particular, is constructed.

Drabble's masterful handling of this material, particularly in certain passages of *The Waterfall*, indicates that female bodiliness cuts both ways. Just as the literal outpourings from the body have always, cross-culturally, been used to oppress women—since their fluids have usually been seen as "contaminating"—Drabble sees that a twist on this from a feminist standpoint results in a revalorization, while still making it obvious that portions of women's lot in male-dominated societies seem almost inevitable. On her first account of how she came to have James as her lover, Jane is (in the third person version) aware of the significance of the fact that James is entering into a childbirth bed, and all of the tropes of childbirth, milk, feeding and blood are used effectively to establish the underlying meaning of James' coming to her in this way. The more distanced, first-person account undercuts the authorial narrative of the first version, but in a way that does not do damage to the sort of point that McNay is making. If Jane comes to see herself as somewhat unreliable and self-deluded, this is no doubt partially because she knows that the mystical world that she tried to portray as inhabited by her and her lover does not exist in a public space. In that sense, Drabble is indeed concerned about the "libidinal body"; it is the body at the intersection of the material and its social construction, and it is this body that is the subject of the long discourse provided by Jane at the beginning of the opening chapter.

This tension between different versions of the body is a recurring one throughout Drabble's work. In the 1960s, liberated Chrissie wants to maintain that her affair with Nick is a form of self-fulfillment and rebellion against bourgeois values—and so it is, in the sense that it outrages everyone around her, including her fellow archaeologists on a dig—but the magnetic, transcendental sort of sex that Chrissie is said to have had with Nick ultimately is non-liberatory in the extreme, since Nick proves to be exactly the sort of womanizer that an older, more experienced person would have been able to detect at the start. The social conditioning of female sexuality runs smack up against its lived version, and this type of tension is present in almost all of Drabble's descriptions of love affairs.

All of the foregoing, while it may to some extent problematize Drabble with respect to feminism and the female body, does much to resuscitate a more sophisticated version of her writings that pushes beyond, for example, Showalter's analysis of her work in *A Literature*. Her extended takes on motherhood and sexuality do not simply attempt to redeem these topics; rather, they themselves indicate the complexity of them while still providing marvelous descriptions of sex and sexuality from a female point of view. It may be that sex during the period of Cotterhall Man, for example, can be placed within the scope of some form of goddess worship—certain feminist stances would ask us to do that. But Drabble would never settle for something so easy. Neolithic veneration of the female has very little to do with today, or even (according to *The Peppered Moth*) with why we might find that period particularly important.

A number of general lines of criticism of the "post" Continental analyses have dealt not only with the social construction of various agents, but with a critique of that concept of social construction. According to McNay, Foucault's general stance may be addressed in terms of what it fails to accomplish—it could be argued that the Foucauldian subject has very little merit, precisely because Foucault's emphasis on the construction of the subject leaves little room for actual persons. (A similar line of criticism has frequently been directed at the work of Judith Butler.) But McNay, in her setting out of Foucault, makes it clear that some of his later work goes some way toward the amelioration of this problem. As she claims, "The emergence of a notion of the self into Foucault's work has been interpreted by some critics as representing an abrupt turn-around in his intellectual project."[19]

Whether the change might rightfully be deemed to be as startling as some have claimed is not important here, but what is important is the extent to which Drabble, as a writer, surmounts this problem. The "old-fashionedness" of her novels rests largely on the sense of narrative and storytelling; it cannot be said that there is no plot, and it is not particularly difficult to follow the plot, at least in the earlier novels. So Drabble is not one of those who is guilty of giving us work purporting to be contemporary fiction that is so postmodern—or whatever label is applicable—that it cannot be read. Rather, what we are giving Drabble full credit for here is the extent to which her characters remain agents—and selves—while at the same time signaling the importance of the body and (in Foucauldian terms) the body's significance as a site of oppression.

No one can claim that Jane or Faro is without agency; indeed, as we have seen, Spitzer wants to claim that a character like Jane has not sufficiently recovered from her compulsive efforts at self-deception. But Chrissie and Jane both are women, and the extent to which they are entrapped by their bodies and the social construction surrounding their bodies is a hallmark of Drabble's work. Chrissie cannot resist Nick at least partly for the simple reason that he is an extraordinary lover. But the price attached to this transcendental sexuality—described by Drabble at length, and in detail—is a high one. Men are the aggressors and seducers; women the victims. Men enter the beds; women sleep in them while awaiting their entry. Jane allows James into her bed, but the astonishing sexual experience that is engendered by having sex in a bed of childbirth is one that is paid for by the willing Jane, accomplice and subordinate to the dangerous, "sulfurous" James.

What do these women characters learn? There are no easy lessons. The male characters are allowed the freedom—which simply mirrors the way that things are in various societies—to seduce again and again. Once having touched the sulfur and the fire, it is unclear whether anything of long-term worth can be gotten from the experience. But it is not the case that Drabble fails to ask this question. Rather, like several other areas, the question of the moral worth or worth in terms of self-growth of a sexual relationship is one from which Drabble does not back off. Her investigations make it clear that we, as readers, also have a great deal to learn from these various forays into and with the body.

---

19 *Ibid.*, 48.

Knowing Drabble

Recent work in feminist epistemology has heightened our awareness that matters epistemological can take a variety of guises. Thus if we want to forward the line of argument that there is much that is feminist—in a number of construals—about Drabble's work, we ought to be able to at least examine it with an eye toward epistemic issues.

The importance of the body for Drabble, and the salience of the different forms of bodily sensing that we have already examined with respect to *The Waterfall* and *The Peppered Moth*, signal to us how we might begin to think of Drabble and the epistemological. These concerns might, in fact, be deemed central for Drabble—it is obvious that some form of knowing and/or knowledge is what she is after in a great deal of what she writes.

Jane's relationship with James in *The Waterfall* was, as we have seen, begun in a childbirth bed. As their relationship continues, Jane looks to the past to try to find markers that might have signaled (in her earlier acquaintance with James, her cousin Lucy's husband) some of what was to come. Drabble writes of a sort of instinctive knowledge—born of the body and things bodily—that trumps, in certain situations, rational knowledge. Before she has come to be James's lover, in looking back Jane is able to see that there were marks of things to come in the ways in which they related to each other at various family gatherings. Here the meeting of eyes, the pull of certain intonations, and the hallmarks of some sort of future are much more real than other sorts of knowing.

At one Christmas gathering, James, Lucy, Jane and Malcolm (Jane's husband) had escaped from the older generation and gone to the seashore. Although Jane and James do not know each other as more than familial acquaintances, something stirs.

> At the sea, we stopped and got out.... It was a small bay, with a beach of pebbles and no houses near; the sky was gray, the sea was gray and flat....
>
> There was a post in the water, standing some way out. James threw a stone at it and missed it.... We all threw stones. By some mistaken distribution of providence, I have a good eye: I hit the post each time....
>
> "I could have played tennis well, I suppose," I said, amazed as I was always amazed by my heavenly gift. "But I never cared for it."
>
> "What do you care for?" said James, picking up one last smooth black round stone, circled with a pale eternal streak of whiteness.[20]

Here Drabble employs the trope of the stick in water (a staple of British empiricist philosophy) to a remarkable end. There are types of knowledge—my awareness of sensory confusion, as cited in the standard philosophical examples, is one sort. Then there is the sort of knowing triggered by the body and its awareness of the other. (At a slightly later point in the text, Jane says that she loved James because "I saw his naked wrists against a striped tea towel once, seven years ago."[21]) This sort of

---

20 Drabble, *Waterfall*, 75–76.
21 *Ibid.*, 77.

knowing might be instigated by a tremor due to a remark—and James' "What do you care for?", especially in its context of family conventionality, is precisely the sort of remark that can trigger that awareness. (Perhaps it was at this same gathering that Jane had noticed his bones.)

The tropes of knowing—the philosopher's bent stick, the post against which only those who can "make their mark" have a real chance—are uncannily set up here against this other sort of knowing. For Drabble, it is manifestly clear which is the stronger.

The author pushes us in this direction once again when she says, after finishing the episode in which the stones against the post takes place,

> The narrative tale. The narrative explanation.... Ah, perfect love. For these reasons, was it, that I lay there, drowned was it, drowned or stranded, waiting for him, waiting to die and drown there, in the oceans of our flowing bodies, in the white sea of that strange familiar bed.[22]

How might this sort of knowing be set against the other? One has to do with rationality, words, propositions—it is the male knowing of the logocentric thinkers, and it is the paradigmatic knowing of Western (and, indeed, of many other cultures). This other sort of knowing is part of the *écriture* of which we have written; it is the female, the flesh, the connectedness that is beyond the rational and that, in many cases, cannot be adequately set out in language or in rational terms. Whatever we call this sort of knowing, there is no question that it has not had a ready place in much of philosophy—indeed, its possessors have frequently been derogated or consigned to the ranks of the ignorant or mad. But Drabble's point is to resuscitate it, and in such a way that we are immediately able, as readers, to recognize what propels this kind of knowledge—love, sexuality, childbirth, intimacy.

It is interesting to note that, even within the more standard areas of contemporary philosophical theorizing, there is some movement toward areas that might be recognizably feminine or gynocentric. The current debate over the naturalization of epistemology might at first glance seem to have little to do with these matters, but it is indeed related. Those who have wanted to use our contemporary awareness of cognitive functioning, or of the actual performance of the senses to ameliorate epistemic theory have been participants in at least one strand of the broader debate. The quest for a priori, universalizable principles of knowing—the analogue of the Kantian quest for the imperative—is at bottom a search for principles that have to do with pure rationality only, divorced from the body, its functioning, or advertence to the senses. But many have argued that such theorizing is at best noninstantiable and at worse incoherent.

Standard epistemology with its search for principles is simply the more technical, more tightly-articulated version of a basic epistemology that values the rational, the logocentric and the codifiable over anything that might adhere to any other form of knowing, cognition or emotion. Yet a number of thinkers seem to want to make the assertion that such forms of activity—whether we label them cognitive or noncognitive—are valuable, and are the sorts of experiences that yield "knowledge"

---

22 *Ibid.*

in their own way. Thus the French theorists have valorized that which has been excluded—the bodily, anything having to do with the feminine, and so forth.

A naïve observer might be inclined to state that this debate has little to do with the naturalization of epistemology as it occurs in current professional circles, but naturalization is considered controversial precisely because it does allude to the senses and to bodily functioning. The point is simply that both of these major strands of contemporary thought—continental theory and naturalized theory—point us in the direction of noticing the body.

It is clear that Drabblean knowing can be categorized more easily in continental terms, and we have already alluded to those thinkers whose work might be mentioned in this connection. But Drabble instinctively wants us to go in a direction that is, at bottom, Freudian. James in the childbirth bed recapitulates not only birth, menstruation, and lactation, but the general metaphor of beginnings—and as Jane later tries to explain, this is indeed a rare love. She was, as she says, "faint with love."[23] A love that can lead to a loss of consciousness is a powerful eroticism indeed, and exactly the type of erotic sensation that, traditionally, would be considered to be antithetical to knowing. Drabble's assertion is that it is itself a form of knowledge.

Why Drabble takes this path is unclear, but we can hypothesize that it is related to some of the concerns of her earliest novels. Her protagonists are educated, in typical Oxbridge fashion, and often left bereft in home situations that require that their skills of rational analysis be put aside so that they can engage in caretaking activities. Perhaps a spillover of this sort of stifled force results in a love that makes one ill. It certainly, if not channeled at all, can make one simply ill—which is essentially what happens to Bessie Bawtry in *The Peppered Moth*. What constitutes a way out for a thwarted, thoughtful, intellectually-inclined woman? Discovery of others may result in intense, driven relationships. Then these relationships themselves lead to a form of knowledge—or at least that is what Drabble seems to be telling us. Better that than the living fossilization of the traditional homely life.

The Future

Margaret Drabble has been deemed traditional not only in the ways in which she sets up her texts, but in their subject matter. Until her later novels, there is little reference to the contemporary Britain that is now becoming a staple of commentary—her novels were lacking in the characters drawn from colonial life and its influx that seem to pepper the works of other British writers.

But in *The Peppered Moth* Drabble seems to become more aware of a future with multiple fractures—a society in which gender divisions will cease, perhaps, to have their same importance, because other (ethnic, racial, religious) divisions will be very important as well. *Moth* is a novel with a number of characters of different ethnic backgrounds, and also a number of characters who exhibit personality characteristics at variance with the sort of genteel middle-classness, or even working-classness, that one associates with her work. Faro has a boyfriend named Seb, whose personal

---

23 *Ibid.*, 68.

characteristics Drabble depicts as almost uniformly negative. He is unprepossessing in appearance, careless in personal habits and given to lying and a failure to live up to personal obligations. Yet Faro has a lengthy relationship with him that is only broken off when she discovers one last lie—his claim to be suffering from terminal cancer (and thus in need of her immediate care) turns out to be false, as were many of his other previous claims and statements.

At this point Faro is able to end the relationship, but Drabble is astute in depicting this somewhat sad entanglement as still another occasion for the acquisition of some kind of awareness. As she says, in depicting Faro's encounter with her mother Chrissie, and their thoughts on Seb:

> Chrissie delivers herself of these views with a somewhat fevered panache.... Faro laughs, and takes this maternal interference in good part. She agrees she will have to break off her relationship with Seb. It is, like him, unhealthy. It is doing neither of them any good. He clearly isn't going to die quickly, in fact he may not be going to die at all. She's beginning to suspect that the whole charade really is something of a con trick. If Seb was as ill as he says he is, he'd be having chemotherapy, or something like that, wouldn't he? She treacherously betrays to her mother Seb's ghoulish necrophiliac Egyptian fantasies, and, treacherously, the two women laugh.[24]

Faro has always been attracted to the dark, literally and metaphorically. It is unclear what Seb's ethnicity is, but at several other points in the novel Britons of color are introduced as characters. More important than Seb's ethnicity is the fact that he represents the strange, the occult, even. It is as if there were a sort of pre-contemporary Britain, somehow steeped in old values and discernible well-being, that is starting to come unraveled in the post-1960s atmosphere. Drabble makes sure that we understand that the encounters with this new Britain are difficult for all, but that they represent an important wave of the future. Seb's interest in things Egyptian and the general gloom in which he lives signal Faro's (and everyone's) first acquaintance with a different take, cultural or otherwise. Faro may not like what she has learned, but she has indeed learned.

At Faro's father's (Nick's) funeral, his wives and former lovers come to pay their last respects. This is, indeed, a portrait of the new Britain. Serafina is described in the following: "Serafina had come next in the catalogue, and there she was, still as large and glossy as ever, in full bloom. She was of West Indian descent, and had robed herself for this occasion in some kind of orange and purple toga: her head she had bound up in a tall and elaborate turban, intricately and lavishly swathed. She looked like an African empress, and this was no doubt her intention."[25]

What kind of a Britain is it where an "African empress" is one of the wives of the departed, himself a Britain of East European Jewish ancestry? It is simply the Britain of the here and now—and of course this England is the spiritual and actual heir of all of what has come before, including the Brontes, Romantics and others of whom Drabble is so fond. The new Britain careens along and does not make a great deal of sense much of the time—its forerunner is seen in *The Ice Age*, although there are no

---

24 Drabble, *Peppered Moth*, 338–339.
25 *Ibid.*, 207.

major characters not of English ancestry in that work. But in order for England to be able to function in the new era, it must be able to meld the colonial with the past, and in a way that makes some sort of sense. In a way, Faro's quest to find out about DNA and Cotterhall Man has a great deal to do with these issues, for Serafina and Nick are also the products of their respective mitochondrial strands—and somehow those strands make their way (embodied, as it were) to the United Kingdom.

Closing

In a world filled with literary prizes, it is somewhat surprising that Drabble's work has not received an even greater level of acknowledgement. Her output has been tremendous, and each novel has the carefully-wrought tone that signals a genuine entry in the realm of literature. But it may very well be the case that her initial reputation as a "woman's writer" carried a certain weight, and that this may have precluded others seeing her work in anything like an adequate way.

We have argued that Drabble is indeed a philosophical writer, and there is a sense in which this particular stand does not really require further argument. Her concern for matters metaphysical, seen through an historical lens, shows up in a number of ways, not the least of which is the thoughtful inner discourse in which her characters seem to specialize. (Only a certain sort of person, after all, would engage in Faro's pillow-smothered reflection on the fate of humankind in the middle of a journalistic interview visit.) Her concern for matters more or less strictly historical is, as we have also seen, tempered by a Foucauldian realization of what it is that history, as we conceive it, amounts to. Her other interests in gender, class and, more recently, ethnicity, may not speak to issues that have traditionally been deemed to be philosophical, but they certainly speak to issues that are in the forefront of current feminist philosophical discourse.

Perhaps most interesting, particularly in light of the voice of earlier criticism, is the move that allows Drabble to be seen as standing in the new tradition of *écriture féminine*. Many who remember Drabble's work—or even remember having heard about her from another devoted reader—are most struck by the descriptive passages that speak of the body and bodily needs, such as passages that we have cited here from *The Waterfall* and *The Peppered Moth*. Her ability to evoke the female view in these matters is remarkable and then some—certainly *The Waterfall* alone is spoken of reverently in certain circles for its evocation of the notion of an erotic love that leaves one faint.

This combination of twists, historical, corporeal and otherwise, and a penchant for memorable characters with highly educated sensibilities places Drabble in the same class as writers such as Woolf and Beauvoir. Those who have interpreted her work at a sort of fundamental feminist level—such as, for example, the early Showalter—have not had the chance to compare the later novels, or even, perhaps, to see how different feminine and feminist tropes appear and reappear throughout the course of her work. Drabble is a test case for our comprehension of what makes literature philosophical. In an earlier chapter, we had cited Denis Dutton and Garry Hagberg on the intersection of philosophy and literature. They claim that "Philosophy is about life from the broadest possible human perspective, and so is literature."[26] But they also note that "Would-be peacemakers will be disappointed to see fresh hostilities breaking out just when they thought differences were at last being reconciled."[27] If Drabble provides ground for fresh hostilities, it probably has something to do with her refusal to submit to easy categorization. Her work is not philosophical in the same sense as Pynchon or Barnes—one has to look further. By the same token, her novels are readable enough that they are indeed standard and possibly even popular fare in educated circles. Surely that in itself is an accomplishment.

What counts as a philosophical theme is, as we have indicated, up for grabs to some extent, but it is important, in forwarding the notion that Drabble has philosophical work to do, to contrast what has been said on such topics by others with the apparent threads of her work. In an essay with the title "Existentialism as a Basis for Theory and Practice in Rhetoric," Michael Hyde notes:

> When existentialists ask us to consider how emotion plays a role in human existence, they are not attempting to throw reason and rationality to the wind, nor are they attempting to deny that emotions can be the source of "stupid" behavior.... Rather, an existentialist appreciation of emotion is one that places it in the company of reason and rationality and credits it with having an active and truthful purpose.[28]

We cannot meaningfully classify Drabble as an existential novelist, but it is important to clarify the intensity of her existential themes, and why these themes in particular make the novels philosophical. To reiterate, but in a stronger fashion, Drabble's characters are concerned with the large, classic questions of the meaning of life, its origins, the existence of God, how to be moral, the possibility of morality, and so forth. These are not merely matters that might appeal to the Oxbridge graduate, as some of her early critics seem to want to claim. Rather, obviously, they are questions that occur to almost all thoughtful humans, and are questions of cross-cultural relevance.

---

26 Dutton and Hagberg (2002), "Worldviews," *Philosophy and Literature*, 26 (1), April.
27 *Ibid.*
28 Hyde, Michael J. "Existentialism as a Basis for the Theory and Practice of Rhetoric," in Cherwitz (ed.), 213–251.

Chapter Four

Woolf, Metaphysics and Life

The work of Virginia Woolf has certainly not lacked for commentary, and of a variety of types. Unlike Margaret Drabble, Woolf has had a sufficient number of commentators over a long enough period of time that there can be little doubt about the importance of her work. Feminists, especially starting in the 1970s, have found her essays and novels to be exemplary; critics interested in the rise of modernism have long heralded Woolf as one of the first major modernists.[1]

But a good deal of what has been written elides some of the more interesting moves that might be made with regard to Woolf. The interior section of *To the Lighthouse*, for example, has attracted many because the author seems to be saying something about social class and the experiences that differences in social class bring, but little has been written about Woolf's virtually phenomenological account of time.[2] Rachel Vinrace, in *The Voyage Out*, is seen as the quintessential unformed young woman, upon whom much can be inscribed, but few have commented extensively on the extended interior monologues that Rachel is given virtually from the opening of the book. Drabble, we noted, creates characters who ask themselves complicated questions about the nature of their lives; Woolf is the interrogator in most of her work, framing scenes in such a way that the questions are indeed asked and stand out from the text.

In this way Woolf's work is paradigmatically philosophical, but her style, one presumes, has precluded a great deal of the sort of criticism that the questions she poses would seem to make obvious. Terry Eagleton notes:

> The English-language writer who most strikingly exemplifies Kristeva's theories is James Joyce. But aspects of it are also evident in the writings of Virginia Woolf, whose fluid, diffuse, sensuous style offers a kind of resistance to the male metaphysical world symbolized by the philosopher Mr. Ramsay in *To the Lighthouse*.[3]

Eagleton goes on to call Woolf's writing "semiotic," but more to the point is the fact that, semiotic or not, it raises and addresses a number of ontological and generally philosophical issues.

Woolf typically poses these issues in at least two general sorts of ways. Like Drabble, she has her characters ask themselves questions that are bound to frequently move a great deal beyond daily concerns. Mrs. Ramsay's well-known self-questioning at the dinner table is one such example; Rachel's thinking back to

---

[1] This sort of criticism very much precedes the more recent feminist commentary, and was already a staple during Woolf's lifetime.
[2] See my "Virginia Woolf, Time and the Real," in *Philosophy and Literature*, 2005.
[3] Eagleton, *Theory*, 164.

what she takes to be the oddity of her aunts' habitual style of conversation at the opening of *The Voyage Out* is another.[4] But perhaps more pertinently, Woolf will, in the guise of narrator, point us in the direction of these philosophical statements or queries at various places in the text. Shortly after depicting Rachel as wondering why her aunts are incapable of expressing any genuine emotion or feeling, Woolf writes:

> Let these odd men and women...be symbols.... Reality dwelling in what one saw and felt, but did not talk about, one could accept a system in which things went round and round quite satisfactorily to other people, without often troubling to think about it, except as something superficially strange.[5]

It is Woolf's relentless attempt to try to limn that "Reality" that places her in the ranks of philosophical novelists.

Both *To the Lighthouse*, and her first, somewhat underexamined work, *The Voyage Out*, are remarkable for their depiction of time as a construct that is both human and outside of human endeavors. In *Lighthouse*, the real has to do not only with felt interiors—in the depiction of which Woolf is almost unsurpassed—but also with felt conceptions of change, time and growth. When Mrs. Ramsay muses on her children's lives, she knows that part of what makes the world entrancing for them is their ability to become caught up in the moment—an ability that many adults have lost. James feels as if he has been waiting to go to the lighthouse forever, because, of course, almost any wait is an extraordinarily long wait for a six-year-old boy. But Mrs. Ramsay also reflects on Cam's inner life, and Cam is several years older:

> They were happier now than they would ever be again. A tenpenny tea set made Cam happy for days.... They had all their little treasures.... And so she went down and said to her husband, Why must they grow up and lose it all?[6]

Time is handled in a similar fashion in *The Voyage Out*. It is not only Rachel's somewhat naïve response to questions that signals to us that she is about to embark on a formidable period of growth; it is her response to unstated time and unstated or implicit commitments about time. Richard Dalloway is spectacular, by Rachel's standards, because he has passed his life in an extraordinary way. When she is in his presence, she feels herself pulled, and yet time seems to slow down. Woolf writes:

> "Please—tell me everything." That was what she wanted to say. He had drawn apart one little chink and showed astonishing treasures. It seemed to her incredible that a man like that should be willing to talk to her.... She stirred her tea round and round. The bubbles which swam and clustered in the cup seemed to her like the union of their minds.

---

4 Woolf, Virginia (1965), *The Voyage Out*, London: Hogarth Press, 34–35.
5 *Ibid.*, 35.
6 Woolf, Virginia (1955), *To the Lighthouse*, New York: Harcourt Brace and Co., 65.

The talk meanwhile raced past her, and when Richard suddenly stated in a jocular tone of voice, "I'm sure Miss Vinrace, now, has secret leanings toward Catholicism," she had no idea what to answer, and Helen could not help laughing at the start she gave.[7]

Rachel experiences time in a different way from the others, because she is thoroughly engrossed in the moment, and in the reverie that has been started by the unexpected pleasure of Richard Dalloway's attention to her. In that sense, she is like Cam—and yet she is much older. Phenomenological accounts of time have been a staple of some recent Continental philosophy (including perhaps neglected portions of Simone de Beauvoir's work), but they are very important parts of Woolf's work because it is impossible to give an accurate impression of psychological interiors without demarcating the felt passage of time. That this is part of Woolf's genius has not been fully appreciated.

In presenting us with stream-of-consciousness as a style, Woolf leaves the door open to somewhat awkward plot structure. But then again, plot is not what drives Woolf's writing—it is, rather, a combination of the psychological states of the characters and a focus on their shifting circumstances. For a depiction of these states and circumstances, her style is unsurpassed insofar as it allows the reader access to what in philosophical terms might be called epistemically privileged states.

Those feminist critics who have focused on work such as *Three Guineas* and *A Room of One's Own* have often left readers with the impression that Woolf is quintessentially a feminist writer, but this is far from the case in the standard sense, or the polemic sense. Rachel Vinrace in *The Voyage Out* is an unfinished character: it is her growth, however truncated, that interests Woolf. Richard's kiss amazes and frightens Rachel—as one of the other characters notes. Woolf writes: "Helen could hardly restrain herself from saying out loud what she thought of a man who brought up his daughter so that at the age of twenty-four she scarcely knew that men desired women and was terrified by a kiss."[8] Although Rachel may be in the process of growth, she is far from a standard female protagonist at the novel's opening. Rather, she is one who experiences, and in her striving to ascertain what is real (and to escape the stultifying Richmond world of her aunts) she is emblematic of much of what Woolf wants to get across. The sweep of Woolf's vision is both explicitly and implicitly philosophical, but it is left to the reader to try to make out these strands. They are part not only of her style, but of the very questions that she raises in the course of setting out her remarkable sequences of time, thought and change.

Mind, Reason and Woolf

Woolf's depiction of the shifting of time is important not only for the ontological stance it takes, and her phenomenological account of it, but also because in the course of such depiction she frequently presents an account of rationality. This is perhaps a more important feature of her work than has been acknowledged—the Bloomsbury atmosphere undoubtedly exposed her, even if only fleetingly, to a great

---

7   Woolf, *Voyage*, 60.
8   *Ibid.*, 90.

deal of the English philosophy of the time, and portions of it appear at intervals in the completed novels.

In trying to think about the mental themselves, her characters often grapple with questions about the nature of rationality, and what an "account" of something would mean. But they will not be easily bought off—it is clear that the artist, for Woolf, has a much more vivid and impressive take on an object than could be gleaned by mere philosophical reflection of whatever recondite sort. Lily Briscoe, in *Lighthouse*, tries to get clear on what sort of intellectual work it is that Mr. Ramsay actually does; Andrew has told her to "think of a kitchen table when you're not there."[9] Woolf writes:

> So now she always saw, when she thought of Mr. Ramsay's work, a scrubbed kitchen table. It lodged now in the fork of a pear tree, for they had reached the orchard. And with a painful effort of concentration, she focused her mind, not upon the silver-bossed bark of the tree, or upon its fish-shaped leaves, but upon a phantom kitchen table, one of those scrubbed board tables, grained and knotted, whose virtue seems to have been laid bare by years of muscular integrity, which stuck there, its four legs in the air.[10]

This is not, of course, what is intended by Andrew's gloss on the philosophical account—but the standard account is not important. Lily, the artist, lives in the felt moment, and the fact that she now sees the table stuck "in the fork of a pear tree" signals to us that that vision is all-encompassing for her and is constitutive of what is real at any given moment.

In *The Voyage Out*, Rachel suffers from a similarly artistic take on reality, but one that in a sense is less polished than Lily's. While Rachel is staying with Helen Ambrose, she is (at least by Helen's lights) in the process of acquiring some polish and sophistication. She does an immense amount of reading, but it is in the middle of one of her post-reading reveries that Woolf has her undergo the following experience:

> She was next overcome by the unspeakable queerness of the fact that she should be sitting in an arm-chair, in the morning, in the middle of the world. Who were the people moving in the house—moving things from one place to another? and life, what was that? It was only a light passing over the surface and vanishing, as in time she would vanish, though the furniture in the room would remain.... She was overcome with awe that things should exist at all.[11]

This sort of dissociative state, minor though it may be, is an altered state of consciousness, and certainly, in its own way, not a standard or normal state. But in a vein similar to Lily's attempt to grapple with the notion of the kitchen table, Woolf has Rachel's dissociated state stand in itself for a certain sort of knowledge, or awareness. It is, in fact, quite philosophical, as there is reason to think that works such as Descartes' *Meditations* are at least partially the result of such experiences—

---

9 Woolf, *Lighthouse*, 25–26.
10 *Ibid.*
11 Woolf, *Voyage*, 145.

here all we have to go on is anecdotal evidence and the sheer odd structure of the *Meditations* itself.

Interestingly enough, Mitchell Leaska mentions that Woolf was hard at work reading *Principia Ethica* while she wrote the first version of *The Voyage Out*, known as *Melymbrosia*.[12] The text does, in fact, allude to G.E. Moore at one point, but the larger concern here has to do with the running-up of these altered, perhaps more artistic states against standard rationality. This is ultimately what Woolf is after—the carefully reasoned sort of work (or life) is one thing, the vision of the sensitive and thoughtful expressionist another. It is clear that Woolf takes the latter to represent some sort of truth. She is, of course, fully aware that this is not the way in which an educated person might be inclined to use that term, but that is precisely why she takes the trouble to try to set something up against it.

Helen Ambrose is aware of Rachel's potential and her rather unplumbed depth, so she has asked Rachel's father for permission to let her stay on with the Ambroses while her father continues his own journey. Helen had been concerned, chiefly, with Rachel's virtual complete lack of experience—this is why the kiss and passionate declaration of Richard Dalloway caused so much consternation. But the passionate life is only one of the many directions in which Rachel is now headed. She also is much more aware of her own questioning with respect to the nature of reality itself—and this is no mere play idea for her. She can see that her old pattern of wanting to lose herself in music probably owed something to this sort of quest.

It would be easy to say that the Woolf of *Three Guineas* is at work here, although that particular piece was written much later. What can be said, however, is that there are a number of ways of dealing with the world, through both cognition and senses, and Woolf is trying to make clear what the ramifications are of those various modes of so dealing. The propositional knowledge mode—the standard philosophical mode, about which G.E. Moore is concerned, and the mode that is so frequently associated with paradigmatic rationality—has its purposes, but for Woolf knowledge conceived in this way lacks both a sort of accuracy and a sort of special access. The access that Woolf is concerned with is no mere standard epistemic access—it is clear, as we have said, that Woolf values altered states, because those states seem to push us in a certain direction of being "in touch" with things. Woolf no doubt realizes that the rational mind might certainly challenge some of these states—Rachel's dissociated state might, for instance, be though to be exemplary of psychopathology rather than of great insight.

But for Woolf our conceptions of reality are simply what they are—and they themselves help to constitute and define a reality for us at any given point. Thus Rachel, lost in music, existed in a mode for which music was ultimately real (and very little else). Her dissociative experience allows her access to a certain sort of questioning—Why anything rather than nothing? Why this?—which is manifestly philosophical even though it does not express itself in the philosophical structured statements of someone like G.E. Moore.

---

12 Leaska, Mitchell (2000), *Granite and Rainbow: the Hidden Life of Virginia Woolf*, New York: Cooper Square Press, 134–135.

Whether we can go so far as to maintain that these different styles are gendered is something else again. A work like *Three Guineas* propels us in that direction; because both Lily and Rachel are female, we might be tempted to make this claim. But these startling, non-professional experiences are those of the artist. In that sense, they are not gendered. Perhaps Woolf's critics have been tempted to make this claim because so many of her artists are female.

The force of the interior and the interior reality is manifest again in *Lighthouse* when Cam complains of not being able to sleep. Cam and James are afraid of the shadows cast by a pig's skull; it is an unusual object, and Woolf uses this episode to great effect.

> It was nailed fast, Mildred said, and Cam couldn't go to sleep with it in the room, and James screamed if she touched it.
>
> Then Cam must go to sleep (it had great horns, said Cam)—must go to sleep and dream of lovely palaces, said Mrs. Ramsay, sitting down on the bed by her side. She could see the horns, Cam said, all over the room. It was true. Wherever they put the light (and James could not sleep without a light) there was always a shadow somewhere.[13]

Just as Cam can get lost in her tea set, she can also be derailed by shadows. But for Cam, and James, the shadows are real and everything else is not.

Woolf refuses to valorize propositional knowledge because it is inconsistent with the artist's vision. For Woolf the vision is everything—and this sort of knowing is itself a goal at which one can aim, if one is so inclined. When Lily says "I have had my vision," we realize that the artist has achieved a certain sort of closure with her work.

Woolfian Criticism

Although Mitchell Leaska has authored both a biography of Woolf and volumes of criticism, some of the most telling work, with respect to the points we are trying to develop here, comes in his biography, *Granite and Rainbow*.[14] Leaska is a superb articulator of this strand of Woolf's visionary process that we have just examined; contra the lines of criticism that have been developed by some feminist writers, Leaska admits to the difficulties with the Duckworths, but does not give them centerplace in his work. Although *Mrs. Dalloway* and *To the Lighthouse* are most frequently cited as being the volumes that show Woolf's intense impressionistic desire to capture the moment, Leaska concurs in the judgment that this desire is present from her early work on, and is seen in *The Voyage Out*. Drawing on her letters and notes to friends (such as Violet Dickinson) and reported conversations remembered later by Clive Bell, Leaska assumes that Woolf began to think seriously about trying to get to the root of things by fully articulating lived impressions around the time that she began *Voyage*. According to Leaska, beginning *Melymbrosia*, and visiting Italy, meant for Woolf:

---

13 Woolf, *Lighthouse*, 126–127.
14 See fn. 12.

[I]n Perugia her attention was caught by the frescoes.... The impulse to record her impressions seems to have been triggered by her comments about Meredith's faults as a novelist. He was not satisfying; he was flimsy.... Then she inspected the frescoes of Perugino and noted how everything in his vision of the world gave way to the expression of beauty. But was his way the only way? Wasn't there another kind of beauty?... How did she as a writer achieve symmetry and wholeness, this finished state she called beauty? And was it of the same order as the artist's?... [S]he could say with some certainty only that her own scriptural beauty would be achieved "by means of scriptural discords" and "shivering fragments.[15]

Here we see a critical assessment of the commencement of Woolf's attempts to render internal states so as to get at "wholes." This is not, of course, nearly as pronounced in *Voyage* as it will later become, and yet it is remarkable how much of it does appear in this early work. The opening lines of that work are:

As the streets that lead from the Strand to the Embankment are very narrow, it is better not to walk down them arm-in-arm. If you persist, lawyers' clerks will have to make flying leaps into the mud; young lady typists will have to fidget behind you.[16]

These lines were written by someone who was not only a careful observer— they go beyond mere observation and notation. It is the "flying leap" and the "fidget[ings]" that capture the reader's attention, for those leaps are what moves the attention of the arm-in-arm walker as he or she proceeds down the streets and has a moment of absorbed attention. And these moments of absorbed attention are not, of course, unrelated to Woolf's conceptions of the real and of time—rather, as we have argued, they have everything to do with what is ultimately real for her. In the phenomenological moment, the leaping lawyer's clerk garners all of the attention before the mind, however briefly, races on to other things. It is Woolf's special gift that she has a virtually unparalleled capacity to express these moments.

Leaska has expressed for us the way in which Woolf's attempts to depict time in its shards and fragments expresses the philosophical. In a passage immediately after the one cited in *Granite and Rainbow*, he wrote, "[S]he said in her journal that she distrusted description in writing, surface matter, external appearance.... Her aim was to discover 'real things beneath the show.'"[17] Part of what enables Woolf to do this, as Leaska contends, is her ability to turn streams of consciousness into "fragments." But it is not merely consciousness that is depicted in this kind of way. Aiming at the "things beneath the show," Woolf in *Lighthouse* constructs a recounting of the passage of time in the well-known interior portion. Here she relies not so much on the sensation of time as internally experienced; the point of this passage is that time, itself becomes an actor, or agent. But this, of course, is part of the reality beneath the appearance. The actors in this section are gusts of wind and currents of air, but their activity is not inconsequential:

---

15 Leaska, *Granite*, 136.
16 Woolf, *Voyage*, 1.
17 Leaska, *Granite*, 136.

> The house was left, the house was deserted. It was left like a shell on a sandhill to fill with dry salt grains now that life had left it. The long night seemed to have set in; the trifling airs, nibbling, the breaths, fumbling, seemed to have triumphedThe saucepan had rusted and the mat decayed. Toads had nosed their way in.[18]

Now the kitchen-table-when-you're-not-there has become an entire house; the activity depicted, however, is precisely what does happen to uninhabited buildings over a period of time. Woolf strips away appearances in two fundamental sorts of ways: her stream-of-consciousness technique allows her to depict reality-as-it-is for the experiencer, and her what-actually-takes-place-over-time portrayal gives us a glimpse of reality without an experiencer. In both sorts of cases, as Leaska claims, Woolf was striving to "achieve wholeness through 'infinite discords.'"[19]

Showalter sees Woolf's use of this technique as being gendered; it is unclear how far this argument goes. In a sense, Woolf simply employed techniques similar to those of, for example, James Joyce. But it is true that a great many of the characters in Woolf's work who exhibit the sensitivity that allows her to make these sorts of moves are female. While citing Woolf's own description of her technique as "The mind receives a myriad impressions...an incessant shower of innumerable atoms,"[20] Showalter also wants to claim:

> In one sense, Woolf's female aesthetic is an extension of her view of women's social role: receptivity to the point of self-destruction, creative synthesis to the point of exhaustion and sterility. In *To the Lighthouse*, for example, Mrs. Ramsay spends herself in repeated orgasms of sympathy....[21]

Tying together two main lines of argument, it may very well be the case that it is a gendered temperament, in general, that sees to the bottom of things—as we have said, propositional knowledge seems to be largely a male domain. But, more straightforwardly, it is simply a certain way of seeing; in theory, it could be had by anyone. That is to say that it could be had by anyone who was interested, as Leaska says, in trying to see through appearances. Only a few, of course, will fit in that category.

Although Lyndall Gordon is strictly engrossed in biography in *Virginia Woolf: A Writer's Life*, she, too, finds Rachel's stream-of-consciousness passages in *The Voyage Out* very important.[22] Gordon, of course, is anxious to let us know how closely these passages mirror Virginia's own growth and maturity, but she does say that "Virginia Stephen adapted her theory of biography to fiction, to find in Rachel's random life a definitive shape, and to follow, in her obscure case, what is fugitive in the mind."[23] What is fugitive in the mind are precisely those moments, already set out here, where Rachel's detachedness, thoughtfulness and occasional dissociations

---

18 Woolf, *Lighthouse*, 155.
19 Leaska, *Granite*, 136.
20 Woolf, cited in Showalter, *A Literature*, 296.
21 Showalter, *A Literature*, 296.
22 Gordon, Lyndall (1984), *Virginia Woolf: A Writer's Life*, New York: W.W. Norton & Co., 98.
23 *Ibid.*

provoke the seeing through. As she says to Hewet, in answer to his question about what it is that she is looking at while she lies on the grass atop their picnic hill, "Human beings."[24]

Although critics have tended to focus on Woolf's stream-of-consciousness *simpliciter*, her feminism, or even her history of abuse as a child, it is clear that Woolf was provoked by what are essentially philosophical questions and that, cast in literary terms, she gave philosophical replies. The felt moment of intensity is not only more real than the analytic philosopher's dry account of it; it is also more real than many other mundane, and less deeply felt moments, however "important" they may seem. This is why, for the Ramsays, Mrs. Ramsay can wryly observe the alleged importance of the academic prizes that her husband and the other men around her so crave. Those moments are not as real as James' desire to visit the lighthouse, or the fact that—believing that he will go—a picture of a refrigerator is, briefly, "fringed with joy."[25]

Feminist Overviews

The classic feminist commentary on Woolf comes, of course, from Showalter's *A Literature of Their Own*.[26] This comparatively early work succeeded in grappling with the Woolf of *Three Guineas* and *A Room of One's Own*, but it is unclear how much of Showalter's main argument translates into the classic Woolfian texts, such as *Lighthouse*, *The Waves*, and *The Voyage Out*.

Phrased succinctly, the crucial question revolves around the fact that the argument itself is susceptible to a strong counter. Showalter sees Woolf as trapped between the two gender identities of her day: a sort of Edwardian version of the "Angel of the House," and the male scholar's life. Thus she is able to construct for Woolf what she terms an "androgynous" identity; on the other hand, this argument could be flipped back on itself, so to speak, and the terms reversed. If we think of "artist" as a more-or-less gender neutral category, then it could be argued that Woolf is the female artist par excellence, and that this description also applies to such characters as Lily Briscoe and Rachel Vinrace. If, as has been argued here, the quest for interiors and for reality is one that pushes the artist—and if it is the case that this is, at bottom, at least a somewhat philosophical quest—then Rachel, for one, is already embarked on this quest before she begins her spell under Helen's tutelage. Showalter claims that "In Virginia Woolf's version of female aestheticism and androgyny, sexual identity is polarized and all the disturbing, dark, and powerful aspects of femaleness are projected onto maleness."[27] Although one can readily understand the point of Showalter's remarks, another view should be articulated. We might term this general artistic/philosophical quest "androgynous" only in the sense that it is more or less

---

24 Woolf, *Voyage*, 157.
25 Woolf, *Lighthouse*, 4.
26 Showalter, *A Literature*, 263–297. An entire chapter of this work is devoted to Woolf; its title is "Virginia Woolf and the Flight into Androgyny."
27 *Ibid.*, 264.

gender-neutral; Rachel's quest, for instance, starts out with many feminine or female markers, which themselves become important parts of what Woolf is after.

Rachel is originally depicted as lost in her music; it provides a solace for her and an escape from the solid conventionality of her aunts' life in Richmond. Woolf intends, of course, that we see Rachel in a certain sort of way. But her intention that Rachel be the female artist is by no means devoid of the usual gender markers—and it by no means devolves into something without gender markers. As is the case with Lily Briscoe, Rachel wants to capture something, and the something that she wants to capture is not unrelated to her femaleness. When Helen Ambrose first comes to feel that Rachel has had contact with Richard Dalloway, she attempts to draw her out.

> [S]he wished to know what the girl was like, partly of course because Rachel showed no disposition to be known.... Rachel followed her indifferently. Her mind was absorbed by Richard; by the extreme strangeness of what had happened, and by a thousand feelings of which she had not been conscious before.[28]

This is not, of course, something that has happened to Rachel just this once—the experience with Richard, although different from other experiences (she has just experienced sexuality for the first time), is still just one of a number of things that Rachel catalogues, mulls and then expresses musically or in some other way. This accounts for her cut-offness; the artist is not interested in the conventional and is, in fact, bored by it. But the female artist has few avenues of expression; perhaps this is why so much of the expression is not externalized.

As part of her argument with respect to "androgyny," Showalter wants to recount Virginia's alleged inadequacy—or felt inadequacy—with respect to Vanessa and childbearing. This particular recitation is probably accurate; the difficulty is where one is to go with it. Showalter writes:

> The inadequacy Virginia felt when she contrasted the sexual side of her life with Vanessa's was compounded by Leonard's decision that they should not have children. The sources of this decision are rather obscure. According to Quentin Bell, Virginia had happily anticipated having children...[29]

But if Virginia did indeed feel the lack, insofar as both mothering and a conventional female sexuality were concerned (she is reported to have had difficulty achieving orgasm after marriage), it is probably a mistake to think that lines can be drawn that demarcate that lack as an area of androgynous growth. In *Lighthouse*, both Mrs. Ramsay and Lily Briscoe are, in a sense, artists—it is that they have taken their artistry and depth in different directions. Mrs. Ramsay, who is able to make everything right—from Cam's fear, to James's longing, to Mr. Ramsay's perceived needs—is the artist transformed in a sort of parenting, motherly way. But one can't help but think that Lily is simply Mrs. Ramsay in a different guise, as it were; Lily is the artist herself, without the conventional female roles. One could interpret this as

---

28 Woolf, *Voyage*, 88–89.
29 Showalter, *A Literature*, 272.

a form of androgyny; one could simply say, as we have attempted to say here, that this is the woman-as-artist.

In the same way, even the philosophical strands that Woolf weaves into her work are probably not devoid of feminist interpretations. If Woolf is the novelist who speaks to us about time, the felt moment, and the import of experience-as-felt, even some of those strands of her work may reflect a certain sort of female-centered view. In general, when Woolf portrays such moments, she does so through the trope of self-and-others. There is a sense in which her play with time in *Lighthouse* reminds us of Simone de Beauvoir's comments about time in *Old Age*; in that work, Beauvoir writes:

> How far does memory allow us to retrieve our lives? The images...are far from possessing the richness of their original object. An image is the seeing of an absent object by means of an organic and affective analogue.[30]

Although one could argue that this is simply one philosophical slant on time, Beauvoir's use of "organic and affective" may have overtones of feminist theory. It is not clear, in fact, how often images are actually cast in this direction; many images probably have little associated affect. But it may in fact reflect gender, in some sense, to make this statement—that is certainly one reading of Beauvoir that is available to us. And so Woolf's own use of a similar highlighting of elements of the phenomenological may be interpreted in the same way; the moments that Woolf intends to capture almost always have important affective components, and of course one is tempted to make the claim that these components might not have been available to (or used by) the male writer.

In sum, there are a number of ways in which Showalter's classic take on "androgyny" could be construed. If the artist is a figure who is quintessentially male—and this has certainly been the case historically—then Woolf's call toward art does indeed, in a sense, make her androgynous; it is clear that she cannot have the kind of life that Vanessa had. But if we think of the tradition of female writers and artists that certainly predates Woolf in Great Britain (and that has, in any case, been around for a long time), then a better feminist take on Woolf is that she is the woman artist who expresses, in some profound way, at least a few strands of the female or the gynocentric in her writing.

Here, again, we have to think of Woolf's Lily. Much has been made of the use of triangles and apparently Cubist techniques in Lily Briscoe's canvasses, as described by Woolf in *Lighthouse*. These techniques themselves inevitably call to mind an array of male-identified images—Picasso at work, Diego Rivera studying in France and then returning to Mexico to work publicly to the delight of Frida Kahlo and others. But Lily makes these techniques her own. She does, in fact, use them to try to depict Mrs. Ramsay, and to recall those scenes that, ten years later at the novel's close, stay in her mind. Regardless of the techniques—and we could think, for example, of

---

30 de Beauvoir, Simone (1996), Old Age, cited in Mary Warnock, *Women Philosophers*, London: J.M. Dent Everyman, 147.

another Lily who did conventional watercolors—the point is that we have no doubt about the gender of the artist when we read Lily's "I have had my vision."[31]

Woolf is, then, the female artist, and although it may be pushing the point too far to talk about her desire to demonstrate connectedness, now a staple of most feminist literature, it is not pushing it too far to indicate that androgyny is only one reading of Woolf. Vanessa had painting and children both; Woolf had literature, Vita, and Leonard, among others. But they both were female artists working in their time whose work spoke of female concerns.

A Continental Slant

As was the case with Drabble, it would not be difficult to use the work of Kristeva, Irigaray or Cixous to try to make the case for Woolf as one whose interest in the bodily can be described theoretically. But Woolf does not do what Drabble does. This is partially related, of course, to the limitations on novelists during the time in which she was publishing; one must remember that both Joyce and Lawrence had prohibitions on their work in the United States until the 1950s.

But there are other, more straightforwardly important reasons for this. Woolf's interest in the interior and the moment-as-felt experience mark her use of visual images, and some of that use probably speaks to concerns that could not, under ordinary circumstances, be articulated in the way in which Drabble has done. Woolf would, for example, write about Alison's relationship with Anthony, or Jane's with James, in a different vein. Her handling of Rachel's first kiss, from Richard Dalloway, indicates that what we would get here is the inner thought process; Drabble gives us thought and exterior, but marks the exterior in such a way that it gains ground, ultimately, in the descriptive process. Some of the most arresting writing in which Drabble engages in her description of the beginning of Jane's relationship is a markedly exterior narrative, but with stunning images: the sheets, the notion of deep waters, and so forth. Her interiors are often used to offset her exteriors: Jane's "It won't do" signals to us that the preceding description may be a highly idealized version of what Jane would like to think of as the commencement of her relationship.

But for Woolf, exteriors are often just another way of giving us the interior—this is evident in many, or even most, of her descriptive passages of places, circumstances and situations. Thus Woolf's focus on the interior readily lends itself to psychoanalytic theory and, as it happens, the Hogarth Press was one of the first to publish Freud's work, and Woolf herself was a frequent discussant of his ideas in her meetings with the Memoir Club and in other venues.[32] The oddity of Woolf's overt relationship to psychoanalytic theory is that, on the surface, she was superficially resistant.[33] And

---

31 This is the last line uttered by Lily in *Lighthouse*.

32 Ward Jouve, Nicole (2000), "Virginia Woolf and Psychoanalysis," in Roe, Sue and Susan Sellers (eds.), *The Cambridge Companion to Virginia Woolf*, Cambridge: Cambridge University Press, 245–272.

33 Jouve cites several instances of Woolf's criticism of James Strachey and others for their interest in this subject matter, 254–255.

yet there is no question that Freud himself, without advertence to Lacan or Kristeva, is perhaps the Continental thinker most helpful in reading Woolf.

Nicole Ward Jouve notes that Woolf, despite initial reticence, began to think that overt discussion of sexuality was helpful. She writes:

> The first meeting of the Memoir Club in March 1920 marked the reunion of the Bloomsbury group that had been scattered for the duration of the war.... Some were attracted to psychoanalysis, some hostile: Virginia Woolf lined up with the hostile ones, the art critics, Roger Fry and Clive Bell. Yet it was to the Memoir club that she shared her memories of her sexual abuse at the hands of her step-brothers: '22 Hyde Park Gate,' as mentioned above.[34]

Perhaps the most helpful take on Woolf and her relationship to this opening up of memory, sexual and otherwise, is that it is clear that she was headed in a similar direction all the way along. In other words, stating it flatly, portions of *The Voyage Out* are no less psychoanalytical in their construction than much of what she wrote later, even though we can date her overt involvement in these issues to a later point.

Her evocation of interiors is itself a way of describing the forceful push into consciousness of repressed material that happens during times of trauma, or even during times of sudden insight. Thus Rachel's reaction to her first kiss in *Voyage* is, although she does not know it, inevitably conditioned by repressed and semiconscious or unconscious memories of childhood intimacy, now evoked at a time when, as an adult woman, she is capable of a much more mature sexual response. Here is the relevant paragraph in *The Voyage Out*:

> "You have beauty," he said. The ship lurched. Rachel fell slightly forward. Richard took her in his arms and kissed her. Holding her tight, he kissed her passionately, so that she felt the hardness of his body and the roughness of his cheek printed upon hers. She fell back in her chair, with tremendous beats of the heart, each of which sent black waves across her eyes.[35]

The telling feature of this passage is its canny intermingling of the psychological and the physical. Apparently Rachel knew nothing of sexuality: its force—much of which, of course, derives from the unconscious—is such that it sends "black waves across her eyes." But in the next two pages of the text, this force recurs in different ways: being driven to bed by Helen Ambrose, Rachel then experiences a series of terrifying dreams, including one where she is trapped at the bottom of a tunnel-like opening with a "deformed man" who is "gibbering." Woolf writes:

> Light showed her the familiar things: her clothes, fallen off the chair; the water jug gleaming white; but the horror did not go at once. She felt herself pursued, so that she got up and actually locked her door. A voice moaned for her; eyes desired her. All night long barbarian men harassed the ship; they came scuffling down the passages, and stopped to snuffle at her door. She could not sleep again.[36]

---

34 *Ibid.*, 253.
35 Woolf, *Voyage*, 84.
36 *Ibid.*, 86.

There can be few evocations of the emergence of repressed sexuality in contemporary literature as forceful as this passage from Woolf's first novel. Freud himself wrote, "We have learnt from psycho-analysis that the essence of the process of repression lies, not in putting an end to, in annihilating, the idea which represents an instinct, but in preventing it from becoming conscious."[37] What is most remarkable here, however, is that, given the number of drafts of *Melymbrosia* attempted by Woolf, and its appearance at an early point in her own chronology of work, it is obvious that a great deal of what we can articulate theoretically here occurred to Woolf naturally, as it were. Pre-Memoir Club, and perhaps pre acquaintance with Freud's writings, Woolf hits on the mechanisms of repression and denial that drive so much of female behavior in the Edwardian period, and that will only be lifted much later.

Those who have claimed that Woolf chose this direction largely because of childhood abuse may not be entirely wrong, but it seems simpler and clearer to assert that Woolf saw through things because, ultimately, her gifts were in that vein. Sexuality, of course, is not the only arena that is at stake here: Mr. Ramsay's drives, somewhat understood—and also somewhat resented—by Mrs. Ramsay in *To the Lighthouse* are also seen through, though many of them might be described in ways other than the overtly sexual.

Woolf's work lends itself to Freudian theory precisely because it is so clearly about that which lies immediately below the surface, but which can be brought up at odd moments. As we have seen, Woolf did not herself always agree with whatever Freudian interpretation she heard about during numerous discussions. It is not so much that Woolf moved in this direction, then—the movement was itself quasi-conscious or perhaps unconscious, because it expresses the "vision" that drove Woolf's art. Not only love and sex, but familial ties, moments of epiphany and insight, transcendental points—all of these are expressed by Woolf in that style that allows for the felt reality of the moment to be greater than any account of surroundings of the mundane.

After Rachel finishes playing for the dance about mid-way through *Voyage*, she returns to her room in an altered state. The next day she borrows some books that have been recommended by Hirst. Then, Woolf writes:

> "What is it to be in love," she demanded, after a long silence; each word as it came into being seemed to shove itself into an unknown sea. Hypnotised by the wings of the butterfly, and awed by the discovery of a terrible possibility in life, she sat for some time longer. When the butterfly flew away, she rose, and with her two books beneath her arm returned home again, much as a soldier prepared for battle.[38]

The "terrible possibility" is sexual love, unfelt by Rachel before due to her very sheltered life, but certainly more than a possibility for a young woman of twenty-four. Those altered moments, for Woolf, define a certain reality itself.

---

37 Freud, Sigmund, "The Unconscious," in Cazeaux (ed.), 506–518.
38 Woolf, *Voyage*, 207.

Philosophical and Then Some

Woolf's use of altered conceptions of time and the real speak to a sort of phenomenological account of things even if (in a similar vein to our remarks on Freud) Woolf would not have acknowledged that this was what she was doing.

Many philosophers, such as Beauvoir, have written about our internal sensations of time because awareness of these states is part of what drives a notion of human beings as inquisitive and philosophical creatures. Our awareness, for example, that we have a completely altered conception of the future at seventy—as opposed to thirty—is itself the source for some philosophical reflection, and gives rise to a number of ways of looking at reality. In other literature that is avowedly philosophical, such as Sartre's *Nausea*, the sort of altered state that is signaled by such pathological conditions as derealization and depersonalization again becomes the focal point for philosophical reflection. Roquentin's famous encounter with the tree is part of Sartre's way of demarcating that which is in-itself from for-itself. In ordinary daily waking states, the facticity of the world is taken for granted, and provides the backdrop for our functioning. Other sorts of states painfully cause us to ask (as Rachel did in a portion of the text cited earlier) why there is anything rather than nothing. Woolf's texts routinely do this, and in addition to that sort of reflection, her sheer play with time and the senses often pushes the text in that direction.

Again, Jouve lets us know that much of what Woolf writes is both philosophical and, as we have said earlier, anti-logocentric. The "shivering fragments" of which Woolf is fond are the very things that let her indicate the break-up of the standard, mundane ontology, and the articulation of her special view. This may not be separate from some conception of either the mad or the mystical, but it certainly is indicative of its own sort of metaphysics. Jouve notes with respect to this:

> What is here happening around the name of Bernard [in *The Waves*] ... is a characteristic feature in Woolf's fiction. Clarissa Dalloway 'would not say of any one in the world' 'that they were this or were that.' As he falls asleep amid the eddies of his cigar smoke, Peter Walsh's 'thinking' dissolves and fuses: 'I shall try and get a word alone with Elizabeth to-night, he thought—then began to wobble into hour-glass shapes and taper away; odd shapes they take, he thought.' Being 'oneself,' to Mrs. Ramsay, is being 'a wedge-shaped core darkness.' There is some shape at least to this image from *To the Lighthouse*, but in *The Waves* instability and dissolution are potent.[39]

The core of the self is, on some philosophical construction, related to concepts of time and continuity, but as we have seen, Woolf's writing is fixated on capturing moments of time in such a way that they emphasize a discontinuity. That disconnection or discontinuity, although it very much assists Woolf in capturing the moment—such as James's joy, which surrounded the cut-out picture of the refrigerator—also works to destroy a coherent conception of the self. It is for these reasons that Woolf's art may reflect not only her madness, but other madnesses as well. For the ultimate breaks—as the therapists term them, the dissociative episodes—are, if prolonged or

---

39 Jouve, "Psychoanalysis," 258.

frequent, themselves a form of emotional illness, and taken at peak they will prevent functioning.

What is the self? What is time? What is the nature of reality? These specifically philosophical questions, introduced as core questions of metaphysics to beginning students, are thus part and parcel of the material with which Woolf has to work. It could be maintained, as has been said here, that this material is not being introduced on the conscious level for precise sorts of philosophical reasons, but then again that simply underscores the point that Woolf, seen psychoanalytically, hits at our cores.

Summarizing Woolf

Woolf's work would not be as important as it is today were it not for an interest in both modernism and feminism that overtook theory to some extent in the 1970s. Appreciation for the full force of modernism as a movement seemed to resuscitate the reputation of those who might originally have been dubbed "minor" moderns, Woolf among them. Then the push for a feminist turn in criticism ultimately meant that Woolf was the modern whose reputation was perhaps, the greatest recipient of valorization—it being understood that authors such as Joyce and Eliot had received their fair share of recognition and then some all the way along.

Still another push for recognition of Woolf came with the publication of Louise De Salvo's work on abuse and Woolf's childhood in the 1980s.[40] The paterfamilias Leslie Stephen had already been a problematic character in Woolf's work—he clearly is the model for Mr. Ramsay, and his relationship with Woolf's mother is also obviously something about which Woolf was concerned and that she had taken the trouble to limn. How much the Duckworth brothers could be said to have altered Woolf's life course is unclear; what is clear is that Woolf, as a child, suffered from a number of episodes and incidents that today would be considered abusive. Whether these episodes—even if alluded to indirectly in her literature—genuinely amount to something that is constitutive of a sea-change in her work is, again, unclear.

With the resuscitation of Woolf's reputation came, as we have seen, lines of criticism like Showalter's that see Woolf as the heir to a type of English literary tradition, and that also see her as "androgynous," a term that she used herself. But the important fact is that Woolf is so much more than simply an heir to a tradition that it does her a grave disservice, in some ways, to even begin to conceptualize the situation in that way.

As Showalter knows, Woolf is the heir to Bronte—or Eliot—only in the sense that she is female and an English writer. In other ways she can scarcely be said to be writing along the same lines at all.

In viewing the totality of Woolf's work, it is helpful then to try to demarcate the priestess of modernism, as she has sometimes been called, from the writer who attempted to grapple with fundamental questions. As has been said here, it is not so important whether we categorize most of her output as "androgynous;" what is

---

40 De Salvo, Louise (1989), *Virginia Woolf: the Impact*, New York: Ballantine Books.

important is that we try to come to grips with why she dealt with the problems that she did, and what sort of response she made to them.

Seen in this vein, the philosophical Woolf takes precedence over other labels that might be created for her. When Lily has "had her vision," she has seen clearly and fundamentally into profound areas.

In an important essay titled "Woolf's Feminism and Feminism's Woolf," Laura Marcus reveals some of the contradictions inherent in the assumption of a feminist identity for Woolf.[41] She writes:

> If the feminisms of the second half of the twentieth century have found in Woolf one of their most significant forerunners, it is at least in part because her writing and thinking were so intertwined with the feminisms of the first half of the century. Her responses to the feminist ideas of her time were, however, complex and often contradictory.[42]

Marcus then goes on to describe Woolf's "reluctant" and "short-lived" period of suffragist activism. The delineation of this episode provides us with further grist, for it perfectly typifies a great deal of what drives Woolf the author. Political causes, however well-motivated, are very much too simplistic and too close to the surface for Woolf's artistry or for her liking. Her need to capture the depths cannot really be sustained by a cause like that for the women's vote; that is why, in trying to align Woolf with any sort of feminist theory, some psychoanalytic constructs virtually cry out for inclusion.

Marcus moves in this direction at a later point in her essay, and citing both Jacobus and Abel she indicates that Woolf is caught up in the "pre-Oedipal realm of the mother–daughter dyad."[43] Part of that dyad can be evoked by some of the very passages that we have already investigated with respect to conceptions of reality. Looked at carefully, the passage in *Lighthouse* about Cam and the pig's skull is also about the importance of the mother:

> It was nailed fast, Mildred said, and Cam couldn't go to sleep with it in the room, and James screamed if she touched it.
> Then Cam must go to sleep (it had great horns, said Cam)—must go to sleep and dream of lovely palaces, said Mrs. Ramsay, sitting down on the bed by her side. She could se the horns, Cam said, all over the room. It was true. Wherever they put the light (and James could not sleep without a light) there was always a shadow somewhere.[44]

Now the import of a certain sort of feminist criticism, leavened with Freudian theory, becomes apparent—Mrs. Ramsay is the one who has the power to create and shape realities for the children. Just as the pig's skull is immediately real for Cam at that moment (in a sense similar to the one in which Mrs. Ramsay had described the "ten-penny tea set"), an alternate reality—lovely palaces—can be created by Mrs. Ramsay by the sound of her voice and the soothing effect of her words ("must go

---

41 Marcus, Laura, "Woolf's Feminism and Feminism's Woolf," in Roe and Sellers (eds.), *Cambridge*, 209–244.
42 *Ibid.*, 211.
43 *Ibid.*, 238.
44 Woolf, *Lighthouse*, 126–127.

to sleep".) This, indeed, is the intensity of the mother–daughter dyad, and, for that matter, the first dyad for all human beings. In this pre-male world—the world of the semiotic—meaning is experienced in a tactile and non-symbolic manner. Woolf, with her "shivering fragments," captures that intensity.

Chapter Five

The Body *à la* Woolf

Any feminist analysis of Woolf, as we have seen, immediately moves into territory of some depth because of Woolf's obvious entanglements with psychoanalytic issues, and because of the clear nature of the woman-to-woman linkage that occurs throughout Woolf's work. In addition, the Continental theorizing that has come to the fore in the last two decades meshes perfectly with a great deal of what Woolf has done, since theorists like Lacan and Kristeva are addressing issues that are paramount for Virginia Woolf.

Elizabeth Abel's *Virginia Woolf and the Fictions of Psychoanalysis* is a work that more than demonstrates the relevance of all of these lines of theory to Woolf criticism.[1] Using the language of contemporary poststructuralism, Abel shows how it is that Woolf's quest intersects profoundly with other narratives, such as the Oedipal narrative, or mother/daughter constructs. Abel indicates that Woolf's use of structure in narrative—and even her sometimes unconventional punctuation—along with her focus on the visual all lend themselves to analysis in Continental terms. Here is Abel, for example, on some of the issues surrounding the actual writing of *To the Lighthouse*:

> Comparing the production of her text to a psychoanalytic catharsis, Woolf insists that what has been released is the mother of infancy—central, majestic, "there...from the very first" ... No unconscious syllabling engenders the paternal text, which is to be construed incrementally "between tea and dinner till it is complete for writing out." Rather than selecting between the narratives determined by these images of origin, Woolf distributes them among the second generation of characters, inscribing through the different tales of James, Cam, and Lily a literary version of the psychoanalytic intersection drawn by Freud and Klein.[2]

By contrast, unconscious syllabling does engender the maternal text—and in a quote from Woolf's "A Sketch of the Past," Abel notes that the entire process felt to Woolf as one of "my lips seem[ing] to syllab[le] of their own accord."[3]

This sort of analysis is at the center of the more recent scholarship on Woolf, and some superb work has been done that makes manifest the connections between receptivity, closed-offness, voyages, separations and ruptures that permeate a good deal of Woolf's written work, and that certainly appear as early as *The Voyage Out*. Although not all of the feminist scholarship is in this vein, there is no question

---

1 Abel, Elizabeth (1989), *The Fictions of Psychoanalysis*, Chicago: University of Chicago Press.
2 *Ibid.*, 46.
3 *Ibid., ibid.*

that some of the most important work attempts to use poststructuralist and other contemporary theory to make the points with respect to Woolf's work that probably should have been made all the way along.

Along with *Mrs. Dalloway* and *To the Lighthouse*, it seems to be generally agreed that Woolf's third major work is *The Waves*. There also seems to be a consensus that this may be her single most difficult work: in any case, as Lyndall Gordon has said, "For the unprepared reader the first hundred pages can be as baffling as an unknown code."[4] Because *Mrs. Dalloway* is now the subject of what seem to be innumerable rereadings and reappraisals—including recent films and novels based on the work itself or its structure—it may not prove as rich a vein for mining as some of her other works. But just as *The Voyage Out* is frequently seen as a first and immature novel, and hence overlooked, the sheer difficulty of *The Waves* can be offputting. Nevertheless, there is real reason to believe that it is itself susceptible to strong feminist analysis, and in a way that may be even more striking than *Lighthouse*.

If we may think of the moderns as making use of the structure of the unconscious in whatever sorts of ways became available to them, then contemporary feminist theory and current continental theory merge in lines of analysis with respect to the more difficult and apparently impenetrable of Woolf's novels. If the "fragments" that appealed to Woolf can be set out—as they can, with some difficulty, for *Lighthouse*, and with greater ease for *Voyage*, then *Waves* makes a challenging text for interpretation. In trying to be precise about Woolf's structure, Gordon said:

> To find the common contours of six lives Virginia Woolf synchronizes them—the six are exact contemporaries—and removes the obscuring clutter of biographic trivia. We are not told where Rhoda lived or with whom Jinny flirted at her first ball. Instead, she takes cross-sections of the lives at nine points in their span. Her method at each stage is to examine nature under a particular angle of the sun and to let that dictate human parallels. The italicized nature interludes link the stages of human development so that they may be considered as part of a continuum. Virginia Woolf also blends stage into stage by an overriding rhythm that takes its rise, at dawn, from the ocean's waves and pulses like the blood from end to end.[5]

This attempt to limn being by taking "cross-sections" and setting them up against "overriding rhythms" is itself susceptible to strong feminist analysis, and seems to be a culmination of the methods that Woolf employed all the way along. The dissociated moments of Rachel, Lily's epiphanies, Mrs. Ramsay's memories—all of these are stages on the way to a work that will be a fully realized compendium of such moments. Rather than a master narrative, Woolf was always attracted to a method that would allow her to grasp reality in its infinitesimally small parts. In addition to *The Voyage Out* and *To the Lighthouse*, *The Waves* is a work that is quintessentially Woolfian in its character and structure.

Following along the lines of Showalter's analysis in the 1970s, some feminist criticism of Woolf has more or less stopped with the discursive texts that reveal strong (overt) feminist stances, or with an insistence on attempting to assess the

---

4 Gordon, *Writer's Life*, 206.
5 *Ibid., ibid.*

damage done to Virginia Woolf by sexual abuse in her childhood.[6] But the lines of criticism, like Abel's, that make a genuine attempt to see how the enormity of Woolf's style can be pitted against lines of demarcated theory, may very well be the most valuable feminist stances. The remarkable feature of Woolf's work for the female reader is that she is one of the few authors—male or female—who does not force a woman reader to have to identify against herself. For that very reason, disclosing the core feminist arguments about her texts is crucial; it helps uncover what makes her work so special for so many women readers, and at the same time it reveals key points and central features of her work.

To recapitulate, feminist concerns with respect to Woolf can move in two major directions. The first and most obvious has to do with overt feminist strands in the more argumentative, essay-driven texts—but this ground has been adequately covered many times. The second, and more recondite, has to do with feminist and female tropes in the novels, and their resonance with gynocentric theory. This line of argument itself divides into two parts, for one part can focus on, for example, the mother–daughter linkings between Mrs. Ramsay and Lily Briscoe, while another can focus on Woolf's innovative style and the way in which that style manifests itself structurally. All of these lines of argument are useful, but the richest vein seems to be the second—as Abel has argued, there is an enormous push in Woolf toward Kleinian psychoanalytic material, even if Woolf denied the obvious influences of Freudian theory. Uncovering these influences and the places in which they appear in the text can be a daunting but extremely rewarding task for the feminist theorist.

As Abel says, for example, "Clear analogies link the tensions that Abel introduced into psychoanalytic discourse and those that fracture Woolf's major narratives. The challenge *To the Lighthouse* poses to the Oedipal story of James Ramsay (who is modeled on Adrian Stephen) is echoed two years later in a piece of literary criticism written by Adrian's analyst…"[7] Perhaps more so than the lines of criticism that ask us to examine Woolf's childhood abuse, or those that see her more as Modernist par excellence, the feminist psychoanalytic line illuminates our reading of Woolf not only in a gender-related way, but in an historical way. Part of Abel's argument will be that it is no accident that Woolf wrote what she wrote at the time that Freud's work came to the fore. Our task will be to uncover the connections.

Feminist Concerns

A take on Woolf's work such as is given by Elizabeth Abel in *Virginia Woolf and the Fictions of Psychoanalysis* helps us to situate Woolf historically and contextually. It is not only the case that Hogarth Press was a publisher of Freud; Melanie Klein gave lectures at 50 Gordon Square, the home of Adrian and Karin Stephen.[8] However resistant Woolf may have felt to some of the theses of psychoanalysis, she could not help but have been affected by it, and she would already have been aware of the

---

6   However controversial the work of Louise De Salvo, there is no question that it drew a great deal of attention upon publication.
7   Abel, *Fictions*, 20.
8   *Ibid.*, 13.

influence of women analysts like Klein who recast the theory in different gender-laden terms.

Woolf, with her constant emphasis on submersion, rupture and reparation, must have felt that Klein was on to something, so to speak, right from the beginning. Abel characterizes this situation, relying on Woolf's notes on meeting Klein, as "Klein's psyche, in this rendition, is isomorphic with her representation of the psyche; primitive forces work underground; a Minoan-Mycenean civilization, more tumultuous than Freud's, threatens to engulf a superstructure (and perhaps the viewer as well)."[9] (Woolf had remarked that Klein had "something working underground.")[10] Further acquaintance with Klein's work, with its emphasis on the mother, probably accounts at least partly for Woolf's own insistence on mothering and the desire to return to the mother as one of the central foci of her work. Mothering, its presence or absence, is not only a part of *Lighthouse*; in *Voyage* it makes itself felt for Rachel by its very lack.

The Waves, with its complexity, recapitulates the core of infancy and the mothering that in the other novels is touched upon but not really attempted as an experience. As Lyndall Gordon says, the sea in this work is "Wordsworth's immortal sea which brought us hither."[11] The first sentences of *The Waves* are attempts by Woolf to recapture the moments of infancy and early childhood; in a sense, as Woolf knows, they cannot really be expressed in language, but then again no other attempt to capture them is likely to be able to portray them as well. Introducing the six characters around whom the novel revolves, Woolf writes as her opening:

> "I see a ring," said Bernard, "hanging above me. It quivers and hangs in a loop of light."
>
> "I see a slab of pale yellow," said Susan, "spreading away until it meets a purple stripe."
>
> "I hear a sound," said Rhoda, "cheep, chirp; cheep, chirp; going up and down."[12]

These efforts at delineating first experience are in the vein of all of Woolf's prose, with the crucial exception that it is obvious that Woolf will no longer settle for a mere recalling of the past. This effort to get at the world of infancy is a sort of Freudian/Kleinian move on Woolf's part; as Abel notes, the entire Woolfian project may be summed up as "Against the flux of the present, these scenes, 'representative, enduring,' yet not accentuated, provide backdrops whose distance from the present character's backward gaze solicits us to bridge."[13] But *The Waves* is an explicit attempt to do more than simply present a backward gaze—it is, in fact, a summoning. The concern is to re-establish the muted pre-Oedipal world.[14]

This deeper, more resonant sort of feminist analysis is, as we have said, reliant upon turns in psychoanalytic theory that themselves are subject to debate. Klein's turn destabilizes Freud's overtly patriarchal narrative, with its emphasis on the

---

9   *Ibid.*, 19.
10 *Ibid., ibid.*
11 Gordon, *Writer's Life*, 206.
12 Woolf, Virginia (1950), *The Waves*, London: The Hogarth Press, 9.
13 Abel, *Fictions*, 1.
14 *Ibid.*, 29.

Oedipal crisis, and with its (obvious) difficulty in accounting for the developmental paths of women. Thus Freud's own acknowledgement of a polymorphously desiring sexual world precedes—both theoretically, and, in Freud's articulation of it, chronologically—the more overtly dramatic developmental sequence of the Oedipal. But in order to make the female narrative parallel that of the male, Freud has to emphasize a displacement of eroticization for the female that has always been seen, at best, as a sort of limping progress, perhaps too overtly mimicking the male path. Klein moves toward the "Minoan" past which is, of course, the world of the mother and of the semiotic. In this world, it is simply easier to construct a comparatively genderless set of stages for development, since the original object for all infants will be the mother. Abel's insight that Woolf is reliant in many ways on a sort of Kleinian object relations theory for her insights and for her setting out of them is valuable insofar as it pushes strands of analysis well past the more superficial and easier to limn analyses of abuse, madness and derangement.

The loss of the maternal world and the harsh oppression of the patriarchal world are constant features of Woolf's work. Some of the dialogue of *Voyage* is a veritable flat statement of these themes; for that reason, the characters, seen in and of themselves, are perhaps less believable than we would like.

It might seem trite or repetitious to allude to the prevalence of many of these themes in straightforward feminist theory—not necessarily concerned with literature—but a great deal of the work done in the last twenty to thirty years in feminism across the disciplines bolsters the importance of the sort of Kleinian-object relations theory ties that we have analyzed as being relevant to Woolf's writing. Two areas, neither of which might seem superficially to be related to literary topics, come to mind. The first is the large amount of work done in feminist epistemology and philosophy of science that makes use of at least some portions of object relations theory to make its general point. Evelyn Fox Keller's work is a classic in this regard: in her well-known essay "Love and Sex in Plato's Epistemology," Keller ties the notion of the quest for transcendence on the part of the male thinker to a denigration of all things female, and, ultimately, to relationships with females.[15] This argument, of course, can be turned on its head (and is by a theorist such as Klein). Female–female relationships recapitulate the force of the original mother–daughter dyad, and also retain the intense connectivity and groundedness that is associated, metaphorically and otherwise, with the realm of the feminine. Thus Abel's analysis of Lily's relationship to Mrs. Ramsay, although an instance of this sort of thinking cast in literary terms, is but one more example of a relationship devoid of the master transcendental gaze that Woolf associates with male thinking, and that in her essays is spelled out as being quintessentially male.

Another line of research, however often it has been alluded to, is the line that culminates in Gilligan's developmental psychology work—work that in itself recapitulates a good deal of the psychoanalytic thought to which advertence has already been made. Although Gilligan's *In a Different Voice* can no doubt be

---

15 Fox Keller, Evelyn (1985), *Reflections on Gender and Science*, New Haven: Yale University Press. Keller's work is among the most intellectually sophisticated of those who attempt to take this sort of line.

criticized from the standpoint of psychological fieldwork, there is no question that the material that she presents is still another version of the same sort of theory.[16] Any reader who can readily recall the examples of Amy and Jake in this text understands why Gilligan uses the notion of different voices, and what it is that those voices ultimately amount to.

From Showalter's take on Woolf's androgyny to Abel's much more theoretically developed Freudian/Kleinian line, feminist criticism of Woolf has found very fertile ground, for it is obvious that her work meshes with feminist theory to an even greater extent than is the case with many other women authors. Fortunately for the analyst who would be inclined to try to make use of Continental thought, or of the notion of *écriture feminine* to which we have already alluded in analyzing Drabble, many other related intersections present themselves. The work of both Lacan and Kristeva is of obvious use here, and is itself an offshoot of the type of theory we have described. Woolf is to a greater extent an inhabitant of the realm of the semiotic; she understands that the important male world of the "symbolic" is precisely that which has done so much damage. *Jouissance* is something that her writing about Mrs. Ramsay puts the reader in mind of, and is perhaps precisely that "truth" that Lily refers to and is aware of.

How one might go about detailing the foci for an analysis of Woolf in terms of Kristeva or Lacan could scarcely be more relevant.

Writing the Body

There is a sense in which one of the most appropriate theoretical stances for reading Woolf is Kristeva's notion of abjection. Although it might appear preliminary that abjection has only to do with bodily disgust and revulsion, Kristeva makes it clear that one form of abjection involves the very same dissociative states that Woolf is so gifted at depicting. As she writes:

> It is no longer I who expel, 'I' is expelled. The border has become an object. How can I be without border? That elsewhere that I imagine beyond the present, or that I hallucinate so that I might, in a present time, speak to you…it is now here, jetted, abjected, into 'my' world….
> The abjection of self would be the culminating form of that experience…[17]

Some dissociative states, brought on by whatever trauma or reverie, are remarkably similar to those episodes of disgust (some involving vomiting or other bodily reactions) that are frequently the result of confrontation with the physically repulsive. In other words, mental or bodily fight are clearly two manifestations of the same type of avoidance, and may even occur simultaneously—some episodes of vomiting, for example, may temporarily induce an odd or unusual mental state.

---

16 Gilligan, Carol (1982), *In a Different Voice*, Cambridge: Harvard University Press.
17 Kristeva, Julia, "Approaching Abjection," in Cazeaux (ed.), 542–562.

The abject is in fact the polar opposite of the sort of merging that fluid ego structures associate with mothering and infancy. The abject is "being opposed to I."[18]

But what these two sorts of episodes have in common is precisely that shakiness of ego structure—one harkens back directly to semiosis; the other is semiosis reversed, so to speak.

In Woolf this set of notions has more to do with the uncanny but Kristeva mentions that "uncanniness" is related to her construction of abjection. The "massive and sudden emergence of uncanniness"[19] can, in fact, be a form of abjection. For Woolf, this seems to be a common occurrence, and it is remarkable how often this experience or something very like it recurs even in *The Voyage Out*. Even Terence and Rachel's declaration of love for each other is accompanied by a similar experience:

> The silence was then broken by their voices which joined in tones of strange unfamiliar sound which formed no words. Faster and faster they walked; simultaneously they stopped, clasped each other in their arms, then, releasing themselves, dropped to the earth. They sat side by side. Sounds stood out from the background making a bridge across their silence; they heard the swish of the trees and some beast croaking in a remote world.[20]

The intensity of their emotion itself creates an experience of the uncanny, and alters their sense of time, since they are very late returning to their group and are roundly chastised by Mr. Flushing. This particular stream of time is not, of course, an instance of abjection, but what is remarkable about it is that it is very similar to some of Rachel's earlier dissociative states, and also similar to the number of instances in the text that are marked by repulsion, a sense of the uncanny, or both.

Abjection clearly comes from some sense that categories have been mixed and that there is something inappropriate. Although Kristeva's account of abjection emphasizes the physical disgust that surrounds many of these states, it is clear that there is such a thing as a sort of mental disgust. Because no line can adequately be drawn between the states, they meld together and give rise to a more powerful account of the phenomenon in question.

Kristeva is, in a sense, the Lacanian theorist par excellence, and her work has an edge and precision to it that is perhaps somewhat lacking even in the writings of other French thinkers. But there is a slide—a definitive move, in fact—from the concept of abjection to some of the other concepts available in the French trove. Abjection is that defilement, dissociation or turning away from the semiotic of the bodily; it is the converse of *jouissance*. Woolf's entrancement with the world of the mother is obvious; Lily feels Mrs. Ramsay's lack because only Mrs. Ramsay has the capacity to make things right. (In *Voyage*, Rachel is depicted as having been motherless.) What many of the French theorists have in common is an acknowledgement of the importance of the semiotic (however it is labeled), and a concomitant importance attachable to the patriarchal *langue paternelle* that, in developmental sequence, moves away from the mother. Kristeva and Irigaray have in common the notion that

---

18 *Ibid.*, 542.
19 *Ibid.*, 543.
20 Woolf, *Voyage*, 332.

to enter the male order is to enter the realm of the symbolic, and that realm is, for Woolf, an unattractive and alienating place.

In the introduction to her *Irigaray Reader*, Margaret Whitford notes:

> Playing on the idea of the mirror, she [Irigaray in *Speculum*] points out that Lacan's mirror can only see women's bodies as lacking, as a 'hole'; to see what is specific to women, he would have needed a mirror to look inside. The mirror, of course, is the mirror of theory or discourse, and although Lacan is not named, *Speculum* is as much a challenge to Lacan as it is to Freud and to Western philosophy.[21]

The world of theory or discourse, which falls apart under Kristeva's abjection, is the very world that Lily and Rachel abhor. Rhoda, of *The Waves*, will be another cast in the same mold. While Lily struggles to see Mr. Ramsay in any terms other than those that he has created for himself, Rachel can appreciate Terence Hewet only when he is away from St. John Hirst. In fact, Hewet away from Hirst is a different figure. Woolf portrays Hewet at the crossroads, so to speak, when he has already become aware of his attraction for Rachel, but is forced to endure more of St. John's company:

> She did not see that Hewet kept looking at her across the gangway, between the figures of waiters hurrying past with plates. He was inattentive, and Hirst was finding him very cross and disagreeable. They had touched upon all the usual topics—upon politics and literature, gossip and Christianity. They had quarrelled over the service, which was every bit as fine as Sappho, according to Hewet....[22]

With the trope of Hirst having, improbably, worked on Sappho during a boring church service, Woolf forces the colliding worlds of maternal and paternal toward each other. As Hewet finds himself engrossed in Rachel, Hirst's usual talk becomes unbearable; the difference is that Rachel has found their usual talk unbearable all the way along.

As we have seen, several lines of theory, both Continental and non-Continental, propel us toward a realization that, whatever conflicts Freud might ultimately have deemed Oedipal, the crucial relationship for both males and females is initially the mother–infant relationship. This intense bonding, especially if sustained and not truncated at an early point, creates a semiotic of longing that recurs in the unconscious and that can become a dominant force at other points in one's life. It is precisely because Freud recognized the strength of this pull that his theory postulated a very difficult move for the little girl, given the need for a transference to desire for the male. The merging that all humans recall in this bodily and unconscious fashion is easily achieved when the male has a sexual relationship with a woman (and, in fact, may be so powerful that it accounts for the somewhat abrupt nature of many of these encounters, seen from the female point of view). But it is not easily achieved for the female when she has a sexual relationship with the male. The desire, both conscious

---

21 Whitford, Margaret (ed.) (1991), *The Irigaray Reader*, Malden, MA: Blackwell Publishers, Inc., 6–7.
22 Woolf, *Voyage*, 29.

and unconscious, to be able to recapture moments from infancy and early childhood is a driving force for both genders throughout their adult lives.

Woolf's feminism, then, may be seen through many lenses; those of *A Room of One's Own* or *Orlando* have been extensively developed in the literature. But what is needed is a more careful look, as Abel has done, at the psychoanalytic constructs that manifestly underpin Woolf's main novels.[23] It is here, one is tempted to say, that the most fruitful paths for feminist theory are found, and it is also along these lines that new meldings and mergings with other theoretical stances can be created.

Post Again

If the work of Julia Kristeva can be of assistance to us in reading Woolf, it is clear that the same may be said of the work of Lacan. However impenetrable his prose, we are fortunate that there now exists a body of commentary, and that the relatively straightforward ties between Lacan and Kristeva may help push us along.

Clive Cazeaux comments of Lacan that "Difficulty is cultivated because the reader is compelled to endure the action of constraint which, it is claimed, represents the passage to understanding and new interpretation."[24] In any case, with effort it is possible to make something of Lacan, and to use one's understanding toward the illumination of other issues. Because of the extent to which her work recapitulates Freudian or psychoanalytic themes—some of which we have just analyzed—Woolf's work can also be analyzed along specific concepts introduced by Lacan, such as the gaze. Although this particular conceptual apparatus is employed by many Continental thinkers, Lacan's use of it is structuralist, or involves structuralist themes, in the sense that he wants to make a statement about how the ego or sense of self develops against its objects. Woolf's constant harking to the past, and her use of memory and certain selective introjects as a way of delineating personality, make her fertile ground for the use of Lacanian theory.

In the work taken from a series of lectures originally given in his 1964 seminars, Lacan tries to introduce the notion of the gaze as defining not only for the object, but for the subject.[25] As he says, "From the...iridescence of which I am at first a part, I emerge as eye, assuming, in a way, emergence from what I would like to call the function of seeingness."[26] The self is constituted, insofar as the construction of the ego is concerned, by its modes of seeing. Thus the objectification in which the young child engages, as she begins to grasp the difference between self and not-self, also helps to create a self.

---

23 Phyllis Rose hints at this in early work on Woolf when she writes: "But in writing *To the Lighthouse* part of Woolf's exorcism of her personal ghosts was to see them as cultural artifacts, monuments not only of personal history but of the history of us all." Rose, Phyllis (1978), *Woman of Letters: a Life of Virginia Woolf*, London: Pandora Press, 172.

24 Cazeaux, Clive, "Introduction to Psychoanalysis and Feminism," in Cazeaux (ed.), 491–505.

25 *Ibid.*, 497.

26 Lacan, Jacques, "Of the Gaze as Object Petit a," in Cazeaux (ed.), 519–541.

Looked at along these terse Lacanian lines, the various sorts of seeing in which so many of Woolf's characters engage is probably related to their own altering states of ego function versus dissociation. Rachel sees differently because she literally has a different self during her less integrated moments; by the same token the loss of integration is causally connected to the different ways of seeing. Even in *The Waves*, Rhoda exclaims in much the same manner:

> There is this mystery about people when they leave us. When they leave us I can companion them to the pond and make them stately. When Miss Lambert passes, she makes the daisy change; and everything runs like streaks of fire when she carves the beef. Month by month things are losing their hardness; even my body now lets the light through; my spine is soft like wax near the flame of the candle. I dream; I dream.[27]

This Woolfian character, like Lily, Rachel and Virginia Woolf herself, feels herself "losing hardness," become "soft," as boundaries blur and things become progressively more unreal. Yet this special ego state is complexly related to a certain sort of sight; in it, Rhoda sees things "like streaks of fire."

If abjection, in Kristeva's terms, is one way of losing the world, objectification, in Lacanian terms, is a way of gaining it. He also says, "The mode of my presence in the world is the subject in so far as by reducing itself solely to this certainty of being a subject, it becomes active annihilation."[28] The ordinary, structured ego has the capacity to annihilate—complete objectification severs the outer world from the inner felt world of the subject, and boundaries are secure. But Rhoda, in her state of seeing "streaks of fire," has not really objectified Miss Lambert, or even most of the outer objects around her. Things penetrate her; she feels caught up in them and cannot make the adequate separation. This, of course, is the source of much of the artist's mastery. That feeling of total identification with the absent object that allows Lily to call out "Mrs. Ramsay" is precisely what allows her to finish her picture.

Other states can also have this effect; both Rachel and Hewet feel it in *Voyage*. As they go for their walk away from the others in the party traveling upstream, all around them takes on a progressive surreal atmosphere since they are wrapped in an all-encompassing sort of dyadic love. Communication breaks the spell to some extent:

> With every word the mist which had enveloped them, making them seem unreal to each other, since the previous afternoon melted a little further, and their contact became more and more natural.[29]

But without communication, the force of the emotional attraction is overwhelming, and it itself becomes a defining reality.

Writing in the introduction to her compendium *The Portable Kristeva*, Kelly Oliver notes of Lacan:

---

27 Woolf, *Waves*., 45.
28 Lacan, "Gaze," 520.
29 Woolf, Voyage, 344.

Bringing linguistics to Freudian psychoanalytic theory, Jacques Lacan claims that the unconscious is structured like a language. Like language, we need to interpret unconscious processes in terms of syntax and semantics.[30]

This somewhat brief and perhaps oversimplified statement about Lacan does accomplish one thing: it reminds us of the extent to which a writer like Woolf, already more than accustomed to diving into her own unconscious, can pull up some of what she finds there to create a new syntax.

If the self and ego are partly created by objectification, lack of the ability to objectify may signal ego loss and some form of breakdown or psychosis. As Phyllis Rose has said of the portions of *Voyage* that deal with Rachel's illness and death, Woolf is unsurpassed at drawing on her own psychological torment to provide a portrait of the emotionally (and physically) ill. Rose claims that "Woolf's descriptions of the phantasmagoric riot of Rachel's sick brain are, to my mind, the best writing in *The Voyage Out....*"[31] Here the unconscious does indeed have its own syntax—and its syntax is completely at variance with "reality." But this sensation of Rachel's that she is stuck at the bottom of the sea, or that she cannot distinguish individual objects, is precisely linked to a sort of floating sensation that overtakes her during her periods of wakefulness. This is not the dissociation that we have linked to Rachel's artistic qualities, or even to the notion of abjection. This is the plain takeover of the mind by the unconscious, and yet, as Woolf indicates (and as Lacan claims) it has a language of its own.

Whatever the origin of Woolf's ability to apparently dissociate at will—and also involuntarily—it served her well in her art. The "shivering fragments" and her ability to record them are related to this sense of the uncanny that apparently overtook her on a regular basis. That Rachel is indeed the young Virginia Woolf seems to be asserted by all commentators, with the caveat that Virginia herself may have been slightly more assertive and less hesitant than the portrayal of Rachel would suggest.

But Rachel's dreamy dissonance is the cognitive state of the artist, and her response to Richard Dalloway's kiss, and the perplexity into which it throws her, are the precursors of the sort of mania that, at its peak, gave Woolf her intense creative power. Although afraid of sex, and of men, Woolf feels the effects of male desire in the well-known passage where Rachel accidentally winds up in Dalloway's arms. As Woolf writes, "Her head was cold, her knees shaking, and the physical pain of the emotion was so great that she could only keep herself moving above the great leaps of her heart."[32]

The unconscious also has a syntax of its own when it is moved by sexual passion, and it is inevitable that the syntactical breakthrough will be somewhat frightening, if not actually terrifying, the first time it is felt. It is in sections such as these of her various works that Woolf excels at both the syntax and semantics of the unconscious, or at detailing to dissolution of the ego—an experience that some artists seem to have on a regular basis. In this sense, Woolf has few peers in her craft.

---

30 Oliver, Kelly (1997), "Introduction: Kristeva's Revolutions," in Oliver (ed), *The Portable Kristeva*, New York: Columbia University Press, xi–xxix.
31 Rose, *Woman*, 72.
32 Woolf, *Voyage*, 85.

Knowledge

Feminist epistemologists, and feminist theorists in general, have often written of ways of knowing that might be gynocentric, or that at least are not forcedly male-dominant. Even within the Anglo-American analytic vein, much new work has tried to articulate a point of view that spells out connectedness, reliance on a community of knowers, and reliance on evidence taken from the senses in a way that might be more than merely empiricist as part and parcel of the project of a feminist epistemology.

Woolf's modernism and the fragmentary nature of her view do not readily lend themselves to any cut-and-dried analysis, but that does not mean that there are not ways of addressing Woolf's particular forms of knowing. What seems to be important for her is the immediacy of the experience, and the knower's sense of it. Thus the work that we have already done on time and the concept of building an ontology through slices of time points in the direction of something that we might deem fit to call a Woolfian epistemics. Ironically, much of what Woolf attacks as "male" in her work is, in fact, the product of a Cantabridgian overview, and some of that product is specifically philosophical (for instance, the work of G.E. Moore).

Woolf's focus on knowing and that which might be known—and here we have to use these terms in ways that might be antithetical to a great deal of professional philosophy—is such that immediacy and reality-within-the-moment are the defining factors for her. Thus, as we have seen, Lily's artistic vision allows her knowledge within a certain framework in *Lighthouse*, but it is certainly not propositional knowledge, and not even knowledge that can be constrained within most developed and articulated feminist views.

What Rachel, Lily and Rhoda have in common in the three novels by Woolf in question is that their altered states—dissociated, the product of illness, or simply "artistic" movements—give them something that, for lack of a better term, might be called a special epistemic access. While Woolf claims, at different points, that this amounts to a special sort of Truth, she probably does not claim that it amounts to a special sort of Knowledge. Yet the two are inevitably linked. Something of what Woolf is up to at a later point in time is spelled out by Phyllis Rose in *Woman of Letters*:

> The style of conversation which Moore fostered... she regarded with amusement. Rather than adopting the styles and values of the Cambridge men, she seems to have defined herself against them, insisting on the value of a distinctively "feminine" and even untutored approach to life: "They sit silent, absolutely silent, all the time," she writes Violet Dickinson in 1905.... "However I don't think they are robust enough to feel very much. Oh women are my line and not these inanimate creatures!"[33]

The latter line says a great deal insofar as Woolf is concerned, and it is noteworthy that even her male characters, such as Terence Hewet, who might be said to feel much in the same vein are seen by critics—and indeed by the author herself—as having many female characteristics.

---

33 Rose, *Woman*, 39.

A pertinent question, however, is why we should think of Woolf's handling of the knowledge-of-the-moment as in any sense feminist, despite her remarks that "women are my line." Here we come to a core that may be susceptible to more standard feminist philosophical analysis.

It is not only the case that the modes of knowing that have been labeled "androcentric" in the literature might be solitary or expressible in propositions—much more to the point is that the sort of empiricism that is standardly philosophical has always been that which led to generalizations over repetitions of experience. Woolf's emphasis on the moment, the special state, and the "shivering" nature of the fragments is, if anything, more phenomenological, although Woolf would probably not be happy with that label, either. What all of Woolf's work attempts to do is to present us with a special sort of epistemic that values the translucency of the given moment, even if it cannot be expressed in words, and even if the moment itself is one that later generations might label a form of illness. Thus Van Gogh's vision—or Gauguin's—also falls under this rubric, although both artists were male, and it would seem unfair to think of Gauguin's vision as anything other than a decided attempt to experience non-European cultures and to escape from bourgeois France.

What is "feminine" about most of the foregoing is along metaphorical lines; in the culture in general, what Woolf wants to depict is a bit like what used to be called, in former times, woman's intuition. But this is not intuition set up to serve a homely task—everyone except for Hewet in *The Voyage Out* is surprised that Rachel will marry, as she does not strike anyone as being a conventionally attractive woman. Rachel is the artist, and most of Woolf's artists are women. Woolf seems to want to associate this special access with a feminine world, even if she has many counterexamples available to her.

If there is a sense in which there is anything at all standardly epistemic about Woolf's forms of knowing, as depicted in the many instances in her work that we have cited, it probably has something to do with the visual. Much of the description that we are given of the "special states" has to do with either striking visual experiences, a sort of disjointedness (especially with respect to time), or a statedly artistic take on the experience, such as we get from Lily's descriptions of what she sees prior to painting.

Traditionally, of the five senses vision has been by far and away the most important for a philosophical construction of knowledge. Indeed, we might say that all of the others are given very short shrift—one might naively imagine that there would be many philosophical accounts of knowledge by touch or by sound, but there are few, and the other two senses are simply, for the most part, ignored.

Woolf's special access, then, is not unrelated to the visual. It is simply that Woolf makes new use of the visual—she moves it in directions completely different from the standard philosophical directions. There are passages in Woolf, of course, with more or less mundane depictions of outer life, of the sort that—again, following tradition—might be used for propositional knowledge. But these are not the sorts of descriptions that interest Woolf; they are clearly stage setting so that she can move on to the real thing. What does interest her, insofar as the external world is concerned, are the slightly jarred or altered descriptions made available to the agent by the strength of the emotional experience.

Thus Terence and Rachel both see things differently while they are in love, and some of this is manifest simply in a sort of somewhat more intense visual experience. Clearly, again, this experience is not unrelated to standard epistemological accounts: it is simply that for Woolf what counts about it is the change, and not the raw data. Here is an exemplary passage:

> Not only did the silence weigh upon them, but they were both unable to frame any thoughts. There was something between them which had to be spoken of. One of them had to begin, but which of them was it to be? Then Hewet picked up a red fruit and threw it as high as he could. When it dropped, he would speak. They heard the flapping of great wings; they heard the fruit go pattering through the leaves and eventually fall with a thud. The silence was again profound.[34]

In this short passage, several features are comparatively marked. The silence is heavy; this is repeated. The red fruit is not only a standout in color, but it is thrown to a great height. Rather than merely hearing birds, they hear the "flapping of great wings." When the fruit falls, it does not make an ordinary noise.

All of this is, of course, partly because of the strangeness of their environment to them, but it is clear from context that Woolf does not mean for that to be the deciding factor. Rather, it is the emotional tension between Hewet and Rachel that changes what they perceive, and that creates an unusually heightened sense of the external for them. Other factors could, of course, create such awareness—and other factors do, for Rachel is perfectly capable of having such experiences by herself, and does in fact have them at an earlier point in the novel. But it would not be too much to say that the greatest changes here are because of the emotional state that Rachel and Hewet find themselves in, one entirely contingent upon their relationship. In that sense, Woolf supersedes the merely epistemic and moves on to new territory.

Movings Out

The sort of modernism of which Woolf is held to be an expositor has now been passed over by various other movements, postmodern though they may be. We are so accustomed to hearing about the virtues of the moderns, and how their breakthroughs represented major achievements in a given time, that it is very difficult to get enough distance on them to be able to make any genuine assessment. Like Joyce, Woolf is handicapped as a writer (now) by the fact that we can scarcely approach her with a fresh sense of expectation.

There is one feature of Woolf's writing, however, that stands out and pushes us on, even if it makes us uncomfortable. Woolf refuses to make things easy for the reader, and her refusal to do so itself stands out, even among the other moderns. It is not, in particular, her word choice; we might give the nod to Joyce here. It is certainly not her subject matter, which in most of the works is simply English life in its various permutations. It is rather, a sort of strained intelligibility that seems to be precisely related to her descriptions of internal states, as we have just outlined.

---

34 Woolf, *Voyage*, 331.

At an earlier point we cited some of the opening of *Voyage*, the first full sentence of which is: "As the streets that lead from the Strand to the Embankment are very narrow, it is better not to walk down them arm-in-arm."[35] But where one would ordinarily think that the following sentences do, in fact, have something to do with couples proceeding along the way, the paragraph turns out to be about (if it may be said to be about anything) "eccentricity." This opening, and its lack of conventional relatedness, is not at all unusual for Woolf.

In fact, David Bradshaw has argued convincingly in an essay titled "The Socio-Political Vision of the Novels" that this opening, with its mention of the Embankment, leads to nascent Woolfian concerns with egalitarian issues.[36] Woolf's construction of the Ambroses and their world makes it obvious that she does not have to mention the inner, hidden side of London, but Bradshaw notes that this concern is very much manifest in *Voyage*, as well as being part of, for example, the "Time Passes" section of *Lighthouse*. As he writes:

> Moreover, even though the novel has barely got started, many of Woolf's readers in 1915 would have noted that she makes her 'voyage out' as a novelist by having her characters follow a well-trodden eastwards path. The Ambroses' journey from the Embankment to the benighted quayside of Wapping in London's East End calls to mind the previous transits of numerous social investigators, missionaries and philanthropists, not least because Helen stops to register some of the key sites of 'Outcast London.'[37]

Bradshaw convincingly argues that Woolf's concern for the "skeleton beneath" theme recurs throughout the novel, and is a trope for more than one kind of concern. It can, of course, signal those states that Rachel, in her artistic giftedness, is so fond of visiting—states that seem to allow her access to some kind of definitive take on the real. But it can also signal a concern for those whose lives, hidden from comfortable London, also constitute the inner skeleton of the city. These are the same sorts of lives chronicled by Dickens, for example—but we may be surprised to read Woolf in such a way that concern for the unfortunate is brought to the surface.

The link between the rejection-of-propositional-knowledge Woolf and these other concerns has been made many times. As we have seen, it is part and parcel of her "feminism," not merely in the sense that it is spelled out in the discursive texts, but that the androcentric worldview is clearly rejected, or at least found lacking, in *The Waves*, *The Voyage Out* and *To the Lighthouse*. The artist is unlikely to be able to engage in the unexamined patriotism of those who constantly glorify the British Empire: that would be inconsistent with the artistic desire to see. But a great deal of what is seen remains, perforce, ugly. It is "deformed," "gibbering," as Rachel dreams in *Voyage*; it is, as Bradshaw claims, tuberculous and ill.[38]

---

35 *Ibid.*, 1.
36 Bradshaw, David, "The Socio-Political Vision of the Novels," in Roe and Sellers (eds.), *Cambridge Companion*, 191–208.
37 *Ibid.*, 192.
38 *Ibid.*, 201–202. Bradshaw provides a superb analysis of the relevant portions of *Lighthouse*.

Now, in an era when there is a great deal more concern about social conditions manifest on a daily basis—or at least what passes for concern—it would be too easy to read Woolf as holding such issues paramount. They clearly are not paramount, because Rhoda, Rachel and Lily do not come from the sorts of circumscribed backgrounds that would inhibit their own development. But what is quintessentially feminist in Woolf is the melding together of the female artist's vision with the desire to see the "skeleton beneath," whatever that may be. That "skeleton" is inconsistent with the vision of reality trumpeted by the Oxbridge dons and their like, and it is not a vision that can be captured neatly in propositional analysis.

Ends

Scholarship on Woolf has tended to emphasize, as we said at the outset, either the interpersonal relations in her early years between the Duckworths, Julia and Leslie Stephen, and Leslie's daughter Laura from a previous marriage, or Woolf's statedly more feminist views as developed in *A Room of One's Own*, or other essays. Bradshaw has argued that *The Voyage Out* is "undervalued," and no one who has made a careful attempt to read *The Waves* will disagree with the contention that it is, in fact, quite difficult to work through.[39]

If careful scholarship on these two works is lacking, the same cannot be said of *To the Lighthouse*, which is Woolf's most criticized work, certainly, with the possible exception of *Mrs. Dalloway*.[40] But even here the difficulty has been that criticism—at least of *Lighthouse*—has tended to emphasize Woolf's play with printerly conventions, or to respond largely to the admittedly triadic structure of the work. Other areas that would seem to cry out for attention, such as her emphasis on time and the interior life, have probably not received the attention that they have deserved. Yet it is these aspects of Woolf's work (also seen, as has been argued here, in *Voyage* and *Waves*) that allow for all of the other areas that do receive commentary: as Bradshaw has said, part of seeing what is beneath is Rachel's take on "the black ribs of wrecked ships" in the depths of the sea.[41] Only someone like Rachel would care to look in the first place.

If Virginia Woolf's admittedly severe mental difficulties—whatever their origins—also have their place in the development of her vision, it is probably because they intensified and allowed full rein to that distanced, altered view of things that she seems to have had on and off from her early childhood. If, as Phyllis Rose has claimed, some of the best writing in *Voyage* is the sections that describe Rachel's illness, then it may very well be the case that Woolf owed her ability to depict this fantastic sickness to her own debilitating attacks of illness.

The point is that Woolf retained her vision, whatever its source, and developed it in a way that allowed her to depict the inner worlds of others. Whether her depiction is of the thought processes in the here and now, which tends to be the case in, for

---

39 Bradshaw, "Socio-Political," in Roe and Sellers (eds.), 196.

40 As this is written, the current mania for the latter work has culminated in a film based on *The Hours*, itself grounded in Woolf's novel.

41 Bradshaw, in Roe and Sellers (eds.), 192.

example, the third section of *To the Lighthouse*, or whether it is the drawing in of the past (Mrs. Ramsay at the dinner party), or at the inner world of the gravely ill (Rachel), all of these states allow for a special sort of vision, and Woolf is consummately gifted at presenting that vision. Then the outsider's take on things allows him or her (frequently a her) to enter sympathetically the world of others, and it is that world that Bradshaw, for one, is concerned about in his insightful essay on Woolf. But even Ridley and Helen Ambrose—although not so flatly in Helen's case—lack that capacity to move beyond the mundane or the overt social structure, and to reach out to others in the process. In delineating these characters, Woolf reminds us of her own voyage from Kensington Bloomsbury, and of the price attached to it.

Laura Marcus indicates that Virginia Woolf's relationship with feminism is a "symbiotic one."[42] While it is clear that Woolf drew on feminism in a variety of ways—and in some sense, simply by having so many women characters whose lives were central to the various novels—it is also clear that latter-day feminism has drawn on Woolf. What remains at the core of her writing, however, as has been adumbrated here, is a sense that the woman artist is primarily an artist, and that the visionary's peculiar take on things needs to be set out. Where the artist is a woman, complexity transpires.

---

42 Laura Marcus, "Woolf's Feminism and Feminism's Woolf," in Roe and Sellers (eds.), 209–244.

Chapter Six

Beauvoir's Philosophy and Literature

Simone de Beauvoir suffers from a sort of reversal-of-fortune change with respect to her writing; for years, she was thought of primarily as a novelist and essayist, and scarcely as a philosopher, but more recently her philosophical work has come to be emphasized over her novels.[1] It is the case, however, that even with a naïve formulation one would expect less difficulty in making out the philosophical strains in her work than, for example, in the work of Drabble.

Why this is the case goes beyond the simple facts of her association with Sartre and her authorship of the heavily conceptual *The Second Sex*. It is also a matter of style. At times, Beauvoir's style is weighty and even ponderous—but this is precisely what allows her to bring up philosophical problems with ease. In the case of Margaret Drabble, it could be argued that her ironic twists hid a great many conceptual issues that were available only on re-reading or on a very careful first reading. Woolf's modernism is an exemplar, but the path through much of her work—particularly the most celebrated novels—is sufficiently tortured that many simply give up.

By comparison, Beauvoir's work, even in translation, is easy to read, and it would not be fair to characterize her as someone for whom style is paramount. Indeed, if there is any feature that marks her novels, it is the lengthy dialogue in which her characters engage, sometimes at the expense of comprehension.[2] But this dialogue, happily, is rife with philosophical and conceptual problems: what is the role of the artist? What is the nature of the best society? What is an ideal love relationship (from the standpoint of either gender)? If Beauvoir is sometimes a bit heavy-handed—many of the most complex dialogues go on for pages, with scarcely a break—it is clear that she is attempting to deal with the sort of material that we usually associate with large questions, and that her mode of dealing with it is transparently philosophical.

Indeed, the sort of existentialism with which Beauvoir and Sartre were both associated favors the notion of the committed artist, and Beauvoir is nothing if not committed. From her essays, such as *The Ethics of Ambiguity* and the later *Old Age*, one can see philosophical positions full blown: novels such as *The Mandarins* and

---

1   That this is so is due largely to the efforts of such philosophers as Margaret Simons. It is worth noting, however, that it is not really possible to neglect Beauvoir's literature, even by the standards of the canon. *The Mandarins* won the Prix Goncourt in 1954.

2   The back jacket of the Norton paperback edition of *The Mandarins* contains a blurb from Time magazine, apparently written around the time of the book's original translation into English. The blurb says, in part, "Anyone wanting to know what interesting people like Sartre, novelist Albert Camus, Arthur Koestler and others were thinking at war's end...." will find the answers within the novel's pages. But the fact that a work is indisputably a roman à clef does not usually speak in its favor, nor does it make it much easier to read.

She Came to Stay allow us to examine the playing out of these positions in daily life. Taken in all, it might be said that the chief problem with which Beauvoir is concerned is that which is also investigated in *Ethics of Ambiguity*, the problem of the "other." If the other's reflection for me of myself is negative, or certainly less than positive, how does this change my own opinion of my project? Do I then see it as less worthy? How can I maintain a committed political stance in the face of lengthy debate and argument, and assault from other parties and/or points of view? These are questions, along with the sorts of puzzles mentioned earlier, that work such as *The Mandarins* examines at length.

Beauvoir also clearly sets out the paradoxes of gender in many of her literary works, even if the reader finds them occasionally a bit flat. Anne Dubreuilh, although a trained psychotherapist and a woman with an independent life—not to say an independent past—experiences problems with a notion of liberation insofar as it conflicts with commitments that she thinks that she has made to others. One of the best-known sections of *The Mandarins* is the part where Anne meets the "Lewis Brogan" (Nelson Algren) character in Chicago; what is remarkable about this section is that, for all of Anne's attempts at free-spiritedness, it is clear that she feels some guilt about the relationship. In her essays, as opposed to her novels, Beauvoir sometimes does an even clearer job of setting out the oppositions. *A Very Easy Death* has been cited not only because of the clarity of its writing, but because of the comparative transparency of some of the philosophical thinking. But the careful reader will note that another feature of the text is the author's guilt and conflict over her role as daughter. Toward the end, she remembers that her mother had had to hear her (Simone) spoken of as "the family's disgrace."[3] She is constantly reminding the reader that her sister, Hélene (Poupette) had a better and more cordial relationship with their mother than she did. It is not difficult to discern that this has everything to do with Simone's personal failure to follow convention.

If we can be more comfortable with the straightforward assertion that Beauvoir's work is philosophical in a way that pushes beyond both Drabble and Woolf, our task is to try to see how it is that we can also see Beauvoir as a successful novelist and writer, aside from the constant promulgation of philosophical problems and categories. This second task is perhaps not so simple.

It may be best to think of her work as having two major divisions—the novels (our primary concern here), and at least a few essays which, although having some conceptual content, may be viewed partially as pieces of craft (*A Very Easy Death* is obviously one of these). If we think for the moment only of the novels, what stands out as a feature of her work is probably the dialogue: the intricately constructed conversations, although sometimes laborious, do an excellent job of transmitting the notion of a certain sort of oral culture, one that certainly permeated post-war intellectual France. In addition, Beauvoir hits hard at another area, and one that in our analysis we have associated with Woolf. Although it does not stand out as much from the text—probably because of the lengthy passages of dialogue—Beauvoir also has a gift for capturing those altered states that seem to signal some sort of cognitive change, or some sort of pronounced change in levels of awareness. Anne,

---

3   de Beauvoir, Simone (1965), *A Very Easy Death*, New York: Pantheon Books, 103.

for example, seems to feel those states on a regular basis. Beauvoir, like Woolf, has a strong capacity to realize that the altered state changes the way in which the artist sees things, and that the ability to alter a mode of seeing is crucial to the creation of art.

The recent upsurge of interest in Beauvoir means that it is now difficult to read her novels as works of literature. Whereas before the alleged or purported difficulty was in making Beauvoir out to be a philosopher, we now have some difficulty in constructing literary merit. Clearly, Beauvoir is someone who has done both. But the same is said, on a regular basis, of Sartre himself, and, at least in some circles, of Camus. We have to ask ourselves why it is that the insistence on placing a thinker in one camp or the other seems to hit so hard on Simone de Beauvoir.

In examining her work, we are once again struck with the difficulty that Beauvoir remains one of our quintessential "female" figures from the annals of twentieth-century thought, even if we would like to feel that we have moved beyond such categorization. This may make her, as a thinker, more vulnerable to the transitory nature of categories in general, and it certainly means that, whereas for Sartre and Camus, there seems to be little or no difficulty in seeing them as philosophers, novelists, essayists and even dramatists, there does seem to be a difficulty in seeing Beauvoir as a figure of many camps. Perhaps, ultimately, part of the problem is our reluctance to acknowledge the lingering disparagement of women intellectual figures that pervades the culture, and that no doubt has something to do with our difficulties with Beauvoir.

Nevertheless, we need to give her work a fair appraisal, and for our purposes her work is exemplary since, as we have said, there is no question that her literary work is overtly philosophical. But Beauvoir's philosophical interests manifest themselves in ways that might well be deemed to be different from the expected. We might hazard a guess, were we unfamiliar with her work, that a more straightforward addressing of metaphysical issues than is the case with many writers would evidence itself. Our argument here will be that—although Simone de Beauvoir does unquestionably address some of these issues—much of her literary work is concerned with the problem of the "Other," an issue that, in *The Ethics of Ambiguity*, she called a crucial philosophical issue.

In *The Mandarins*, Anne Dubreuilh is by profession, interestingly enough, a trained psychotherapist. This gives her character a certain resonance with this issue, and, as we shall see, Beauvoir handles it deftly in virtually every section of that work.

Metaphysics and Beyond

If one of Beauvoir's chief philosophical interests is the relationship between the self and others, she, like Sartre, has an intrinsic interest in depicting the "mirroring" that the self finds in relationships with other selves. In *A Very Easy Death*, the reader is moved by the extent to which Beauvoir's awareness of the bodily frailty of her mother actually changes her attitude toward this rather staid bourgeoise. She writes:

Mama went to sleep. But in the morning there was all the sadness of a defenceless animal in her eyes. When the nurses made her bed, and then made her urinate with a catheter, it hurt her and she groaned: in a faint voice she asked me, 'Do you think I shall come through?'[4]

What one would take to lead to objectification—the seeing of the human body in all of its naked degradability—in this particular case leads to an alteration in her relationship with her mother. The mirroring that Simone finds is all to the good; she is perceived as a helper and caretaker of the frail (even if she did not originally want this role), and it is a mirroring that she has not previously had available to her.

For Anne in *The Mandarins*, the chief mirrors are Robert, Nadine and her eventual lover Lewis Brogan. But each of these mirrors not only alters Anne's conception of herself, they provide the basis for altering philosophical reflection.

With Lewis, Anne is in some sense able to create the mirror that she desires—he sees her as a woman, and responds to her in the sexual and overtly bodily fashion that she craves after years of marriage and motherhood. But precisely because Lewis' mirroring is so important to her, any breakdown or slight change in it leaves her distracted and frantic. Robert's mirroring is positive in a sense, but the difficulty is—as the text makes clear—that Robert himself requires a mirror, and this is the function that Anne has always served for him. Nadine's function, as so frequently happens in the case of the adolescent offspring, is to serve as a negative mirror, and this is part of what makes her mother's relations with her so painful.

The Other, then is someone whose borders we can never completely surmount but who, by reflecting us back to ourselves, so to speak, makes a difference in our daily lives. Thus, as we have seen, Simone de Beauvoir's relationship with her own mother changed when she saw her mother in a different way. As Elizabeth Fallaize says in a study on Beauvoir's novels:

> Anne of *The Mandarins* is a turning point. She has charge of her own narrative... and uses monologue to express her suffering as well as offering an account of recent events in the past historic. Anne also has a negative double in the suffering Paula....[5]

Doubles and mirrors serve much the same function, although standard literary usage (particularly when we think of such authors as Dostoevsky) may mean that the notion of the double is a bit more familiar. But, as we shall see, Beauvoir uses these notions, whether we think of them as being interchangeable or not, in new and exciting ways.

If, in phenomenological terms, part of the difficulty with the Other is that he or she makes manifest another "for-itself," then the facticity of the surrounding world may itself call into question our own being, or more properly our reason for being. Sartre, famously, wrote a novel on this very theme: *Nausea*. Roquentin's distress—a sort of severe breakdown of a depersonalized type—leads him to a greater awareness

---

4   Ibid., 65.
5   Fallaize, Elizabeth (1998), "Narrative Strategies and Sexual Politics in Beauvoir's Fiction," *Simone de Beauvoir: a Critical Reader*, in Fallaize (ed.), New York: Routledge, 192–202.

of the contingent in-itselfness of the rest of the world. The chestnut tree appears to him as totally unnecessary in its being, and yet completely there. Similarly, although probably with less emphasis on this aspect of the ontological, Beauvoir has Anne and some of her other main characters engage in strong questioning of metaphysical issues in *The Mandarins*, but it is Beauvoir's particular gift that she is able to make this internal querying seem a natural part of the existence of the thinking human. Thus there is no part of the novel that leaves one with the uncanny and forceful sensations that one gets from reading *Nausea*, but it is obvious that Beauvoir means for us to question our freedom strongly.

Even Anne's relationship with Lewis promotes a sort of metaphysical questioning, since Anne experiences the relationships as something of an immediate intensity even when she is not in Lewis' presence. The transatlantic traveling and necessity for her to resume her relationship with her own family once she is back in France seem to make her even more aware of the fragility and futility of all things human. Reading Lewis' letter to her, she feels his presence, as it were, but knows that she cannot see him again for months.

The opening sections of *She Came to Stay* are perhaps paradigmatically revelatory of Beauvoir's overall philosophical take on things and are, in the main, somewhat opaque with respect to matters other than the philosophical. In the very first chapter, in which Francoise has a long conversation with Gerbert about the future of their dramatic production, Beauvoir sets the stage for the notion of otherness and also discusses human existence in general. For the philosophically naïve reader, the book may, in its opening, be nearly unintelligible—but the ontological stance is there for those who can discern it. Here is an exemplary passage:

> Francoise hesitated; she felt very strongly about this; the corridors, the auditorium, the stage, none of these things vanished when she closed the door on them, but they existed only behind the door, at a distance....
>
> "It's like a lunar landscape," she said. "It's unreal. It's nothing but hearsay. Don't you feel that?"
>
> "No," said Gerbert. "I don't think I do."
>
> "And doesn't it exasperate you never to be able to see more than one thing at a time?"
>
> Gerbert thought for a moment. "What worries me is other people."[6]

Here two of Beauvoir's classic areas of concern come together. The textbook philosophical problem of the existence of the rest of the world independent of my awareness of it—a Berkeleyan sort of problem—seems to be something that genuinely perplexes Francoise. This somewhat unusual character has her match in Gerbert; he reveals himself as not only worried about other persons, but he is especially concerned about "someone who's living his own life and who doesn't even know that I exist."[7]

---

6   de Beauvoir, Simone (1999), *She Came to Stay*, New York: W.W. Norton and Co., 16.

7   *Ibid., ibid.*

Perhaps Beauvoir strains for literary effect here, as it strikes one as decidedly odd, not to say evidence of a dissociative disorder, that Francoise is actually concerned about the existence of objects not in her view or in the reach of her senses. But the existence of other persons—as Gerbert tries to indicate—is problematic on still another level. They represent a conceptual problem in the same way that the tree does when one is not present (or as Virginia Woolf had said in *To the Lighthouse*, "think of a kitchen table when you're not there"), but the greater level of the problem is that they appear to possess a consciousness like one's own, and yet it is a consciousness at which one can never get. And in the sense that one needs one's existence confirmed by the gaze of the other (Gerbert again), when the other is not around, one's existence is a good deal less confirmed.

This triad of problems—the solipsistic puzzle, the existence of others as consciousnesses, and one's own existence *qua* object of the other—is a grouping with which Beauvoir will continue to be concerned in all of her work. In the later novels it is seldom so explicitly brought to the fore, but *She Came to Stay* has the merit of being written in such a fashion that it is no exaggeration to say that philosophy is foregrounded.

It is no doubt for these reasons that, as we have said at an earlier point, criticism of Beauvoir as a novelist has not really been separated from criticism of her other works. It is not at all unusual to find a critique of the novels in the same essay as an extended appraisal of *The Second Sex* or *The Coming of Age*; indeed, it is rare to find the literary work addressed separately. But if those who have attempted to write on the novels feel frustrated, their pain puts Beauvoir in good company, for the same sorts of difficulties also infect appraisals of the work of Camus and Sartre.

Criticism

Although much of what has been written about Beauvoir has focused on the philosophical, there is now a body of at least putatively literary criticism that attempts to find a place for Beauvoir in the canon.

Elizabeth Fallaize has organized a reader with criticism of both the philosophical and literary work, and her take on the novels is a refreshing glance at them from a more standardly critical point of view. What is remarkable about at least one of her appraisals, however, is how little she is willing to concede to Beauvoir as a novelist who is writing from the female point of view. Fallaize sees all five novels or longer works taken in toto—*She Came to Stay*, *All Men are Mortal*, *The Blood of Others*, *The Mandarins*, and *The Woman Destroyed*—as a sequelae that does little, if anything, to establish an authorial voice for the female narrator. There may very well be something to Fallaize's argument, but the fact that it is made certainly undercuts any line that would attempt to mesh, for example, the sort of view found in *The Second Sex* with the novels themselves. Fallaize writes:

> The story of ... Beauvoir's fictional writing is the story of an ever increasing reduction of this plurality of voice, and a loss of authority conceded to the female voice.[8]

---

8 Fallaize, "Narrative," in Fallaize (ed.), 194.

Although Fallaize is willing to concede that someone like Anne in *The Mandarins* definitely embodies a point of view, Fallaize's stance on this particular novel is that Anne's narrative is a "narrative of the past," and that it is "constantly invaded by a present-tense monologue which does not so much narrate events as raise perspectives of suffering and death."[9]

If there is anything to Fallaize's overall line, there is no question that the intelligent woman pays a great price in Beauvoir's novels for her intelligence. Her place in the world seems to be one that is manifestly more affected by "Othering" than is the male's but at the same time the female characters are more aware, as gender circumstances might demand, of their commitments to the larger scheme of things. The upshot of all of this is that Anne is perplexed and bothered by relationships in a way that Robert is not; nor is Henri. Henri's vague attraction to Josette is nothing like Anne's attraction to Lewis, and this is no accident, for even though Anne feels that she cannot make a commitment to Lewis, she worries about her relationship with him in a way that the male characters simply do not.

In other words, at least from the standpoint of Fallaize's writing, being female seems to be problematized for Beauvoir in her novels, and part of Fallaize's point appears to be that this is something we would not expect. A similar line of argument comes from Jane Heath, who also sees feminine identity and strength as problematic in the novel sequence, and who writes that there is "a masculine economy represented by Pierre and Francoise" in *She Came to Stay*.[10]

A matching line of argument is constructed by Hazel Barnes, another one of the comparatively small circle of critics who have chosen to address Beauvoir's novels. Barnes' work was one of the first done in this vein; she is concerned largely with the notion of the "Other," and it is indeed an easy way to begin to address Beauvoir's work.

Barnes is explicit in seeing *She Came to Stay* as dealing with the notion of the Other in more than one way. Although Xaviere is admittedly in a position to serve in the "Other" capacity for both Pierre and Francoise individually, she also serves as a "Third" in their bonding relationship. Barnes writes:

> [A threat exists] to Francoise's relation to Pierre. In part this is simply the Sartrean disintegration of a dual relation under the Look of a Third. Before Xaviere's lofty disdain of human bonds, their mutual; dependency begins to appear ridiculous. More seriously, Francoise is forcibly reminded that she and Pierre had not really been one. Although they had scrupulously respected each other's freedom, still Francoise, at least, had come to believe that they not only shared all experiences with each other but that either one could penetrate to the unspoken thought of the other.[11]

Barnes' rather complex analysis takes off from the fact that the epigraph to the novel is taken from Hegel, and the admitted obviousness of the constant theme of the self-vs.-other in the work. Barnes reads the novel as an attempt to make clear that

---

9 *Ibid.*, 195.
10 Heath, Jane, "She Came to Stay: the Phallus Strikes Back", in Fallaize (ed.), 171–182.
11 Barnes, Hazel, "Self-Encounter in She Came to Stay," in Fallaize (ed.), 157–170.

consciousness does indeed yearn for the annihilation of another—and that this can take multiple forms. As Xaviere's influence on the dyad grows, the baneful force of a third becomes all the more obvious.

It may be a shortcoming of most of the criticism done so far on Beauvoir's novels that there is a tendency to read them in a rather limited way. But this is partly because of the way in which they are constructed—as mentioned earlier, it might be thought to constitute a rather awkward opening for a work of literature that it is so blatantly philosophical as to sound a bit like a textbook. However, by *The Mandarins*—written a decade or so after *She Came to Stay*—Beauvoir's style has altered, and, aside from some of the dialogues, the philosophical context is not as strong.

If consciousness and otherness are two of the main foci of Beauvoir's novels, the critics also agree that politics is still another. Simone de Beauvoir's focus on a committed existentialist politics is a crucial part of *The Mandarins*, and again it has ties with the perennial questions of philosophy. Henri and Robert, for example, frequently ask themselves how they can function in a world where many are starving. They feel a necessary commitment to the left, because only the left can put into place the alterations in social practice that make a difference for the masses. But at the same time they have a difficulty deciding which strand of the left requires their commitment. Key parts of this novel revolve around Communism as opposed to some other social movement, and one of the crucial scenes in the novel involves the break between Robert and Henri over what it is that Communism can actually do. In a sense, Henri, even with all of his defects (a character who clearly represents Camus) can be seen as the existential hero, since he makes the decision early on to publicize the camps of the Soviet Union—revealed to them by an informant—despite the fact that to do so is in a sense a betrayal of all that they stand for. Robert makes the somewhat standard argument that this will be a sell-out to the Right. These debates, and others like them, are crucial parts of *The Mandarins*.

As we saw in our analysis of the work of Margaret Drabble, many have been unable to see her as anything other than a novelist who is engaged in pushing forward the lengthy British effort at the "traditional" novel; Woolf has been seen as one of the major moderns, but in many instances criticism has focused on style rather than content. With Beauvoir the situation is the other way around. So much of what has been written about the novels focuses so exclusively on their admittedly strong philosophical content that it is difficult to find criticism that speaks to their literary merit, or to their construction as novels.

Although the early novels may be somewhat weak, seen purely from a literary point of view, it is generally agreed that the same cannot be said of *The Mandarins*. This prize-winner was a best-seller in France and in English-speaking countries; there is no question that certain portions of it—especially the descriptions of the affair with Lewis Brogan—stand well in any field of literature. But along with the obvious emphasis on philosophical considerations has come another strong emphasis—it has been difficult for some critics to read the novels as anything other than works involved with "feminism." That these two lines of argument—the statedly philosophical and the decidedly feminist—would seem to merge is no doubt due to the fact that one can always point to *The Second Sex* and try to read the novels as efforts to elucidate not only a sort of existentialism, but a sort of feminism, or a sort of understanding of woman's role.

This line of criticism applies more straightforwardly to *The Mandarins*, a later work, and one written after *The Second Sex*. But it is important to clarify how a number of those who have written on Beauvoir have tried to interpret her work with respect to feminist themes.

La Femme

Jane Heath has written of the feminine as a force for the disrupture of the masculine economy, and there is no question that this is at least one obvious reading of *She Came to Stay*. Xaviere represents something irrational and beyond the closed world of Pierre and Francoise, a world that is, of course, dominated by Pierre. As Heath writes,

> My reading of Xaviere as a destabilising force in Francoise's orderly life is so far reductive in that I have not emphasised the importance of Xaviere as the locus of the feminine within the text, the feminine being defined as that which is problematic to a phallic economy and which always exceeds any attempt at containment. I am arguing that the case of Xaviere exceeds both her construction in the text as a rebellious contestatory child and as 'other' with a small 'o', Francoise's adversary in a Hegelian confrontation.[12]

How much sense does it make to see the Beauvoir of the novels as essentially masculinist in her identification, even given the proximity in time of some of the later novels to her writing of *The Second Sex*?

This sort of query is not as out of place as it might initially seem. From those who have experienced difficulty with her constant valorization of Sartre as "the philosopher," to those who have noted her own identification with masculine values, many have seen Beauvoir as less than fully female-identified.

A bit of recapitulation may be in order here, since there might initially be a difficulty with the notion of a masculine economy. All of the cultural constructs traditionally brought to bear on the masculine/feminine split are needed here: the time-honored association of masculinity with reason, the notion that relationships are more important, typically to women—these constructs help us make sense of Heath's argument, or any stance similar to it. If woman has traditionally been the body, and man the mind, many of Beauvoir's female characters, insofar as they themselves participate in the masculine thought patterns that drive the intellectual world, are also men. Thus Francoise has so closely identified with Pierre that she has ceased, in some sense, to fulfill the female role. (The same might also be said of Anne Dubreuilh, although perhaps to a lesser degree.)

So Xaviere—or even Nadine of *The Mandarins*—represents a libidinal economy that is enmeshed in the body. As Sartre himself might have phrased it, they are "contingent viscosity." To push the argument in this direction does, of course, indicate that Beauvoir has perhaps valorized a certain sort of traditional view, without doing

---

12 Heath, "Phallus," in Fallaize (ed.), 173.

much to promulgate any other sort of view that might be thought to be "feminist." It is for these reasons that feminist criticism of her novels has found them so difficult—they are not necessarily redemptive along feminist lines. Xaviere, far from being a sympathetic character, strikes one as manipulative and crudely narcissistic; although Nadine (Anne's daughter) is too young to be subject to the same lines of commentary, her character is not a sympathetic one on first reading.

What, then, can the feminist critic make of the novels? *The Mandarins* is perhaps the best target of sustained feminist criticism, because here Anne makes some moves as a character that might help forward a feminist view. Initially, Anne, like Robert, does little that does not reflect a sort of male-identified view of the French intellectual. She appears to live a life that is thought-filled; when she is not actually at work as a therapist, a great deal of the rest of her time is spent in helping Robert to sort out the problems that he has (with Henri and others) in creating his new political party, the S.R.L.

But Anne's relationship with Lewis Brogan changes all of that. We are given to think that this is the first time that Anne has genuinely experienced a type of sexual pleasure that had previously been unavailable to her. It is unclear precisely what is different about her relationship with Lewis—she admits that it has a great deal to do, at least superficially, with the cultural differences of America. But other passages descriptive of the relationship—her focus on the details of Lewis's room, the blanket, and so forth, call out a different sort of sensuality. In this sense, Lewis, although a very traditional male character in a number of ways, is the catalyst for a type of feminine/feminist growth in Anne.[13]

Beauvoir's depiction of her women characters would not have achieved the problematized status that it does achieve for commentators such as Heath were it not for the fact that there is a pronounced tendency to read the author of *The Second Sex* as if all of the female characters created by her were somehow intended to make some sort of statement, a la Gina Sanseverina of Stendhal's *La Chartreuse de Parme*, a work often cited by Beauvoir for its view of women. Because of the conflation of the novels with works that might be thought to be more overtly philosophical, it has been difficult to read the novels in an even fashion.

In an essay on *The Woman Destroyed*, which is more properly speaking a collection of short stories, Anne Ophir has made the point that the women characters seem to experience a need to recreate their own lives, through writing or other means. This, in at least a small sense, may represent a part of the male economy that Heath mentions in *She Came to Stay*, and in any case it does appear to be relevant to an analysis of Anne in *The Mandarins*. Writing of the relationship between Monique and Maurice in the title story of *The Woman Destroyed*, Ophir notes:

Writing is, from the beginning, a defence, a talisman.... Monique writes to fight for her survival.... She could also select particular elements and deliberately rearrange them in

---

13. As Heath also says, "Xaviere's interrogatory stance has dramatic consequences for Francoise..." (172). Although Lewis is certainly not interrogatory in the same kind of way, he does produce changes in Anne.

a way not corresponding to the reality experienced, thus creating if not a work of art, at least an imaginary universe.[14]

If writing has this function in this particular story, it is not too much of a stretch to note that involvement in the arts, writing, and the male world of the mind in general is a hallmark of the lives of Francoise and Anne, characters in the major novels. But although it might make sense to provide an analysis of the sort that Heath has of Xaviere—especially since the polarized tension between these two female characters is so explicit—other complexities come into play in, for instance, *The Mandarins*.

Anne, although functioning in the realm of the professional—her original purpose in going to Chicago is to attend a conference on psychoanalysis—moves more fluidly back and forth between masculinized and feminized identities in *The Mandarins*. This is what makes the sections of the work where she stays with Lewis so intriguing: not only is it clear that Lewis in a sense opens up her world as a woman, but Beauvoir employs numerous strategies in these sections to try to signal to us that this relationship is a turning point for Anne. In the latter parts of the work, the encounters with Lewis take place in Mexico, and Beauvoir leaves Yucatan as an exoticized and even fetishized region where Anne's and Lewis' lovemaking achieves unparalleled heights. (It is interesting to note that the blanket described as being in Lewis's room in Chicago is marked in the text as a "Mexican blanket.") Although Lewis is nominally a writer, he is not an intellectual in the same sense as Robert, Henri and Anne's Parisian friends. In fact, by contrast Lewis is himself feminized—he is given to moody outbursts, irrational statements, and, in what must be an implausible sequence of events to many women, is the one in the relationship who keeps declaring his love and asking for commitment.

Thus Anne moves from the more male-identified world to one largely of her own creation, and in that sense the novel does make a powerful statement that is not out of line with some politicized view of feminism, or with the burdens placed on Beauvoir by her having authored *The Second Sex*. The waves of criticism over the years having to do with Beauvoir's own pronouncements to the effect that Sartre was the "philosopher" and that she was not are probably not unrelated, at least in terms of authorial notions, to the putative difficulty in the texts of moving from male to female identification.

Structure and More

As it happens, among the commentary that has been generated that addresses Beauvoir's novels in specific terms, one of the most salient pieces is by Merleau-Ponty. In an excerpt from *Sense and Non-Sense* titled "Metaphysics and the Novel," this Continental thinker makes it clear that *She Came to Stay* is the quintessential philosophical novel—one so filled with attempts to limn ontological views that, as

---

14 Ophir, Anne, "Mythical Discourse in 'The Woman Destroyed,'" in Fallaize (ed.), 183–192.

has been said here, it is sometimes difficult reading.[15] Merleau-Ponty's particular take on the work is that it goes a far way toward explicating the concepts of in-itselfness, for-itselfness and the confrontation between self and other, and that it does so in ways that make it particularly pertinent and clear. Starting with a specific example of the in-itself (and one that is similar to many of those noted by Francoise in the opening portions of the book), Merleau-Ponty writes:

> [A]n old jacket on a chair will be a riddle if I take it just as it offers itself to me. There it is, blind and limited; it does not know what it is; it is content to occupy that bit of space—but it does so in a way I never could. It does not run off in all directions like a consciousness; it remains solidly what it is; it is in itself.[16]

This sort of confrontation is a staple of Beauvoir's writing, and examples of it also occur in *The Mandarins*—interestingly enough, some of what Anne uses as a mental stop-gap to wile away her time spent apart from Lewis also has the same quality to it. But part of the reason that Merleau-Ponty devotes as much space to an analysis of Beauvoir's first novel as he does has to do, obviously, with what he takes to be its philosophical impact. He, like Beauvoir herself, cites Balzac and Stendhal as examples of authors whose work is philosophical—but then he moves on to an analysis of *She Comes to Stay*. As he says, "Everything changes when a phenomenological or existential philosophy assigns itself [a] task…"

Like Hazel Barnes, Merleau-Ponty sees *She Came to Stay* as a work that addresses Otherness in terms of its impact on a couple—since the relationship that Francoise and Pierre had initially was supposed to be an "essential" one (as Sartre had said of his relationship with Beauvoir), their duality-as-oneness can be unhinged by another. He closes his essay by making the comment that "[Beauvoir's] book shows existence understood between two limits: on the one hand, there is the immediate closed tightly upon itself, beyond any word and commitment (Xaviere); and, on the other, there is an absolute confidence in language and rational decision…(Francoise at the beginning of the book)."[17]

If the already philosophical commitments of an existentialist view like Beauvoir's make it difficult to cast her work in any other terms, it is noteworthy that Merleau-Ponty notices the sheer fact of encasing in a skin. Each Other is encased in his or her own shell; the shells are impenetrable and we assume the existence of another like ourselves in order to make, so to speak, minimal contact. But if this other erects herself or himself as an implacable, absolute barrier (Xaviere), then the mirroring that transpires in the situation is likely to be deleterious to all involved. This is essentially what takes place in *She Came to Stay*.

Sartre's own work *No Exit* is, of course, about a very similar triangle (indeed, one has to feel that it, too, was inspired by the Olga–Simone–Sartre trio). The issue in *No Exit* might be cast in terms of bad faith: the characters do not want to hear the truth about themselves, and in that sense the philosophical problems posed by the

---

15 Merleau-Ponty, Maurice (1987), "Metaphysics and the Novel," in Elaine Marks (ed.), Critical Essays on Simone de Beauvoir, Boston: G.K. Hall & Co., 31–44.
16 *Ibid.*, 33.
17 *Ibid.*, 43.

play are probably not as straightforwardly metaphysical as those posed by *She Came to Stay*. But what both works have in common is their attempt to address questions having to do with the for-itself, its relationship to the other and, at least in the case of Beauvoir's work, its relationship to that incomprehensible world of the in-itself that is symbolized by Merleau-Ponty's jacket.

Conceptualizing Beauvoir's novels in her own philosophical terms, or any other philosophical terms, also calls into question the very vehicle that she has chosen for the presentation of at least some of her ideas. After all, we already have the overtly philosophical works, such as *Ethics of Ambiguity*, or, some would argue, *A Very Easy Death* or *The Second Sex*. Why bother with the construction of a novel when the ideas involved could have been presented in a more overt way? As Merleau-Ponty himself says, the novel allows the author to present philosophical dilemmas and issues as they occur in the space of living. These ideas, after all, presumably came to thinkers originally immersed in the demands of everyday life. The classic problem of evil, for example, could not have arisen as a philosophical problem were it not for the fact that a careful look at our lives shows multiple examples of what appears to be inexplicable and ineradicable evil. The novelist, then, if she or he wants to show what a philosophical dilemma looks like, has fertile ground if it can be shown to be a problem that would occur to a thoughtful person in an everyday context.

Enclosure-in-the-body is a theme that is found throughout Beauvoir's work, and is one of the hallmarks of the later, nonfiction works such as *A Very Easy Death* and *Adieux*. The intersection of these works is to be found in the somewhat Foucauldian theme—also alluded to, at least implicitly, by Merleau-Ponty—of inscription on the body. If the body is a case that prevents us from meeting the Other, it is also a case that has inscribed on it the facticity of our existence, and the in-itselfness of sheer corporeality. These themes are rampant even in the opening of *She Came to Stay*; they appear to some extent in *The Mandarins*, although in this work they are more obvious in the sections having to do with Lewis Brogan. Following along the lines of Merleau-Ponty, Ursula Tidd notes that:

> In *Une Mort tres douce* and *Adieux*, sexuality, ageing, illness and death are represented as brutal reminders of human corporeality and, unlike maternity, experienced by both women and men. Beauvoir attempts to decipher some of the meanings which the aged body has accumulated throughout a lifetime, which have hitherto been concealed from her.[18]

The novelistic equivalent of these takes on the body occurs frequently in *She Came to Stay*: here, of course, they have little to do with aging or illness, but much to do with enclosure and maskedness. (One could always argue, of course, that the stripping away of the mask is part of the theme of aging.)

Xaviere strikes Francoise as willfully encased in the body, and in a way that precludes a "reading" of her will. Paradoxically, this seems to be part of Francoise's attraction to her. Initially secure in her relationship with Pierre, Francoise seems to feel that she can manipulate Xaviere even though the latter's blind egocentricity should signal that this will be no easy task. Frequent visual descriptions of Xaviere's

---

18 Tidd, Ursula (1999), *Simone de Beauvoir: Gender and Testimony*, Cambridge: Cambridge University Press, 157.

face and physical features assure us that Francoise is more than aware of the effect of packaging.[19]

In a sense, Xaviere represents the unthinkable for Francoise: a for-itself that is so impenetrable, in terms of comprehension, that it almost achieves object-like status. This mysterious aspect of Xaviere—however much a product of Francoise's imagination and overconfidence—is precisely what keeps Francoise intrigued. Perhaps we are intended to believe that the meshing of her relationship with Pierre has left her very naïve about other human relationships. It is more than interesting, however, that there are shades of Francoise in Lewis Brogan. His moods, his opaqueness, his stubbornness (at least from Anne's point of view) about their relationship all signal the same sort of attraction.

If the novels can be interpreted as a series of encounters with the Other, it is remarkable that the sort of Other who seems to be most attractive to many of the protagonists is the very Other who most resembles, in many ways, a kind of embodied in-itselfness. Even Henri of *The Mandarins* does not escape: his relationship with Josette is still another version of the same phenomenon. Perhaps the for-itself is most obviously at work in comparatively directed characters like Robert; perhaps we have some difficulty believing that there is a genuine for-itself in the mannequin-like automaton represented by Xaviere. But this attraction to the obliterating force of an Other who in some ways has the frightening qualities of Merleau-Ponty's jacket is a key feature of the novels.

Philosophy

As we have seen, an area of difficulty for both Drabble and Woolf is not at all an area of difficulty for Beauvoir—that is, the sheer question of whether and to what extent the novels are philosophical. Here, rather, we have problems with trying to establish literary themes for the novels that are in any way solidly divorced from the classic philosophical questions.

One area of Beauvoir's literary works that is comparatively unexamined, however, is the political philosophy inherent in them. So much has been written about Otherness and questions having to do with ontology—particularly with respect to the two major novels—that it is not obvious that the political questions have been fully addressed.

Politics is indeed one of the major themes of *The Mandarins*, and the extent to which Robert, Henri, Anne and such other characters as Scriassine and Lambert are driven by political considerations cannot be overstated. The novel is filled with considerations that now seem somewhat repetitious, but that no doubt presented themselves in new and forceful ways in the 1950s—our moral obligations to others on the planet, the sheer multiplicity and numbers of human existence, the nature of the best society, the social structure of justice, and so forth. Beauvoir's work must be

---

19 Some typical phrases from the early parts of *She Came to Stay* include the following: "Xaviere walked faster and faster, scowling and looking wretched." (34) "Xaviere wrinkled her face in disgust." (35) "Xaviere's face suddenly fell limp and all the hardness disappeared." (37)

one of the few during this period to express overt concern over, for example, China's "starving millions," or the possibility that the Stalinist prison camps represented a justifiable feature of the Soviet system.

These particular features of the novels have not received the commentary they deserved, probably because of the understandable emphasis on the notion of the Other, or the explication of the tenuousness of the for-itself. But a nascent political philosophy also is obvious in at least *The Mandarins*—it is a humanistic and socialistic view, one that calls for a redistribution of wealth (and one is tempted to say that Beauvoir sees that redistribution as something that should occur on an international basis). Some of the dialogue between Henri and Robert with respect to these camps is helpful in giving us a look at Beauvoir's political focus:

> Dubreuilh interrupted Henri. "I know perfectly well what we'd say. My conviction is that these camps aren't essential to the regime, as Peltov maintains. They're tied in with certain policies that can be deplored without questioning the whole regime. We'd dissociate the two things: we'd condemn corrective labor, but we'd defend the Soviet Union."
>
> "All right," Henri said. "But it's as plain as day that our words would carry more weight if we were the first to denounce the camps. Then no one could believe we were following a line."[20]

Since the new political party founded by Robert Dubreuilh is also a leftist party, it is easy to see that the political debate here has to do with whether one can be a meaningfully committed leftist without becoming a Communist. At the novel's beginning, this is not such an issue—but it becomes a much larger question later on, once Scriassine has brought an informant who is willing to speak candidly about the network of the gulag, something suspected but not yet documented in Western circles.

The break between Robert and Henri (which, according to almost all commentators, parallels to some extent the break between Sartre and Camus) makes clear the extent to which Beauvoir believes in a leftist political commitment, even if centrists or others can find out damning facts about various leftist states. The key notion is redistribution; a leftist state is assumed to be the most just because it keeps capital from flowing into a few specific hands.

Although there is no question that this political conundrum is at the heart of *The Mandarins*, it is also interesting to note that, in today's terms, some of the rest of the novel fails to exhibit a sensitivity toward "other" cultures. Indeed, the sections on Mexico would not pass muster today; the characters find the Indians "charming," and areas of Yucatan are routinely referred to as if they were at the end of the earth.[21] Nevertheless, Beauvoir's political views are not only extremely progressive for her time, needless to say, but they are also deeply tied to the rest of her thought. Awareness of the for-itselfness of another, no matter how debilitating in certain circumstances, arouses one's awareness of the individual's vulnerability

---

20 Beauvoir, *The Mandarins*, 400.

21 Anne notes, while visiting a site much like Chichén Itzá, "It had left nothing behind it, that civilization which had sacrificed so many lives to its games of building blocks." (Beauvoir, *The Mandarins*, 455.)

and humanity. No thoughtful human can remain unmoved by, as *The Mandarins* has it, the plight of the starving millions: the reflective person would like to be able to participate in some sort of action that would ameliorate the situation. It is for these reasons that so much of the dialogue of the novel revolves around political matters. If the French term is "engagé," then the characters in Beauvoir's novels are nothing if not engaged—and engaged in the most active and profound way. Henri is ashamed to be seen in public with Josette and her family because he considers them to be too bourgeois—the sort of noncommitted Parisians whose lives revolve around conspicuous consumption and the pursuit of pleasure (and this shortly after the end of the war). It is also interesting that Henri is so concerned about Anne's opinion that he actually does not want her to see him with Josette.

Overviews

An intense awareness of our fragile existence, our enclosure in a bodily covering that is itself subject to decay and the vicissitudes of time, and our need for a full engagement (intellectual and otherwise) with these issues motivates the work of Simone de Beauvoir. Her engagement is so intense that even portions of her work that are presumably at least partially autobiographical—and that might have something to do with aspects of her own lived life—delineate a constant concern for these matters. Even in the midst of a recounting of her affair with Lewis, Anne cannot help but articulate these Beauvoirian issues:

> We bought belts, sandals, fabrics. The old woman with the wonderful cape was still there, but I didn't dare approach her. In the café-grocery on the square, a few Indians were sitting around a table and drinking; their wives were seated at their feet.... Two young Indians were half-staggering, half-dancing together; they looked so incapable of enjoying themselves that it touched my heart. Outside, the merchants were beginning to fold their stands;... Their foreheads straining against a band of leather that helped them support their loads, they went off at a dog-trot.[22]

The combination of support for the downtrodden Indians, awareness of their plight, and a sort of general existentially edgy atmosphere pervades a good deal of the overtly descriptive portions of this work. But perhaps the strongest point of her writing is her ability to convey to the reader the notion that these levels of awareness are available to all and that, indeed, someone who has not gained an acquaintance with them is not a fully functioning human.

The intersection of these sorts of issues with a more standardly Beauvoirian concern—the Other—is the focus of much of the critical analysis of the novels, as we have seen. But the whole point of this type of analysis is that the Other can be anyone—although we now have connotations to the term based on non-Eurocentric slants, the original other is simply, someone other than the self. It is this sort of take that drives *She Came to Stay*, and for that reason a great deal has been done on this

---

22 Beauvoir, *The Mandarins*, 459.

first and (according to some) most powerful Beauvoirian work. Here is Hazel Barnes again on the relationship between Xaviere and Francoise:

> Xaviere's emergence as a subject threatens Francoise in two ways. In the first place she forces Francoise to become aware in a new way of her self-for-others and to see herself and her whole life in a different and dubious light. Francoise had developed through her relation with Pierre and her work a quiet contentment. She assumed that one pursued happiness; she had developed a routine to guarantee its future.[23]

It is the first part of this analysis that is crucial for an understanding of the entire Beauvoirian project, and Barnes is a very precise articulator of the issues at hand. The presence of the other—just simply another human being—forces Francoise to see herself and her life "in a different and dubious light." That reflection of the self back to the agent through another consciousness (another for-itself) is key to what it is that is the chief focus of Beauvoir's concern, and it might well be said that virtually everything else springs from that.

To attempt to weave together, at least minimally, the non-literary works and the novels, *A Very Easy Death* may be construed along the same lines, with perhaps a couple of twists. We have already seen how the body's fragility and vulnerability signals something to Simone de Beauvoir as she watches her mother dying. But in addition to this part of the work, the focus of much of the commentary, there is still another way in which the otherness of her mother and her own otherness to her mother can be analyzed. Some of her mother's comments, ill though she may be, remind Simone of the very sorts of disputes and tensions that had unhappily marked their relationship all the way along. At one point, when Simone tries to explain that there will be alternations between her and her sister's visits, her mother remarks to her, "You frighten me, you do."[24]

This particular comment sets in motion a train of memories having to do with Beauvoir's failure to conform to bourgeois culture, her mother's confusion over her life and writings, and her somewhat weak and acrimonious relationship with her family, no doubt fueled by what was viewed at the time as a scandalous, albeit intellectual, lifestyle. The point is that, once again, even her very ill mother has made her feel less-than-something, and this memory of all of the other times that she felt less than something (especially during adolescence) leads Beauvoir on an extended reverie about the self and others, this time, of course, with the crucial relationship being the very relationship that developmentally is most important for humans.

---

23 Beauvoir, *She Came to Stay*, 160.
24 Beauvoir, *A Very Easy Death*, 67. Interestingly enough, at a later point in the text when Beauvoir reminds her mother that she had made the remark, her mother has no memory of having said it (71).

Chapter Seven

Écriture and the Other

If it seems accurate to say, as has been maintained here, that there is a paucity of criticism on Beauvoir's literary work, and an abundance of material that addresses either *The Second Sex* or works such as *The Ethics of Ambiguity*, the peculiarity of the criticism that does exist is that it either takes for granted that a feminist analysis of the literary works is required, or fails to make one. *She Came to Stay*, for example, is often addressed in a way that precludes anything other than an analysis along the lines of "the Other," but it is obvious that the relationship between Francoise and Xaviere is ripe for feminist commentary.

The contemporary feminist has another sort of problem, and that is—as was mentioned in our commentary on *The Mandarins*—that portions of the literary works that today might plausibly be interpreted in the light of "third wave" or multicultural feminism do not really lend themselves to these efforts, except perhaps in a negative sense. Thus the sections on "underdeveloped" nations reflect a sort of colonial and Eurocentric superiority that is today completely out of date, and yet, to be fair to Beauvoir, there is very little reason to think that it would have been possible for her to write in any other kind of vein during the 1940s and 1950s when that work was being composed.

New work on Beauvoir however, even in areas that resemble historical excavation more than criticism, begins to develop lines that are both feminist-friendly and contemporary. For example, it is now obvious that Beauvoir, Sartre and Richard Wright had an interesting relationship in France during the period of Wright's residency there; although both Beauvoir and Sartre might seem somewhat naïve on the subject of Black American culture, the very fact that the relationship existed—and that Wright, for one, seemed to profit from it—is food for thought in any feminist analysis.[1] Still another take on the corpus of Beauvoir's work that requires feminist analysis is the line, developed originally by Margaret Simons, that asks us to look at the relationship between Sartre's theoretical work and Beauvoir's own writings. Much evidence points to key passages in *Being and Nothingness* as having developed from ideas that were first present in the work of Simone de Beauvoir; a complex and tangled question of identification between these two thinkers helps to elucidate the relevant strands here.

From the standpoint of any kind of feminism, several questions immediately come to mind in reading the central Beauvoirian novels. Why is there so little actual development, in many cases, of the female characters? If Anne, for example, is the independent woman that much of the test of *The Mandarins* makes her out to be,

---

[1] Richard Wright wrote a novel, somewhat underappreciated, titled *The Outsider*, and clearly based on an existentialist overview.

why does she find herself so emotionally beholden to Lewis on the one hand, and so actually melded to Robert on the other? What is there about Xaviere's "immanence" that exercises such a tremendous pull on Francoise in *She Came to Stay*? Why, in *The Mandarins*, is Henri besotted with Josette, a paradigmatically vacuous woman?

It would seem that it might be desirable to try to tread a middle path between those who have seen Beauvoir's feminism as deeply problematized, and those (few) who seem to see little or no difficulty. Among those who opt for the position that Beauvoir identifies more with males, and therefore is problematic as the feminist savior she has sometimes been made out to be, some voices have been clear articulators of what the problems are. Mary Evans, for example, in an article in the Marks anthology, notes:

> Accolades from feminists, have been so generously heaped on her work that some of its short-comings have been obscured. I would like to suggest here that whilst de Beauvoir claims that much of her work is concerned with the overall condition of women, she turns away from many of the issues which are central to women's lives and in particular accords very little place in her epistemology to areas of human experience which are not immediately amenable to rational understanding.[2]

The emphasis on rationality and the denial of the bodily is indeed key to the difficulties that some have had with Beauvoir's feminism, and these particular areas are well delineated in both *The Mandarins* and *She Came to Stay*. Anne exhibits an almost masculine carelessness in her relationship with Lewis—despite the fact that we are repeatedly told that Anne is in love with Lewis, he is the one who feels hurt and rejection in the relationship, and not Anne. Indeed, Anne cannot seem to understand why it is that Lewis might want a relationship with a greater degree of commitment, or why he would think it odd that a married woman would have little apparent difficulty in negotiating a long-range affair. Here Anne is the rational manipulator and Lewis, at least to some extent, the betrayed one. In *She Came to Stay*, Francoise feels an almost masculine sense of intrigue in Xaviere's impulsivity, devotion to a sort of bodily definition of life, and refusal to follow any one course. As mentioned earlier, Xaviere has been said by one commentator to be sunk in "immanence." If that is an adequate description of Xaviere, it has little to do with Francoise, whose original aim in saving Xaviere, as she thought of it, was to introduce her to the intellectual life and delights of Paris.

As Evans also says, a perusal of Beauvoir's personal relationships and her life with Sartre reveals still another way in which she may be said to have ignored a more fully feminist view of things. Evans claims that, "The accounts given by Beauvoir of these various instances of personal anguish and misery [affairs, including her own with Nelson Algren] reveal, I would argue, one of the central weaknesses in de Beauvoir's view of the world: the supposition that personal, and highly charged emotional relationships are always amenable to rational control and organization and that human beings are capable of the rigid compartmentalization of their emotional

---

2 Evans, Mary, "Views of Women and Men in the Work of Simone de Beauvoir," in Marks (ed.), 172–184.

and intellectual worlds."³ What Evans is trying to say is that, in today's terms, a more feminist-friendly appraisal of relationships and their importance in life might very well eschew the somewhat androcentric "compartmentalization", and foreground the relationships themselves. But, of course, it could very well be countered that Beauvoir did not have this particular luxury in her time—and to be able to write about these issues at all, she had to be in a position to take whatever stand occurred to her, although there is no question that many of her stances do not accord with the later gender feminism.

Intriguingly, Evans reads a great deal of the rejection of the body that is inherent in Beauvoir's stance as having to do with something like shame at her own sexuality—and she also sees this as being at the core of the rather easily truncated sexual relationship between her and Sartre. (As is clear from all her work, their relationship quickly evolved into a purely intellectual, but intense, friendship.) Evans seems to feel that what Beauvoir experienced was an actual revulsion against sexuality—an actual sensation that sexual feelings were some sort of toxin. She writes:

> Thus we find, in her account of the early years of her relationship with Sartre, that de Beauvoir describes sexual passion as a "poisoned shirt" and a "shameful disease."… The reader is left with the distinct impression that the physical self, and particularly so in the case of women, is liable to lead only to uncontrollable, threatening passions and the destruction of all peace of mind.⁴

These lines of argument further the contention that, in all, Beauvoir has a view of the world that we would now label "masculinist," a view that seems to be recapitulated in many of the female characters in her novels. As we have seen, this is certainly the case with Anne Dubreuilh, and accounts, at least partially, for the somewhat jarring sensation that the reader has in poring over the scenes in the text that have to do with what we are supposed to believe is the love of Anne's life.

But Beauvoir is nothing if not complex, and it is important to try to see through any easy analysis of her texts. Francoise may be pushed over the brink by Xaviere, but another analysis is that these capacities were inherent in her all the way along. A feminist analysis is crucial to the recovery of this material.

Feminisms and Beauvoir

Elaine Marks reads Beauvoir as feminist largely in terms of her influence. This may, in fact, be one of the most helpful modes in coming to grips with the ways in which she may be said to interact with the label. Marks, like other critics, acknowledges the difficulties with Beauvoir's texts, and reiterates the contention made by many that one of her chief interests seemed to be in preserving and forwarding Sartre's reputation. Marks notes that Beauvoir's life is "exemplary," and states that it is not

---

3 *Ibid.*, 174.
4 *Ibid.*, 175.

farfetched to make a comparison between her and such influential (in terms of life-modeling) figures as Rousseau.[5]

In other words, whether or not her legions of admirers may in some sense be making some sort of mistake about Beauvoir, they see her in such a way that one cannot help but trot out most of the tropes of feminism with respect to any assessment of her accomplishments. Marks notes:

> It will take at least another twenty-five years before scholars can determine the extent of the influence of Simone de Beauvoir on her many readers, not only those who wrote her regularly asking for advice, but those more reserved women, and I suspect some men, for whom her journey was unique.[6]

Here the point is that it matters little, for example, what can be said about "immanence" in the novels, the behavior of Anne, or even what might be said about *The Second Sex*.

Mary Evans, as was said earlier, has written a trenchant critique of the extent to which any sort of contemporary feminism can be read into Beauvoir, and her essay makes crucial points. Her focus on Beauvoir's denial of the body takes her past the denial of physical pleasure—a denial which, in any case, is by no means consistent, because it does occur from time to time in the novels. More profound, according to Evans, is the lack of emphasis on or, again, the denial, of roles that are deeply important to most women, such as those associated with mothering. It is not simply that these roles are insisted upon by society; it is that current strands of feminist theory frequently address these roles because they have to do with the core issues that caused oppression to women in most societies in the first place: menstruation, lactation, and so forth. Evans comments:

> De Beauvoir, having argued that maternity is the basis of woman's dependence is much concerned to demonstrate that no "natural" desire for motherhood exists. If women would refuse to be duped by the social construction of false maternal instincts, they would no longer be mothers and hence no longer dependent. In short, they would be able to act in all respects as men act, free from social and sexual constraints and, in a quite literal sense, masters of their own fate.[7]

It is urgent to try to be precise about the ways in which this view, articulated by Evans (and with genuine specificity) differs sharply from so many of the views that we now think of as comprising strands of contemporary feminism.

Because they are so frequently taken for granted, it is now difficult to remember that the major points of what we call "gender feminism" would once have been controversial. Carol Gilligan and Dorothy Dinnerstein, among others, did us the service of showing how object relations theory, itself a strand of Freudian thought, pushed lines that could be useful for feminist theorizing.[8] If it is the case, as this sort of theory implied, that girls typically develop closer bonds and relations of

---

5 Marks, Elaine, in "Introduction," in Marks (ed.), 1–13.
6 *Ibid., ibid.*
7 Evans, "Views", 177.
8 Gilligan, *In a Different Voice;* Dinnerstein, *The Mermaid.*

connection, then we might expect this to be reflected in later life choices for girls, and we might also expect what Chodorow called "the reproduction of mothering" to be a relevant social force.

Evans' point is that Beauvoir writes as if these forces did not exist. Evans must be one of the few critics to have noticed and to have seized upon a very salient fact in Beauvoir's fiction: the lack of almost any allusion to a staple of human existence, families and family life. Indeed, the fact that Anne is a mother in *The Mandarins* marks one of the very few instances in Beauvoir's work where anything like such a relationship occurs, and Robert and Anne are nothing if not unusual parents. With respect to this, Evans says:

> One direction in which it [heterosexual love] does not lead is towards the establishment of domestic and family life. Both the characters in her novels and the friends and acquaintances she describes in her autobiography are nearly always both unmarried and childless. Women...do not express any desire for children, neither do they demonstrate any interest in their existence. [9]

Evans quite rightly sees all of this as evidence of still another level of denial of the body: the combination of the emphasis on rationality, the independence exhibited by so many characters like Anne (however admirable in some ways), and the push away from standard human relations combine to make Beauvoir perhaps much less sensitive to issues having to do with what we would now demarcate as gender feminism than many writers who would not, in any case, be labeled feminists. Evans closes her essay by noting that acceptance of certain parts of the female body and its concomitants must, in some sense, have something to do with feminism; such acceptance she sees as being utterly lacking in Beauvoir's work.

Pushing the analysis a bit further, and recapitulating, it is not only the various lacks that Evans cites that are remarkable; again, some female characters display more interest in at least certain aspects of the body and of bodily delights, but then these characters are frequently deranged and irrational, and stand as points against which the other female characters can be developed. Paula has a genuine and devoted love for Henri in *The Mandarins*, but her genuine and deeply felt emotional life leads her to become suicidal and ultimately to be committed. We have already seen how Xaviere is a foil to Francoise; what is worth noting is that Xaviere's intense devotion to herself, her needs, and her inner life (however thoughtless) is obvious almost from the point at which the character is first introduced. It is as if both Anne and Francoise need a female character who embodies certain sorts of characteristics against which they can be measured; in each case, a character is constructed and introduced into the text for this purpose.

Perhaps the chief difficulty with "feminist" analyses of Beauvoir's work is simply that today's feminist theorists are seeing the work through a different lens. What is taken for granted in contemporary theory is, in fact, work to which Beauvoir gave birth by her own productions. In other words, the clear impact of *The Second Sex* and some of her other writings is that they resulted in the very feminism that is now being used to criticize her.

---

9   Evans, "Views," 176.

Reading her novels more charitably, they constitute a breakthrough in issues discussed and manner of address, even if a good deal of the female characters' strength derives from male identification. (As has been said by many critics, we are accustomed now to a wide degree of frankness and an array of topics broached in the novel; in 1954, women authors did not commonly address sexual issues. The sexual passages in her work are therefore remarkable.) Anne may be given to a variety of styles and behaviors that in themselves can constitute a sort of masculinity, but her enjoyment of sex with Lewis Brogan is one of the first descriptions that we have of a woman's view of sexual relations, particularly in a novel published by a major publisher and recipient, as it was, of a major literary prize.

If it was said of Beauvoir when she died that women owe her everything, then it should also be said that a great deal of what is owed revolves specifically around these female characters from her major novels. In that sense, we can have little quarrel with their construction as characters, or with the novels' import.

Bodily Words

Beauvoir is nothing if not provocative, and other critics have seen her work in other ways. At least some of the descriptive passages to which we have just alluded can support an argument that turns the lines of the previous section on their head, and moves forward in a new direction. In other words, it is the thesis of at least some critics that Beauvoir's sexual descriptions constitute a breakthrough. As Barbara Klaw writes,

> It is through the sex and placement of characters who view the events related in this novel that Beauvoir depicts her internal struggle to understand the proper conditions for sexual relations and, in so doing, sabotages Freud's theories concerning penis envy. Violating his discourse, she problematizes sexuality, constructing it as both feminine and masculine for both sexes, and she revalorizes the female sex.[10]

Klaw's set of contentions pushes the argument with which the preceding section was closed; in the context of the time, Beauvoir's work, for its frankness, is new and innovative. Although both Klaw and Evans, for example, see a character such as Anne as essentially male-identified, Klaw sees this is a virtue. She also is explicit about what she sees as the bisexuality of certain texts—this is clearly the case with *She Came to Stay*—and she provides a lengthy analysis of *The Mandarins* wherein sexuality is seen both from Henri's and Anne's perspectives (Henri is the narrator of a large part of the novel) with some surprising twists.

Bodily delight is but one source of growth in the novels, according to Klaw. *The Mandarins* contains a virtual interrogation of sexuality and sexual mores, at least if an examination of some of the more minor characters is included. Nadine's presence in the texts, frequently unremarked upon at any length by readers, is, according to

---

10 Klaw, Barbara (1995), "Sexuality in Beauvoir's *Les Mandarins*," in Simons, Margaret (ed.), *Feminist Interpretations of Simone de Beauvoir*, University Park, PA: Pennsylvania State University Press, 193–221.

Klaw, crucial. Although Beauvoir's work precedes the sort of analysis by Kristeva or Irigaray that has driven *l'écriture feminine*, the freedom and delight in sex exhibited by some of the female characters pushes in that direction. Here is a portion of what Klaw says about Nadine and her discourse on sexuality:

> [T]his character's perspective implies that Beauvoir deplores the fact that society has taught women to exchange their bodies as material goods in return for fleeting attention.... Furthermore, Nadine's boldness in talking about her exploits serves a specific subversive intent. Not only does she praise or criticize her current beau to Anne as society traditionally perceives women do, but she also transgresses the boundaries of acceptable discourse by announcing her sexual promiscuity....[11]

Nadine, in a sense, does describe patriarchal power—she claims that "If I want to go out with them, I have to sleep with them."[12] But having said that, she has no hesitation in indicating that decent round of sex is as pleasing as a fine meal, no more or less, and that she, Nadine, has no difficulty in enjoying either meals or sex.

The fact that Nadine is supposed to be Anne's daughter probably goes a long way toward explaining the positioning of sexuality in her comments. Anne eventually comes to enjoy sex with Brogan—and even to some extent with Scriassine—but she will never have Nadine's casual attitude. But Nadine is supposed to be in her late teens. By having Nadine engage in her (overtly masculine) equation of the bodily delights of sex with that of a meal, Beauvoir paves the way toward the future.

In her work on Beauvoir's literary writings, Fallaize is specific about sexuality and *Mandarins*. Like Klaw, she thinks that a number of lines of argument support the view that Beauvoir's take on female sexuality—and specific descriptions of Anne having sex—is innovative for its time, and the sort of view that promulgates a feminist outlook. Fallaize writes in *The Novels of Simone de Beauvoir* that, despite Anne's wordy intellectuality:

> There are...some lyrical scenes between Anne and Lewis, in which Anne describes a sense of transfiguration, of recovery of the body in its most elemental form, and in which desire, happiness and love mingle.[13]

Although Fallaize in general supports the notion that Anne chooses a sort of rationality over sexual desire, the very fact that her sex life is depicted as it is is a sort of writing of the body.

More to the point are some of the descriptions in Beauvoir's other work, such as *The Woman Destroyed*. In the first story, "The Age of Discretion," sexuality is not invoked—but the body is. The narrator, a woman old enough to be the spouse of someone retired and uncertain of what to do with himself (and herself retired), reflects on her past and remarks to herself,

---

11 Klaw, "Sexuality," 205.
12 *Ibid.*, 204.
13 Fallaize, Elizabeth (1988), *The Novels of Simone de Beauvoir*, New York: Routledge, 107–108.

> Yet still from time to time a bewilderment comes over me. I remember my first appointment, my first class, and the dead leaves that rustled under my feet that autumn in the country. In those days retirement seemed to me as unreal as death itself, for between me and that day there lived a stretch of time almost twice as long as that which I had so far lived.[14]

These passages, reminiscent of the work *Old Age*, show Beauvoir's awareness of the fragility of the body and our enmeshment in it. The narrator also looks at her daughter-in-law at a later point and thinks "those fat, influential, important bourgeois, stinking with money…"[15] It is almost as if the worldview of the bourgeoisie was a part of its corpulence. It is not that Simone de Beauvoir does not notice the body, with respect to sexuality or otherwise. It is that our relations with our bodies are complicated, and, in a sense, speak of our relations to other things as well.

Like Woolf, and to some extent like Drabble, Beauvoir also writes of the altered states that signal another way of seeing, and their import. Such a state precedes her relations with Scriassine, and in Anne's case changes in awareness are almost always related to a heightened state of sensuality. It is true that Anne, ultimately, backs off from a great deal of the sensual content that she experiences, even in Mexico with Lewis. But the fact that she allows herself to experience it leaves the reader with the impression that Anne knows how to be overwhelmed. As Fallaize notes, some of the more straightforward sensual material is omitted from English translations of the novels, whether the scenes have to do with sex or not. As Fallaize says with respect to descriptions of Henri and Paule in bed in *The Mandarins*, "Henri's lack of desire for Paule shifts female sexuality into a grotesque and obscene mode. Paule is metamorphosed into 'a corpse or a madwoman' (omitted in the translation), 'a woman beside herself mouthing obscene words and clawing him painfully'(omitted in the translation."[16] No one can say that, at crucial points, Beauvoir has not managed to capture key aspects of bodily experience.

In the first story of *The Woman Destroyed*, already alluded to, Beauvoir captures aging, but she also captures a visceral fear of death. That fear is, of course, attached to an obvious decline in the functioning of one's body, and one's own perception of it. This somewhat surreal experience is one that Beauvoir can articulate in powerful ways—it is as if one were watching oneself through a mirror or a glass. As she has the narrator write:

> Ahead there were the horrors of death and farewells: it was false teeth, sciatica, infirmity,… Shall I succeed in not lifting my gaze to those horizons?… Will [it be] bearable for us? I do not know. I hope so. We have no choice in the matter.[17]

In other words, it is bad enough that we are all mortal—and aware of it—but before we pass away, most of us will have to live through an inevitable decline, signaled by the failure of parts of the body and the attendant embarrassment. It

---

14 de Beauvoir, Simone (1969), *The Woman Destroyed*, trans. Patrick O'Brian, New York: Pantheon Books, 15.
15 *Ibid.*, 32.
16 Fallaize, *Novels*, 108.
17 Beauvoir, *Destroyed*, 85.

might be argued that Beauvoir's awareness of these issues is not unrelated to her highlighting of, for example, Anne's sexuality. The point is that we are prisoners of our bodies, and that there is no escape. While we are objectified under the gaze of the other, we are also from time to time made very aware of the limitations of not being "pure rationality."

In writing about these issues, Beauvoir achieved a new sort of awareness of the body, and, in many ways, a sort of *écriture* that at least is aware of the feminine.

Detheorizing

Ultimately, it is difficult if not impossible to write about Beauvoir without pausing to examine Sartre. Since their work is so interwoven, he is, in a sense, the Continental theorist whose work is most meaningful when used to extrapolate Beauvoir.

What both thinkers have in common—and it may receive even more play in Sartre—is an interest in the objectification caused by our encounter with another. If it is often written that Sartre is most accessible in his novels and plays, it is an interesting corollary that some of the less successful plays, at least, are the best at getting their didactic points across. One such example is not nearly as well-known as either *The Flies* or *No Exit*, but it is an important point of departure for certain conceptual work—that is *La Putain Respectueuse*.

Lizzie, the protagonist, has very little to hang on to in her small Southern town other than her whiteness. Although Sartre was often faulted for his alleged misunderstanding of American issues, his phenomenological account of race (one shared by Beauvoir, and manifested to some extent in the output of their friend, Richard Wright) is of great use in elucidating some of Beauvoir.[18] The work done by race here—and exemplified in some of the key dialogue of *La Putain*—is crucially important because it draws attention to the notions of gaze, Othering and objectification in obvious and startling ways.

Lizzie has little to sustain her, but in time of trial she can always fall back on race. Much of her dialogue consists of an attempt to mouth old stereotypes whenever it seems that other sorts of remarks will not do. Although from time to time she tries to move beyond these beliefs, the play reinforces the notion that categorization of an Other is crucial to the maintenance of a worldview, something that is manifest in Beauvoir's writings as well.

In *The Respectful Prostitute*, Sartre has Lizzie engage in the following dialogue with a son of Senator Clarke:

> Lizzie: It doesn't bring bad luck, to see a nigger just after waking up, does it?
> Fred: Why?
> Lizzie: I—there's one going past down there, on the other side of the street.
> Fred: It's always bad luck when you see a nigger. Nigger's are the devil.[19]

---

18 An underappreciated work of Wright's, *The Outsider*, is clearly the result of interaction with them.

19 Sartre, Jean-Paul (1989), "The Respectful Prostitute," in *No Exit and Three Other Plays*, New York: Vintage, 249.

Lizzie's initial project of not wanting to testify falsely against a Black man runs afoul of the town's power structure, and, ultimately, of Lizzie's own need for the security of a certain form of bad faith. Part and parcel of that bad faith is the reification of the Other and the continual reliance upon it as a construct. In addition, Lizzie becomes caught up in her relationship with Fred, but Fred only desires her insofar as she can become an object for him, and adhere to the dominant pathologies. As a woman, Lizzie is again trapped in the immanence of the body and its categories. In some sense, she is similar to some of the characters in *The Woman Destroyed*.

An underexamined, but very powerful piece of work by Simone de Beauvoir is the second of the trio of short stories in *The Woman Destroyed*, "The Monologue." It may very well be that critics have found this thirty-some page stream-of-consciousness piece too difficult—it is Beauvoir's take on the worldview of a more-or-less well-off woman who feels that she has been typed by life, and who expresses herself in oddly working class ways. She masterfully captures the self-deception and lack of awareness of the character, and the monologue is one long stream of complaint against the world in general and Murielle's family and friends in particular.

Like Lizzie, Murielle has to hang onto certain beliefs, as they prop her up and keep her going. The fact that most of her beliefs are false or, at best, gross exaggerations, does not seem to occur to her. Elizabeth Fallaize probably speaks for many when she writes of this story that: "Sudden changes of subject and unexplained references to new characters and events constantly hinder the reader and prevent identification with the speaker."[20] But this is not nearly as derailing as Murielle's own conceptual scheme, which consists of almost non-stop blame, objectification and evasiveness. The point of this story—however unappealing it has proven to many—has to be seen within the context of the two stories that surround it. Each of the other tales involves upper-middle class women whose mode of expression (albeit in translation) is much more acceptable to many. But the point, presumably, is that the level of self-deception is the same—Murielle is simply a more obvious exemplar.

Like Sartre's characters, Murielle cannot see beyond her limited range. Although the text makes it clear that she has something to do with her daughter's suicide, she claims to be the best mother in the world. With her one-against-everyone view, Murielle says:

> They are killing me the bastards. The idea of the party tomorrow destroys me. I must win. I must I must I must I must I must. I'll tell my fortune with the cards.[21]

But this theme of lack of self-awareness, bad faith, and necessity for otherizing is a constant one in *The Woman Destroyed*. Because Beauvoir is so good at capturing different voices in this work, this short collection is one of her stronger pieces of fiction. A similar take on things (although certainly not as overtly angry a take) is exemplified by the narrator of the title piece in the last story. She is driven to distraction by her husband's affair, but one of her first responses is to characterize the

---

20 Fallaize, *Novels*, 161.
21 Beauvoir, *Destroyed*, 111.

woman in question, Noellie, as "the incarnation of everything we dislike—desire to succeed at any price, pretentiousness, love of money, a delight in display...."[22]

Some of Sartre's strongest writing about the Other comes in his analysis of the treatment of Blacks. As we have seen, this is to be found in at least one play; it is also found in an essay "The Oppression of Blacks in the United States" that has appeared in his *Notebook for an Ethics*.[23] Although Beauvoir probably has no one example in her writing of analysis of an "Other" that is this severely objectified, both she and Sartre share certain core beliefs about the creation of this other by the for-itself. Crucially, Sartre writes:

> It is also true that there is an initial attitude of the For-itself that freezes the other into an object. With the outcome that the Negro who can read is that Negro over there that I see at this moment, that inferior and half-damned creature, come into possession of a stolen, almost external power that he only knows how to make use of for evil. [24]

Beauvoir's central characters tend to exhibit this "freezing," albeit with somewhat less force. But the crucial notion is the freezing itself, and the objectification is sometimes a defense mechanism (Anne against Lewis, for example), sometimes a mode of being (a near-permanent maneuver of Xaviere) and sometimes a response to a crisis (the narrators of the stories in *The Woman Destroyed*). Insofar as it prevents mutual recognition of the for-itself, these maneuvers signal moral failure and bad faith. Nevertheless it is clear that, however reprehensible, they represent a large part of human behavior.

Since Sartrean work in general—and for the moment we will shove Beauvoir's thought into this category—came to be anathema to the poststructuralist theory of France, it would seem to be an act of consummate bad faith to attempt to analyze her work in such terms. Unquestionably, some of her writing would lend itself to interpretations along the lines of Kristeva or Lacan. But the history of her work with Sartre indicates that it is that particular line of thought—post-war existentialism—that is not only their common umbrella, but the best explicator of some of Beauvoir's writings. Authors such as the Fullbrooks, who would give Beauvoir primacy with respect to the origins of key critical notions, are on to something insofar as the structures of at least the novels are concerned.[25] Much of the literary work of Beauvoir forwards the same sort of analyses in which Sartre engaged, and in a more easily accessible fashion. Whatever the primacy, there is little question that these two projects are united, and part of the beauty of this somewhat dyadic work is that strands of the work of either author can be used to illuminate the writings of the other.

---

22 Beauvoir, *Destroyed*, 140.
23 Sartre, Jean-Paul (1992), "The Oppression of Blacks," in *Notebook for an Ethics*, trans. David Pellauer, Chicago: University of Chicago Press.
24 *Ibid.*, 563.
25 Fullbrook, Edward and Kate (1998), *Simone de Beauvoir: a Critical Introduction*, Cambridge: Polity Press. This work contains a great deal of analysis of the novels and short-story cycles; see also their *Simone de Beauvoir and Jean-Paul Sartre: the Remaking of a Twentieth-Century Legend*.

Knowing

The emphasis on alterity in Beauvoir's work might lead the reader to think that certain sorts of epistemic moves would fold automatically out of her use of notions of othering. To some extent, this may be an accurate statement—in Anne's relationship with Lewis, for example, certain states of awareness seem to produce a sort of knowledge, and the text of *The Mandarins* is full of such examples.

But there is also an emphasis on a more standard form of knowledge in at least *The Mandarins*—and to some extent, for example, in portions of *The Woman Destroyed*—and that sort of knowledge (the label "empirical" would not be a complete misuse of the term) is often put to political uses. What is most intriguing about Beauvoir's thought patterns in the novels is the ways in which these two sorts of knowings seem to mesh.

Because it is clear that the focus of a work such as *Mandarins* is largely political, the characters' epistemic grasp of their situations vis-à-vis and with respect to the world situation is important to get across. At the bottom level, the politically-motivated lead characters of Beauvoir's longest novel gain a great deal of their information from newspapers and media. But in a move that Beauvoir makes in much of her writing, almost all of the characters take that information into the realm of the imagination and extrapolate it. This gives their political pronouncements a great deal of power—and a genuinely felt basis. Fallaize is impressed by the tortured ruminations of Henri and Robert, especially insofar as these lines of thought are fictional entries into the world of the oppressed:

> By the time of Anne's last visit, however, [to America] the political climate has deteriorated sharply. Henri refuses the politically loaded offer of paper for *L'Espoir* made to him by the American Bennet, telling him that America is the country which everywhere and always systematically takes the side of the privileged. In China, in Greece, in Turkey, in Korea, what are they defending? It isn't the people is it? It's capital, it's the big land holdings. When I think that they're supporting Franco and Salazar....[26]

Aside from a trip to Portugal which is described in some detail in the book, we are given little textual evidence that Henri has traveled enough to visualize conditions in, for example, Turkey or China. But a certain form of knowledge, based on extrapolation, observation, and plain accumulation of evidence is clearly at work in many of the more overtly political parts of the novel. Fallaize also cites the lengthy sections of debate over whether to reveal the labor camps in the Soviet Union; as she notes in her commentary on this section, "[For Henri] the consequences of this attitude [that there is a duty to tell the truth] do, however, disturb him; in the past he has felt able to affirm that his duty as a journalist is to tell the truth without regard for what uses might be made of it."[27] The difficulty, as Fallaize notes, for the characters as well as the reader is to discern what is the truth. With respect to the existence of the camps, the characters have only the words of defectors (and not a large number of defectors) upon which to base an opinion. It is entirely possible that the defectors

---

26 Fallaize, *Novels*, 103.
27 *Ibid.*, 93.

are exaggerating, or telling overt falsehoods. But imagination permits one to travel to the camps in one's mind.

It is a combination of this straightforward empirically-derived attitude to the consequences of political action in the world around us and the phenomenological accounts of interaction with the other that provide some of the most intriguing sections of Beauvoir's work. A special sort of knowing is born; the insight that is required to try to face the other, come to grips with the other's point of view, and learn to construct a *modus vivendi* with the other's objectification provides the springboard for a special sort of knowledge.

Thus Anne finds that her attempts to come to know Lewis—danger-fraught and unsuccessful though they may be—give her an epistemic platform from which to imaginatively enter the worlds of others. It is no accident that some of the most poignant writing in the book comes in the section describing Lewis and Anne's trip to Mexico. An intense focus on Lewis, his gestures, his frowns, his moods and his speech has sensitized Anne to the world around her. Now the suffering that in France requires of Anne (or her friends) a highly fictionalized mental journey is presented to her through her own eyes and on an everyday basis. The reader is invited to make the inference that part of what allows Anne to view the Indians, for example, with something less than detachment is directly related to the amount of time and effort that she has just expended in trying to get to know a single human being, namely Lewis.

This section of *The Mandarins* contains several pointed passages descriptive of local poverty, and at later points in the novel these evocations recur in conversation. Anne thinks:

> We did a lot of walking that week. We climbed to the tops of tall pyramids and sailed in flower-filled boats; we strolled along Jalisco Avenue, wandered through its shabby marketplaces, went into its dancehalls, its vaudeville theaters; we roamed around the city's outskirts and drank tequila in its infamous bars. We were planning on staying a little longer in Mexico City, spending a month visiting the rest of the country, and then returning to Chicago for a few days.[28]

When Anne notices the poverty, it seems to strike in a way that is noticeably different from her reaction to Lewis' Chicago of poor homes and seedy bars. In Mexico, Anne is able—at least temporarily—to attempt to see into the other. The writer's life in Chicago is a bit like that of bohemian Paris, but there is nothing bohemian about poverty among Mexico's indigenous. These particular sections of the novel are among its strongest.

Issues that might classically be deemed to be relevant to epistemology seem to attract the attention of commentators with respect to *She Came to Stay*. This difficult to read work, with its tortured characters and overt, somewhat off-putting use of philosophical concepts and language, is justifiably one that can be said to deal with areas of knowledge. There is no question that the first few chapters, with their descriptions of Francoise's reactions first to Xaviere, and then to Pierre's obvious attraction to Xaviere, constitute a *tour de force* of phenomenological writing.

---

28 Beauvoir, *Mandarins*, 464.

Here the questions are more classically philosophical. As the Fullbrooks claim, much of *She Came to Stay* has to do with our assumptions about the thought patterns of others, and our stronger—and often necessary—assumptions that they mimic our own. Edward and Kate Fullbrook write:

> Beauvoir locates the solution to the problem of other minds in the structure of social solipsism. At the beginning of the novel, Francoise personifies this position in her relations with Xaviere. Francoise works at keeping herself persuaded that, rather than apprehending Xaviere's consciousness, she knows of its existence only indirectly through inferences based on sensory observations of Xaviere's body.[29]

But what makes Beauvoir's work so exceptional in *She Came to Stay* is that these sorts of philosophical positions recur, in various permutations, on almost every page. Although Xaviere is less than easy to know—in fact, this is part of the plot—both Pierre and Francoise seem to assume that they can come to "know" her through her highly changeable facial expressions and almost pathological willfulness. But what they come to know is frightening; as the Fullbrooks also say, "The French edition of *She Came to Stay* has an epigraph: 'Each consciousness pursues the death of the other.'"[30] More so than would be the case with most individuals, it is clear from the outset that Xaviere embodies this saying, and that it does not bode well for the other characters in the work.

What both *The Mandarins* and *She Came to Stay* have in common is a focus on how we come to be able to claim knowledge of the consciousness of another, even someone we know well (Lewis, for example, in the case of Anne). We can never be sure of the other; we can only guess in more or less sophisticated varieties of guessing. But the effort expended in the guessing opens us up to other possibilities, and those areas of endeavor may be more beneficial—and pleasing—in the long run.

Beauvoir in the Future

Some of Beauvoir's attempts at social relevance seem dated today, because we are so much more aware of the problems to which she alludes. It is interesting that, mixed with concern for humanity and a genuine interest in the poor, there are passages that allude to the French colonies as a fine dropping off point for those whose lives seem useless in France, and there is, of course, a general awareness in the writing of France's position in the world (and, perhaps not so oddly, a sort of sadness that it seems to have fallen into decline after the end of the war).

If Drabble, as a contemporary novelist, is able to alter some of her work so that the more recent novels genuinely engage the social problems of Britain, we have no such luxury with either Beauvoir or Woolf. What some might interpret as the general arrogance of French culture is by no means missing from the work of Simone de

---

29 Fullbrook, *Critical*, 86.
30 *Ibid.*, 85.

Beauvoir; the question is how to incorporate her many insights with her assumption that French views are of crucial importance.

The strongest parts of her work in this regard are some of those very passages to which we have already alluded—in *The Mandarins*, for example, there are not only many pages of descriptions of Mexico and Guatemala, but genuine wonder on the parts of the major characters about the fate of the planet and about the lives of those who live in China or the Soviet Union. Although Beauvoir frequently writes of "the millions," it is clear that one of the points that separates her intellectually-oriented characters from those like Claudie Belzunce, who take no interest in such matters, is the very sincerity of their concern.

A strong point for Beauvoir is that the consistency of her focus on "othering" as an issue means that a good deal can be drawn from her novels that speaks to the concerns of, for example, today's multicultural societies. Even a work such as *She Came to Stay* can be used in this regard. In one of the opening chapters, Francoise and Xaviere go to see a performance in a "Moorish café." Beauvoir writes:

> The dancing girl moved toward the middle of the room; her hips began to undulate, and her stomach ripple to the rhythm of the tambourine.
> "You'd think a demon were trying to tear itself from her body," said Xaviere. She leaned forward, entranced.[31]

Although this section is used primarily to highlight the ways in which Francoise tries to penetrate to Xaviere's core—with only intermittent success—the scene can also be used in another way. Beauvoir is, of course, aware of the fact that there is an exotic quality to the dancer and her culture—the shock of seeing the dancer (Francoise admits that, in Morocco, she had seen them "dance naked"[32]) draws out of Xaviere some of the very emotions that Francoise had hoped to see. Thus the entire encounter is a lesson in Otherness writ large; in another context, the dancer herself, or someone from her culture, could be the object of Francoise's gaze and her attempts at understanding.

Thus the focus that Beauvoir has on this particular form of phenomenology can be employed to try to penetrate larger constructions of objectification, even those that are primarily on a societal level. Portions of *The Mandarins*, above and beyond the travel sections, also further these notions. Although Beauvoir is only intermittently successful at getting a progressive point across, her delineations of the characters with whom Lewis surrounds himself, for example, speak to these issues.

In a larger sense, the most progressive portions of Beauvoir's novels are probably those that, although they take place almost entirely in Paris, routinely ridicule the bourgeoisie and its concerns. Henri takes as a lover Josette, whose mother seems driven to constant accumulation of wealth, and whose vacuousness seems to have a perverse effect on Henri. The sections of the novel describing Josette, her family and her lack of an interior life are powerful indictments against the conventionality and stupidity of the bourgeoisie. The following passage might be thought to be typical of this sort of scene, at least in *The Mandarins*:

---

31 Beauvoir, *She Came to Stay*, 20.
32 *Ibid.*, 19.

"It's a triumph!" Lucie Belhomme cried out, rushing toward him as he entered the huge restaurant in which a perfumed crowd was jabbering away. She placed her gloved hand on Henri's arm; on her head a big, black sad-looking bird was poised. "You've got to admit that Josette really looked stunning when she came on in that red dress."

"Tomorrow night I'm going to take that dress, drag it through the mud, and give it a few good rips here and there."

"You have no right to do that. It's an Amaryllis original!" Lucie said sharply. "Besides, everyone thought it was very beautiful."[33]

This set of passages does the situation justice; Henri, who would like to be able to forget about his involvement with Josette, is faced not only with the triumph in a special dress, but with the response of Lucie, of the "jabbering" crowd, who reminds him—when he claims, in good, Bohemian fashion, that it deserves a few rips—that it's an "Amaryllis".

While Henri, Robert and Anne agonize over the position of the intellectual in post-war France and in an atomic world, the *haute* bourgeoisie meanders on in its concern for consumption, effect and display. In her depiction of this group in *The Mandarins*, Beauvoir succeeds in giving us something that not only resonates now, but will doubtless continue to do so. It reminds us of the ugliness of consumption in a world of suffering and pain.

All Said and Done

The heightened awareness of the work of Simone de Beauvoir in the last twenty years since her death has resulted in an outpouring of commentary, but, as indicated earlier, most of it is directed either to *The Second Sex* or such works as *An Ethics of Ambiguity* and *A Very Easy Death*. Then again, attempts to formulate a criticism of her novels are undermined, to some extent, by the very philosophical nature of the works themselves—along with those of Sartre and Camus, Beauvoir's novels and short stories must count as among the most overtly conceptual of the twentieth century.

Nevertheless, literary concerns militate against an easy dismissal of any of the works. *The Mandarins* is not only well-written, with a tightly-woven plot, but it contains extraordinary passages with respect to politics, sex and the detritus of the war. It is compelling in a way that many other novels are not, simply because it is so highly intellectualized, and because so many of its themes are spelled out in great detail. *She Came to Stay*, while difficult to read—and at least in part because of the tortured nature of the relationships, reminiscent of Dostoevsky—draws the reader in, as the reader attempts, also, to penetrate Xaviere and to read her personality. The somewhat overwritten early sections, with their phenomenological bent, are easy to put aside once the tensions between Pierre, Xaviere and Francoise begin to build. *The Woman Destroyed* shows Beauvoir at her best—because the stories are short, they are easy to follow, while familiar points about the sexes and engagement in general are made.

---

33 Beauvoir, *The Mandarins*, 387.

What Beauvoir is not is a stylist. Where Woolf pushes, and the reader attempts eagerly to follow, as if it were a tennis match against a very talented opponent, Beauvoir simply gives one a cascade of words and ideas. Drabble's irony finds no counterpart in Beauvoir, who is rarely ironic, except in some passages of dialogue. The questions that remain about Beauvoir, then, tend to the opposite poles of those that we would ask about the novelists whose work we examined earlier. Where it takes argument to see precisely what might be philosophical about either Drabble or Woolf, it takes no argument for Beauvoir, since the difficulty is that there is rather too much obvious philosophy, rather than too little.

But at this juncture it is helpful to remember that neither Sartre nor Camus seem to have been faulted for the "obviousness" of their philosophical bent—rather, works such as *Nausea* and *The Plague* have been greeted with near universal acclaim, resulting, among other things, in Nobel prizes for the authors, even if Sartre did, in fact, refuse his. One cannot help but ask if the difference in the treatment accorded to Beauvoir's literary work has to do with the author's gender. *Nausea* is awkward, hard to follow, and (like *She Came to Stay*) painfully philosophical. Many readers simply find that they cannot keep going, and the delineation of Roquentin's depersonalized breakdown is altogether too harrowing to work through. In the same way, *No Exit* and *The Flies* are remarkable plays—remarkable, that is, for how little they resemble standard drama. Again, it is clear that conceptual schemes drive these works, and the uninitiated reader may be puzzled and left bereft.

PART III
The New World

Chapter Eight

Toni Cade Bambara and the Black Vision

Toni Cade Bambara is the author of a number of works that have been deemed to be groundbreaking by black and white critics alike. Her most famous work, *The Salt Eaters*, is a novel that is at once Afrocentric, philosophical and progressively feminist/womanist, while dealing in many of the best-known tropes and constructs of black American culture.[1]

Authors such as Alice Walker, Toni Morrison and Gloria Naylor may be better known, but Bambara asks a number of difficult questions about identity while at the same time pushing a sort of postmodern outlook that transgresses boundaries. She was also one of the first black writers to attempt to tie together, in an anthology, black women's writings, and she is one of the few whose work has pushed critics to ask what sort of worldview might be encompassed in her novels. Of her anthology, Barbara Christian has noted, "it is a seminal collection that indicated a black feminist orientation existed."[2]

A great deal has been written about the double oppression of being black and female in America, and of the special worldview that it engenders. Most of those who purport to speak for the black experience in some way are male; most of those who purport to speak for women's experience are white. The black woman has historically been at the bottom of a hierarchy that is so profound as to resist analysis, and yet the epistemic privilege from this standpoint of extreme marginality has not, until recently, has been investigated.

Bambara uses fiction as a device to explore modes of being, but she is also especially sensitive to any one way of constructing reality, or to the hegemony of any one perspective. One of the things that makes *The Salt Eaters* so difficult to read is that it is unclear which take on reality is something like an "actual" take, and in many cases it is unclear whose take is being presented. As John Edgar Wideman has written:

> With the force and freedom of a great traditional storyteller…Toni Cade Bambara takes a lot of chances. Her novel is set in the Black section of a large Southern city…but her characters also inhabit the nonlinear, sacred space and sacred time of traditional African religion.[3]

---

1 Bambara, Toni Cade (1992), *The Salt Eaters*, New York: Vintage.
2 Christian, Barbara (1997), *Black Feminist Criticism*, New York: Teachers College Press, 205.
3 Back jacket blurb, Vintage edition of *The Salt Eaters*.

If Bambara pushes us to think, it is only because Eurocentrism and its concomitant vantage points are so engrained in us that it makes it difficult to conceive of other modes of thought. If time is conceptualized as necessarily linear, then the cyclical nature of time as evidenced by the social patterns of other societies will seem nonsensical when set down in fictional form. If the notion of place is always geographic and not simultaneously conceptual, writing that tries to deal with both simultaneously will seem inaccessible. Bambara asks us to believe that we cannot fully understand the black experience in the Americas until we understand the indigenous thought patterns from which it is derived, patterns that are set out, for example, in such classic works as Robert Farris Thompson's *Flash of the Spirit*.[4]

In *The Salt Eaters*, we learn early on about the conceptual changes that Bambara will ask us to make when we are confronted at the beginning of the book with Velma, a young black activist who is undergoing a ritual healing. Velma sits on a stool in a clinic, but the stool is hardly Velma's place:

> She tried to withdraw as she'd been doing for weeks and weeks…. She wasn't sure how to move away from Minnie Ransom and from the music, where to throw up the barrier and place the borderguard. She wasn't sure whether she'd been hearing music anyway. Was certain, though that she wasn't sure what she was supposed to say or do on that stool. Wasn't even sure whether it was time to breathe in or breathe out. Everything was off, out of whack, the relentless logic she'd lived by sprung. And here she was in Minnie Ransom's hands in the Southwest Community Infirmary.[5]

The "borderguard" is Velma's system of defenses that she has always used to get by—here Bambara plays with our own notions of ego boundaries and borders, and indicates how permeable they can become. Yet if they are too permeable—and the black woman is constantly under multiple assaults—the ego crumbles, the sense of self is fractured, and the individual cannot go on. Velma undergoes a traditional healing in the hands of Minnie and twelve others, but she undergoes this healing in a clinic that, like most contemporary medical facilities, is filled with individuals in white suits. Velma is literally and figuratively out of place. As Minnie, the healer, asks her, "Are you sure…that you want to be well?"[6]

The necessity for a safe space for a black woman is investigated extensively by Patricia Hill Collins in her classic *Black Feminist Thought*, and it is a recurring theme of much black women's writing. But Bambara is more sensitive than most to the notion that this safe space is largely a mental space, and that it can be abrogated at any time. As Collins says, "Behind the mask of behavioral conformity imposed on African-American women, acts of resistance, both organized and anonymous, have long existed."[7] History, sociology and literary endeavors have tended to focus on external, organized resistance—novels by black women writers from *Dessa Rose* by Sherley Williams, to *Corregidora* by Gayl Jones, to *Sula* by Toni Morrison, in general choose the outer context of rebellion as their theme. Bambara is concerned with

---

4 Farris Thompson, Robert (1984), *Flash of the Spirit*, New York: Vintage Books.
5 Bambara, *Salt Eaters*, 5.
6 *Ibid.*, 3.
7 Hill Collins, Patricia (2000), *Black Feminist Thought*, New York: Routledge, 97.

the inner struggle, the construction of an Afrocentric or African-derived conceptual space, and the restructuring of personal cognitive schemes along such lines. The powerful changes of time, place and person that such restructuring inevitably causes the agent to undergo are the most evocative and long-lasting themes of Bambara's literary works.

Because so much of what she has written, especially in her one novel, *The Salt Eaters*, speaks to these conceptual issues, Bambara is easier to categorize in philosophical terms than many writers are. Woolf's use of time signals to us the breakdown in narrative that we find as a hallmark of modernism; it is simplistic, but accurate, to claim that this breakdown mirrors the social disorder of the European world at the time. Bambara's work, however, uses the notions of "sacred space" of the West African cultures, and, as Wideman indicates, she plays freely with these concepts. Using African philosophy as a guide, her work can be unpacked—but the tropes and symbols that she employs are far from Eurocentric in origin.

The history of commentary on black literature is rife with allusions to DuBois' concept of double consciousness, and its effect on black Americans. In an anthology published in the 1960s, Abraham Chapman notes:

[T]he invisibility and denial of identity, the facelessness and namelessness...are actually deeply rooted in the group or folk consciousness of black America....[8]

Black women authors, however, have pushed this line much further than its original instantiation in the works of Ralph Ellison and Richard Wright. In general, the special oppression of black women might be said to yield a triple consciousness—but Bambara is not content to merely portray this in the manner that has been done by a number of other authors. Rather, Bambara's central characters often feel an internal call, a call that is as old and ancient as the cultures of the continent from which their forebears sprang. Bambara refers to the "mud mothers"; her characters seem to connect with them in a visceral way. Bambara's remarkable melding of the here and now, of black community activism and politics with the lure of the past and its African roots, makes her work memorable in ways that are difficult to describe. As Wideman said, the elements of traditional storytelling are all in place in her work, but the tales themselves are far from traditional.

African Ontologies

Contemporary African philosophers have often been at pains to disabuse others of the notion that African thought is non-empirical, or irredeemably dualist. Appiah, for one, asserts that dualism is not at all an adequate term to capture the array of "substances" posited in many varieties of non-African thought; he counts four or five.[9] Still other thinkers have wanted to make the case that a great deal of what counts as traditional thought is empirical in its origins, at least insofar as cause and

---

8 Chapman, Abraham (ed.) (2001), *Black Voices*, New York: Signet, 29–30.
9 Appiah, Anthony (1993), *In My Father's House: Africa in the Philosophy of Culture*, Cambridge: Harvard University Press.

effect are concerned—the point is that it is the observation of the natural world that has led to the positing of forces dubbed by non-Africans as "spirits."

Western philosophical terms do not easily translate into the worldviews of other cultures, and so, in a sense, one is always at a loss in trying to explain beliefs that were originally constructed in Twi or Wolof. But there is no question that the African-derived cultures of the New World display a range of beliefs that tie in to the original views, often in very explicit ways. Robert Farris Thompson writes, for example, of Brazil:

> Eshu-Elegbara became one of the most important images in the black Atlantic world.... Blacks honor him in Cuba where "men and women of African descent pour cool water at crossroads..." And thousands honor him today in Rio de Janeiro, where candles begging Eshu's favor may be lit in the gutters at intersections, in the very shadows of the skyscrapers that line the beaches at Ipanema or Copacabana.[10]

It is this heritage that is evoked in a great deal of *The Salt Eaters*, even if Bambara's indirect style asks the reader to do a great deal of work. One of the most salient features of this evocation is the character of Minnie Ransom, the archetypal healer. Minnie regularly converses with spirits, and her chats with these entities take up a fair amount of the dialogue in the book—in some cases, it is by no means clear with whom Minnie is speaking, so that the assessment that the interlocutor is a disembodied entity comes to the reader gradually. Bambara writes:

> "Quit wrasslin, sweetheart, or you may go under. I'm throwing you the lifeline. Don't be too proud to live.
> "Speakin of wrasslin with pride, Min—"
> "What you say?" Minnie Ransom hadn't been aware of her spirit guide's presence, or of her drift elsewhere.
> "Say she can't hear you, Min. Don't even see you. Henry gal off somewhere tracking herself."
> "Mmm. Hanging on to her's like trying to maneuver a basket of snakes on a pole. Spasms in every nerve center.... What's ailing the Henry gal so, Old Wife? Not that I'm sure I can match her frequency anyway. She's draining me."[11]

The reader who has attempted to follow *Salt Eaters* up to the relevant point in the text may be forgiven for thinking that the second line of dialogue belongs either to one of the observers, or possibly to Velma Henry herself. But Old Wife, Minnie's spirit guide, is an active character in the text and an enormous help in trying to heal Velma.

Kwasi Wiredu has done an excellent job of trying to articulate the intersections of Akan ontological beliefs and some hallmarks of Western philosophical systems, such as the classic distinction between dualism and materialism. As Wiredu indicates, it is not that there are no pertinent analogues—rather, what is the case is that commentators have often failed to use appropriate analogues, or have indicated the parallels in an

---

10 Thompson, *Flash*, 19–20.
11 Bambara, *Salt Eaters*, 42.

awkward and less than useful way.[12] Wiredu, for example, distinguishes between the *okra* (often glossed as "life principle"), the *sunsum* (an "ingredient" of the personality which does not survive death) and the Western notion of "soul." As he indicates, "The difference in ontological character, then, between the *okra* and the *sunsum*, on the one hand, and the *mogya* and the bodily frame as a whole, on the other, is only one of degree of materiality, the body being fully material and the other constituents only partially material in the sense already explained."[13]

As Wiredu goes on to say, if the *okra* is in some sense partially material, then it really is not a particularly apt analogue for the Cartesian concept of the soul, and it certainly would explain why there might be a more cogent explanation for persistence of some part of the individual after death. In any case, it is important in trying to present material from the Afrocentric writing of the 1980s and 1990s to be as precise as possible about the origins of the views in question. Bambara delves into a West African past, and she does so in such a way that she leads the inquisitive reader into the inevitable philosophical tie-ins.

Conceptions of space and time play an enormous role in much of Bambara's work, and particularly in *The Salt Eaters*. As Velma moves into herself and ceases to want or need communication with the outside world, her own concepts of space and time change. The reader is caught up in Velma's view and, again, may have a great deal of difficulty discerning elements of the plot. These points themselves merge with elements of Western thought in ways that might be deemed cosmological. Bambara's shifts in narration are consistent with the metaphysical points that she wishes to stress; although such shifts make the world difficult, they are within the scope of the tradition. Patricia Hill Collins emphasizes the importance of similar points when she writes:

> This belief in connectedness and the use of dialogue as one of its criteria for methological adequacy has African roots. Whereas women typically remain subordinated to men within traditional African societies, these same societies have at the same time embraced holistic worldviews that seek harmony.... Rooted in a tradition of African humanism, each individual is thought to be a unique expression of a common spirit, power, or energy inherent in all life.[14]

As we are introduced to Velma, Minnie, Old Wife, the circle of healers, the Infirmary, and the town of Claybourne, we see each as part of a whole, and experience this in Bambara's attempt to unify all of these features in one undivided *mélange*, rather than introducing them separately. Initial confusion is replaced by understanding as we come to grips with the notion that, in the spacetime shared by Minnie and Old Wife, there are no such "divisions."

Part of Velma's healing is to try to wipe out earlier pain, and Bambara has her undergo a series of flashbacks to make this very point. In one such scene, Obie, her husband, reminds her, "It's got to be costing you something to hang on to old pains....

---

12 Wiredu, Kwasi (1992–93), "African Philosophical Tradition: a Case Study of the Akan," in *Philosophical Forum*, XXIV, (1–3), Fall–Spring, 35–62.
13 Wiredu, "African," 50.
14 Collins, *Thought*, 261, 263.

It takes something out of you, Velma, to keep all them dead moments alive."[15] For Velma, the past is still very much alive, but her psychological struggles merely mirror the actual spacetime past that is coterminous with the present and future on some traditional conceptions of time. These concepts may, in fact, be stronger and more fully articulated in the culture than the Western concepts of a deity who creates or who is outside of time. In a similar vein, Wiredu has noted that "[B]y the very nature of the laws by which he [the deity, or a deity] fashioned the cosmic order he [cannot change the laws]."[16]

A virtue of a novel such as *The Salt Eaters* is that its very mode of presentation signals to the reader that something is going on. In other words, it is not possible to read the book without the sense that one is being presented with philosophical views, however different those views might be from what many readers will expect. To name a novelist from another tradition, some of what Bambara exposes the peruser to is similar to what might be gleaned from the work of N. Scott Momaday, for example. In such works as *House Made of Dawn* and *The Ancient Child*, Momaday takes the reader on a journey constructed through the use of Navajo worldviews. The reader's initial mystification is eventually replaced by understanding, and a fuller and richer comprehension of what is meant by the positing of differences between Native American and European cultures.

Toni Cade Bambara achieves, in *Salt Eaters*, that which many other black writers have claimed as an aim or goal—the setting out of a traditional West African cosmology in the guise of a contemporary set of circumstances. It is for this reason that Wideman labels her work "risky," but the risks that she takes are more than compensated for by her eventual gains.

Bambaran Criticism

Initial critical efforts on the work of Toni Cade Bambara seemed to want to place her as simply another voice in that group currently known as "Black Women Writers." In fact, it is remarkable that, before Gloria Hull's essay on *The Salt Eaters* was published, comparatively little of what was written about Bambara (or Toni Cade, as she was initially known) captured the imaginative vitality of her work. There is a remarkable trajectory with respect to critical commentary on her, and to some extent this trajectory recapitulates other salient features of the categorization of women writing in the Black tradition.

For example, Barbara Christian's *Black Feminist Criticism* mentions Bambara several times, but mainly in group citation.[17] In a passage that starts out about the work of Toni Morrison, Christian writes:

> There are so many fine black Afro-American women writers, including June Jordan, Mari Evans, Toni Cade, Alice Walker, Sonia Sanchez, Jane Cortez, not to mention

---

15 Bambara, *Salt Eaters*, 22.
16 Wiredu, "African" 41.
17 Christian, *Feminist*, 28, 162, 179, 180, 205, 223, 226.

the playwrights.... [T]hey leave us with the diversity of black woman's experience in America, what she has made of it and how she is transforming it.[18]

Similarly, Patricia Hill Collins in *Black Feminist Thought* mentions Bambara twice in a text of some three hundred pages, both times in brief citation. Only one citation mentions *Salt Eaters*; the other notes that "Black women's fiction, such as Toni Cade Bambara's short story 'The Johnson Girls' (1984) and Toni Morrison's novels...is one important location where Black women's friendships are taken seriously."[19]

What is remarkable about this material is that it appears, by its date of publication, to have been composed after *Salt Eaters* made its appearance in print. In other words, astute critical commentary on this work appears to have been lacking—other than in the material actually used for reviews in such publications as *The New York Times*—for several years. This may partially have been due to the novel's obvious difficulty, but another take on this lacuna is simply that critics may have felt that, to make its mark, a "Black" novel should be intelligible to all, and that this longest and most complex piece of work by Bambara failed the test.

An additional level of complexity enters the picture when it is noted that, at least by Christian's lights, Bambara's earlier work (such as her compendium *The Black Woman*) was intended to make a more or less patent political statement. Christian, for example, refers to *The Black Woman* as "a seminal collection that indicated that a black female orientation existed."[20] All of the foregoing indicates that, while it may have been the case that the importance of *The Salt Eaters* as a work indicative of an African worldview and with deep West African philosophical roots was recognized, it was very difficult for reviewers or critics to grasp the work, expound upon it, or make it more palatable for any reading audience.

A sea change in the view of this novel—and in the reception of Bambara—came with the publication of Gloria Hull's essay on the work in the Barbara Smith anthology *Home Girls*. Hull opens her piece by noting that many have thought *Salt Eaters* important, but that they found that they could not get through more than the first few pages. As she says:

> Although everyone knows instinctively that Toni Cade Bambara's *The Salt Eaters* is a book which they *must* read (and they intend to do so), many are having difficulty with it.... They all seem to be waiting for some future time of courage and illumination which will make completing the work possible.[21]

Hull does the hard work of trying to explicate why *Salt Eaters* is so difficult to follow in any traditional sense, and, like Wideman, she has no hesitation in mentioning its obligations to African traditions, and their offshoots in the New World. What is

---

18 *Ibid.*, 28.
19 Collins, *Thought*, 102–103.
20 Christian, *Feminist*, 205.
21 Hull, Akasha (Gloria) (2000), "What it is I Think She's Doing Anyhow: a Reading of Toni Cade Bambara's *The Salt Eaters*", in *Home Girls: a Black Feminist Anthology*, New Brunswick: Rutgers University Press, 124–142.

remarkable about Hull's commentary is that it does more than merely shed light on the work; it valorizes the novel in a way that only careful, sympathetic reading can.

Hull claims that "spiritual matters form one half of a critical equation in *The Salt Eaters*";[22] she also notes that "the literal plot, which takes place in less than two hours, is almost negligible."[23] Hull's point, which she articulates carefully in several sections of her essay, is that all matters and entities are equally real for Bambara, and they all coexist in space and time. As she says, it is "this dimension of the novel's technique which dismays many people."[24]

But part of what goes on in *Salt Eaters* merely recapitulates, to some extent, techniques used in Bambara's shorter fiction. Although *Salt Eaters* remains her only published novel, she has several collections of short stories, the best known of which is probably *Gorilla, My Love*.[25] The title story in this anthology is a perfect example of Bambara's more standard technique, but it also sheds a great deal of light on how that technique—when meshed with the ontological shifts of West Africa—evolved into *The Salt Eaters*.

In the short story, "Gorilla, My Love," the child protagonist recounts her adventures at the cinema where she had expected to see a wonderful King Kong-type film and wound up with a religious movie instead. Told in stream-of-consciousness from the child's perspective, a sort of Piagetian egocentric babble emerges: everything is coequal in memory, from her uncle's refusal to honor the promise that she would be his girl when she grew up, to her disappointment about the film, and her inability to be a map reader in her uncle's car (where the remembering takes place). As the narrator says:

> And we got to hear all this stuff about this woman he in love with, and all. Which really ain't enough to keep the mind alive, though Baby Jason got no better sense than to give his undivided attention and keep grabbin at the photograph which is really just a picture of some skinny woman in a countrified dress with her hand shot up to her face like she shame fore cameras. But there's a movie house in the background which I ax about. Cause I am a movie freak from way back, even though it do get me in trouble sometime.[26]

This sort of passage is not at all unusual for Bambara's short stories, and with its use of the dialect and inner monologue is already difficult in its own way. *Salt Eaters*, however, parallels such passages with the shifts in time, narrative point of view, and place—some of which are dramatic—that Hull writes about. The result is a sort of Afrocentric, psychedelic *mélange* that has a strong grip on the reader, as the somewhat frightened and confused reader experiences a decided through-the-looking-glass quality. It is for these reasons, no doubt, that *Salt Eaters* is not taught with a great deal of frequency.

Hull is right in saying that *Salt Eaters* requires a great deal of effort, but then so do Bambara's short stories. The effort that is required is not merely one of

---

22 *Ibid.*, 128.
23 *Ibid.*, 138.
24 *Ibid.*, ibid.
25 Bambara, Toni Cade (1981), *Gorilla, My Love*, New York: Vintage Books.
26 Bambara, "Gorilla, My Love," in *Gorilla*, 13–20.

attempting to delve into the ontological structure of the piece, or to come to grips with the spacetime notions employed. In addition—and more so than many other contemporary black American writers—Bambara employs a black mindset and a black worldview. In this mode, the white world scarcely exists, except insofar as it impinges on the consciousness of the characters involved—and this does not happen with great frequency. It is not merely a case of trying to articulate the point of view of a black community; it is that in Bambara's world, it is as if the white and Euro-dominant frame does not exist. It is seldom alluded to, and even then only indirectly. It simply does not appear, for example, in many of her short stories. Neither "Gorilla, My Love," nor another story from the same collection, "Talking Bout Sonny," shows any awareness of a world beyond the black community and its inhabitants.[27]

Not enough has been said about Bambara's work, probably because many potential critics have had the same trepidations that Hull ascribes to Bambara's would-be and potential readers. But the startlingly black and Afrocentric views that she presents are an introduction that is sorely needed by many literate and interested parties in a wide variety of places.

Afrocentric Womanism

If Alice Walker is often cited as having first given broad usage to the term "womanism" in her *In Search of Our Mothers' Gardens* and other pieces, Bambara pushes this to new heights, and does so in a way that is deeply Afrocentric.

Patricia Hill Collins tried to address a similar set of issues, at least in terms of epistemology and modes of knowing, in *Black Feminist Thought*. In addition to citing Sidran's work on African-based oral traditions, Collins claims:[28]

> As critical social theory, U.S. Black feminist thought reflects the interests and standpoint of its creators. Tracing the origin and diffusion of Black feminist thought or any comparable body of specialized knowledge reveals its affinity to the power of the group that created it.[29]

Womanism, or Black feminism, is created in a space that makes it the object of white male power, and yet it reflects its roots and does so in a way that leaves it demonstrably marked. From call-and-response to oral tradition to religious worship to holdovers of West African burial rituals, the womanist culture attempts to save and serve the community while allowing the individual black woman a place in which to declare herself. Bambara takes this tradition as it already exists, particularly within the Southern black culture, and uses Afrocentric ontological notions to alter it. The dialogue between Minnie Ransom and Old Wife in *Salt Eaters* is a particularly resonant construct here, as are many scenes and situations from her short stories. Indeed, the narrator in "Gorilla, My Love," variously called Scout, Peaches and one or two other names is herself a miniaturized womanist storyteller.

---

27 Bambara, "Talking Bout Sonny," in *Gorilla*, 79–84.
28 Collins, *Thought*, 261.
29 *Ibid.*, 251.

Hull's criticism, of course, speaks to these very issues, and a combination of Hull's concerns and Collins's articulation of what she takes to be the larger theoretical points does a lot of work here. If we remember that a number of feminist theorists have long maintained that many "traditional" cultures are much closer to the original goddess-oriented worldviews in which human beings originally flourished, we can understand why the import of developing the Africanist or Afrocentric ties to womanism is a pronounced one. Theorists as varied as Dorothy Dinnerstein and Marija Gimbutas have posited the rise in androcentrism as being directly related to cultural dominance achieved at the time of the move from hunting/gathering to early settled agriculture; many African societies, of course, retain much closer ties to hunting/gathering, or are at a very early stage of settled agriculture. Thus one might hypothesize, contra further evidence, that such cultures would be somewhat more gynocentric to begin with.

Work of a number of social scientists and anthropologists in general buttresses this view. Many West African cultures are matrilineal, and although this matrilineality may not translate into overt power, it is certainly degrees away from the intense patrilineality of the European cultures. More important, new work done by African feminists on some West African cultures—one thinks, for example, of the work of the sociological theorist Oyeronke Oyewumi—tends to reinforce the notion that gender simply does not translate as a divide among the Yoruba, for example, in the same way that it does in Eurocentric societies.[30]

If all of the foregoing is the case, then the tropes developed by Bambara in *Salt Eaters*, specifically, are of the utmost importance for the development of an Afrocentric womanism. Minnie Ransom and Old Wife are collaborators in a spacetime warp that is gynocentric and concerned with healing and movement across planes. The world of logic and rationality—which is not only androcentric but, in black terms a white European construct—is not their concern. In fact, it positively gets in the way of the important work that Minnie Ransom is trying to do. Minnie tries to get Velma to be a willing participant in the healing at the same time that Minnie is waiting for directions from Old Wife:

> "You just hold that thought," Minnie was saying again, leaning forward, the balls of three fingers pressed suddenly, warm and fragrant, against Velma's forehead.... And Velma was inhaling in gasps, and exhaling shudderingly. She felt aglow, her eyebrows drawing in toward the touch as if to ward off the invading fingers that were threatening to penetrate her skull. And then the hands went away quickly, and Velma felt she was losing her eyes.[31]

Collins would remind us that such passages have not only to do with the obvious topics of healing, but that they recapitulate the West African concern with what in Western terms is considered to be the "otherworldly." As Thompson has said, it is the same sort of concern that drives the residents of Rio to place "candles begging

---

30 Oyewumi, Oyeronke (1998), *The Invention of Women*, Minneapolis: University of Minnesota Press.

31 Bambara, *Salt Eaters*, 6.

Eshu's favor" near the skyscrapers of Ipanema.[32] In any case, as Collins says, there are certain West African constructs that "pervade African-American culture."[33] There is no question that Bambara is prepared to make full use of them in her work.

Still another aspect of her womanism—and a pronounced series of gynocentric metaphors—has to do with the prevalence, in *Salt Eaters* at least, of allusions to female genitalia, menstruation and menstrual cycles, female fertility and so forth. Early on in the novel, in a passage that has been remarked upon by several commentators, Velma remembers her participation in a civil rights march while she is undergoing the healing from Minnie. The march ends ignominiously for Velma when her period begins as she struggles to make her way to a dilapidated and depressing public restroom at a filling station at the march's end. Bambara contrasts the styles and attitudes of the march's male leaders—who have done comparatively little work—with Velma's finale.

> Mounting a raggedy tampon fished from the bottom of her bag, paper unraveled, stuffing coming loose, and in a nasty bathroom with no stall doors, and in a Gulf station too, to add to the outrage. She'd been reeking of wasted blood and rage…. Knew beforehand that she would squat over a reeking, smeared toilet bowl stuffed with every thing that ever was and prayed through clenched teeth for rain. Some leader. He looked a bit like King, had a delivery similar to Malcolm's, dressed like Stokely, had glasses like Rap, but she'd never heard him say anything useful or offensive.[34]

A few lines above, the leader had moved from the "air-conditioned interior" of a limousine to begin his speech.

Bambara sees how women's work is unrewarded and tied to the everyday needs and lives of those who take such work for granted. Velma even remembers that, at the march, she had purchased cowrie shells from a vendor who had them for sale under a sign labeled "matriarchal currency." As she continued on the walk with her cowrie-shell bracelet, a male colleague had commented on her jewelry as "little pussies with stitched teeth."[35] It is, of course, pussies who should perhaps be baring their teeth who are doing almost all of the work of the march. As Hull says in her analysis, Velma is a "truly dedicated" civil rights worker—and it is her dedication that breaks her down.[36]

An Afrocentric womanism must harken back to societies the roots of which are only partially obvious or known in the United States. That is why *Salt Eaters* is filled with references to the "mud mothers," those primeval beings who are, in a sense, the antecedents of any human society. In a sense, these are also the beings whose images fill santería and vodun, even if it is not always obvious who or what is being made reference to. Not only do shells serve as emblems of these goddesses, but palm fronds, fans and a number of other items that might make their appearance, under any given set of circumstances, in a more mundane way. As Robert Farris Thompson

---

32 Thompson, *Flash*, 19–20.
33 Collins, *Thought*, 261.
34 Bambara, *Salt Eaters*, 34–35.
35 *Ibid.*, 36.
36 Hull, "Doing," in Smith (ed.), 128–129.

says in *Flash of the Spirit*, "Nana Bukuu is the courage and accomplishment of women, sublimed to the form of an orisha. She knows terrifying secrets."[37]

Almost all women know terrifying secrets, at least from the male perspective. And the secrets known to black women have not only been kept away from a shared sort of knowledge by white power, but also, all too often, by black male power. That is why *Salt Eaters* is primarily a novel of black women's knowing, although some male characters are more sympathetic than others. Velma is an older version of Peaches/Scout in "Gorilla"; as she says at the end of that story, "we must stick together or be forever lost, what with grown-ups playin change up and turning you round every which way so bad."[38]

Bambara and the Continental

In an anthology titled *Existence in Black*, Lewis Gordon has tried to find the intersection of contemporary black thought and continental thinking.[39] The essays cover a variety of topics, from Sartre and Richard Wright on the intersection of existential thought and black theorizing, to black feminism and work on such Caribbean topics as Rastafarianism. But perhaps most salient for our purposes is an essay by Joy James titled "Black Feminism: Liberation Limbos and Existence in Gray."[40]

At a crucial point in the essay, James notes:

> The dismissive by some African-American males that black feminisms are handmaidens to Euro (American)-feminisms, or that black feminisms are not black enough, has been widely circulated. Sometimes in their roles as correctives to white racism, some black feminisms have served as the "clean-up woman" or domestic of racial messes and seem overly preoccupied with white, privileged women.[41]

Whatever else she may have constructed, Bambara can scarcely be accused of having constructed a black feminism that is not black enough. Indeed, the difficulty for most white readers of a work such as *The Salt Eaters* is that it is so culturally black that it will be impenetrable to many. If, according to Sartre and others, the African was always the ultimate "other" for the Euro community, then black feminism, as James notes can also serve in that capacity. But Bambara does more than create a set of images with cowrie shells and other, interesting intersections. She has as Hull notes, the Seven Sisters, a touring group of skit players, all women of color, who interact with each other in multifarious ways. Hull claims that "They are simultaneously engaged in myriad projects, always thinking and doing, being political and creative, smart and hip all at the same time."[42]

---

37 Thompson, *Flash*, 68.
38 Bambara, "Gorilla," 20.
39 *Existence in Black*, (1997) in Gordon, Lewis R. (ed.), New York: Routledge.
40 James, Joy, "Black Feminism: Liberation Limbos and Existence in Gray," in Gordon (ed.), 215–224.
41 James, in Gordon (ed.), 217.
42 Hull, "Doing," in Smith (ed.), 136–137.

Thus Bambara seeks to create a black feminism and womanism with much deeper roots than merely a black counterpart to standard mainstream feminist thought. In the spirit of Fanon and most of the Continental thinkers who have essayed to articulate a broad range of issues with respect to persons of color, colonizing, and the effects of Euro dominance, Bambara creates a sort of postmodern, multi-hued feminism that is itself larger than black in many respects. In fact, Bambara could have been taking a leaf from Joy James when she writes:

> Ability to deliver will be largely determined by the political, ethical, and intellectual projects. In limbos, the incompatibility of linearity to overlapping and contradictory relations of dominance are witnessed.... In limbos of our own progressive movements, time is not linear. One bends backwards in order to move forwards....[43]

Bambara is not content with a simple womanism: her Afrocentric vision not only moves back in time, but encompasses a great deal of spacetime simultaneously. She also pushes the post-colonial in her relentless quest to bring a number of groups of color and progressive issues together in one melding.

In a piece that pushes the boundaries of existential philosophy and work having to do with the African Diaspora, Paget Henry, writing in the same volume, tries to link Jamaican Rasta beliefs and existential concerns.[44] Although there are few, if any, references to Rasta in *Salt Eaters*, much of what Henry has to say is still highly relevant to Bambara's overall project. His point is that the complexity of Rasta beliefs arises out of an existential confrontation: the black man is profoundly aware not only of his existence and mortality, but of how his subjectivity in his existence is conditioned by the white man. Henry writes:

> The word most often used by Rastafarians to describe both their subjective and objective condition is "dread." A dread experience is one that confronts or challenges the subjectivity of the Rastafarian.... The dread of the Rastafarians does not derive immediately from such an anxious relation of the self to God or to nature's continuous movement [as was the case for Kierkegaard].... Rather, this dread springs from the dance of social life; from the unjust and impersonal conventions of Jamaican society....[45]

Because the African origins of Rasta belief are clear—and even include reference to things Ethiopian—Rasta as whole can stand as a focus for much of the Afrocentric thinking that Bambara brings to bear in her novel. Part of what Henry alludes to in his analysis is that the peculiar situation of the African-ancestored person in relation to her/his New World life places an edge on what is already the existential dilemma of the human condition. If everyone, from Sartre to an entertainer to a driver in the Sudan, is equally confronted by life's burdens, the question becomes how to make finite life meaningful in an apparently absurd world. This was, of course, the original quest of writers such as Sartre, Camus, and Beauvoir, however little they might be deemed to have had in common otherwise.

---

43 James, in Gordon (ed.), 218.
44 Henry, Paget, "Rastafarianism and the Reality of Dread," in Gordon (ed.), 157–164.
45 Henry, "Rastafarianism," 157–158.

Henry places a twist on this all-too-human conundrum and indicates that the black man in the Western hemisphere feels his existential insignificance most fully when faced with the objectification and distancing of the dominant Euro society. This is, in fact, a fine statement of what drives both Bambara as a novelist and many of her characters. Velma's original illness stems from her work in civil rights, but this is, of course, a task that society forces on her. Although Bambara seldom alludes to the society outside Claybourne, it is the source of all of black Claybourne's problems. This is made clear at many points in the dialogue, especially during conversations between Ruby and Jan:

> Just give me the good old-fashioned honky-nigger shit. I think all this ecology stuff is a diversion.
> They're connected. Whose community do you think they ship radioactive waste through?[46]

One of the main points of using Velma's illness as a metaphor for what ails the black community—not to mention humankind in general—is that it is clear that her illness springs from a political response to a certain kind of oppression. But here "wanting to be well" (something of which others are unsure, as Minnie continually reminds her) means reassuming the burden of consciousness, of blackness, and of the fact of injustice in an unjust and poisoned world. This is, indeed, an existential dilemma. As Henry says at a slightly later point in his paper, in attempting to explain clearly how the fact of blackness can become an existential focus, "In other words, in colonial societies, anxiety in relation to rhythm of social life replaces, or eclipses, the anxiety experienced in relation to the rhythm of cosmic life."[47] But colonial life is, for the black, nothing but the confrontation with the Other, and the mirroring of the negativity placed on blacks by the Other's existence.

These existential takes on blackness harken back to some of Sartre's work, which we have already cited. But Sartre was, of course, looking at the situation from a European perspective. The black existential analysts have, in general, tried to articulate how it is that blackness can confront white existence, and then move on to push itself to subjectivity rather than continuous objectivity. The assumption of subjectivity may involve any number of forms of Afrocentrism—for the Rastas, it involves a complicated belief system revolving around the assumed special status of Haile Selassie, at a time when he was the most visible and dominant African presence on the international scene.[48] The naïve European observer may not understand the connection between an Ethiopian ruler and the blacks of Jamaica, since manifestly they are of West African origin. But that is just the point—all things African are black to the white man, and blacks throughout the Diaspora have understood this.

In explaining to us how the "dread" of the Rastas is a sort of existential dread, Henry has pointed out—much more forcefully than Sartre—the objectified origins of the black dilemma. It is this dilemma that Bambara continually addresses in her

---

46 Bambara, *Salt Eaters*, 242.
47 Henry, "Rastafarianism," 159.
48 *Ibid.*, 159.

work. From Peaches in "Gorilla," to *Salt Eaters*, to Punjab in "Playin with Punjab," the black is up against it. Bambara tries to give her something to hold onto.[49]

Perennial Questions

If strands of Continental thought can be used to explicate Bambara's Afrocentric quest to deal with problems of human existence, black existence in particular, one work done by an American writer stands out as having a parallel motivation. Although it was written before any such concept as Afrocentrism was available to black Americans, Richard Wright's *The Outsider*, like Bambara's work, is infused with an awareness that is easily analyzable in philosophical terms.

Floyd Hayes has examined *The Outsider* in philosophical terms, and finds it infused with a peculiar kind of existential awareness.[50] Bambara pushes her awareness with an array of devices that we have already examined: womanism, allusion to West African cultural constructs, and an awareness of imminent global disasters. Writing at a much earlier pint, and without an awareness of global sensibility, Wright's work moves along another track, but it might well be deemed to be a parallel track. As Hayes writes:

> *The Outsider* is about a black man in urban America who in many respects transcends the assumed limitations of his blackness. In this way, Wright fashions a concept of blackness as a complex system of meanings.... Wright's representation of the complex psycho-political condition of outsiderness is grounded in the everyday life-world of modern black America and yet in some ways is suspended above it.[51]

In a similar fashion, particularly in *Salt Eaters*, Bambara tries to show how the alienation imposed on black women, in particular, meshes with general existential concerns, and pushes individuals out of their trajectories. Any person alive and thinking can ask herself or himself the ancient and obvious questions about the meaning of life and the existence of a divine being, if any. But as both Henry and Hayes are arguing, these questions become more complex for individuals of African ancestry trapped in Euro-dominant societies. For Velma Henry, the questions take the form of a general psychological breakdown that seems to propel her, as an individual, into the sacred spacetime that Bambara uses as the backdrop for the book. A sense of dislocation—Velma's and a general derangement—permeates the text. The past that Velma finds so demoralizing is overwhelmingly a past of black oppression, and yet her relationships, especially those of males, partake of that oppression. Painting broadly, we might say that Velma is, in some sense, the latter-day equivalent of Wright's Cross Damon in *The Outsider*.

In addition to the quest for meaning, the more overtly politicized sections of *The Salt Eaters* present a powerful critique of contemporary American culture, as

---

49 Bambara, "Playin with Punjab," in *Gorilla*, 69–75.
50 Hayes III, Floyd W., "The Concept of Double Vision in Richard Wright's *The Outsider*: Fragmented Blackness in the Age of Nihilism,": in Gordon (ed.), 173–183.
51 Hayes, "Double Vision," 176–177.

we have seen, for example, in the exchange between Jan and Ruby. Similarly, and after having been exposed to the thought and lives of Sartre and Beauvoir, Wright aimed a sharply critical fusillade at the capitalist America of the 1950s. Hayes writes, "Wright identifies the growth of urban life with the process of industrial capitalist development which he describes as a kind of war against all humankind."[52] This growth, of course, cannot be separated from white dominance.

In a collection of essays put together after her death titled *Deep Sightings and Rescue Missions*, Bambara addresses some of these same issues in a straightforward manner. In a particularly poignant essay, "Language and the Writer," she notes that what may well be the attempt of the writer of color to deal with a number of important human themes almost invariably gets shoved under the rubric of "specialized" writing, while white writing on the same subject is normativized. Thus even existential or philosophical twists in writing may not be recognized for what they are. She notes:

> There is no American literature. There are American literatures. There are those who have their roots in the most ancient civilizations—African, Asian or Mexican—and there are those that have the most ancient roots in this place, that mouth-to-ear tradition of the indigenous peoples who were here thousands and thousands of years before it was called America, thousands of years before it was even called Turtle Island. And there is too the literature of the European settlement regime that calls itself American literature.[53]

Concerns of authors of the "settlement regime" are likely to be recognized by critics almost immediately; writers such as Faulkner and Hemingway, Pynchon and Heller have not had any difficulty getting their work accepted and deemed to be of consequence to the most fundamental human concerns. But a similar set of concerns on the part of Richard Wright—or Toni Cade Bambara—is much more difficult for critics to see and articulate, and the more profound among the concerns are frequently not recognized at all.

Change-ups Every Which Way

If, as Barbara Christian and a number of black feminist critics have claimed, black feminism is problematized because of its allusion (by title, so to speak) to standard white feminism, Bambara's feminist work might be deemed to be even more problematic.[54] It is not only black, but it is no stretch to claim that Bambara's work is not black in the same way that, for example, Walker's is, or Toni Morrison's is. Bambara's work is much more black—because she takes so many of the cultural references for granted, it may be difficult for white, or non-black, readers to consume. In a sense, Bambara is writing for a black audience.

---

52 *Ibid.*, 178.

53 Bambara, "Language and the Writer," (1996) in *Deep Sightings and Rescue Missions*, New York: Pantheon.

54 Christian, *Feminist*, 159. As she says, "[There is] a persistent and major theme throughout Afro-American women's literature—our attempts to define and express our totality rather than being defined by others."

Bambara's African-derived cultural expressions are foregrounded in *The Salt Eaters*, but in a sense that work is scarcely any more difficult (though certainly longer) than many of her other published pieces. "Gorilla, My Love" is not easy to read unless the reader is already very familiar with the black cultural style—and the same may be said for any of the other pieces in that volume.[55] Even her critical pieces, such as those in *Deep Sightings*, presume a genuine level of familiarity not only with black literature, but with the debates surrounding it, and with the names of various black artists and filmmakers whose work might not even be known to academics, let alone the general literary public. As she says in her essay "Language and the Writer," "Before we get to the issue of what idiom one should speak in, there is the prior struggle of who may speak."[56]

Bambara's take on who may speak is not one of simply assuming that she herself is the designated speaker for her community, but rather one of insisting that, as a speaker, she speak in the voice of her community. Because her work so accurately captures that voice—and any other cultural tropes that may be relevant to it—it has not, until recently, received the critical acclaim that has been awarded to some other black women writers. As a blurb from Lucille Clifton on the back of *Gorilla* says, "She has captured it all, how we really talk.... She must love us very much."[57]

Bambara refuses to pander to white audiences, feminist or otherwise. A number of critics have long maintained that Alice Walker, for example, has been more popular with white women readers than with the black community. The relationship between Shug and Celie in *The Color Purple* might be thought to emphasize lesbian loving at the expense of cultural blackness, and the epistolary form of the novel is essentially a culturally European form.

There is very little that helps any brand of feminism—other than womanism, as black feminists frequently call it—in much of Bambara's work. Although many of her short stories are simply too terse to play with time in the way that *Salt Eaters* does, they do play with time (and space) in one straightforward way: the reader is simply somersaulted into the story, a black space, and if the reader cannot make her or his way through it, too bad. The opening two or three paragraphs of "Gorilla" are stream-of-consciousness, but the consciousness is that of a young black girl, thinking in the dialect and with the jumps in time that any stream-of-consciousness normally entails. Moving forward with the story (as Hull said of the novel) is a test for the reader.

---

55 Bambara, "Gorilla," 13. The opening sentences of "Gorilla" read: "That was the year Hunca Bubba changed his name. Not a change up, but a change back, since Jefferson Winston Vale was the name in the first place."

56 Bambara, "Language," in *Deep*, 142.

57 Back Blurb on paper edition of *Gorilla*, Vintage.

Chapter Nine

Afrocentric Womanism

Any attempt to describe Bambara's work in terms of womanism—or indeed, a general feminist rubric—must quickly come to terms with the reliance in her work on Afrocentric constructs, and African-derived divination sources.[1] What Bambara accomplishes, especially in *Salt Eaters*, is to create a world filled with West African metaphors, and leave it to the reader to try to unpack the various cultural references. We might, for example, think that Bambara had been a student of Robert Farris Thompson, for much of the descriptive material in *Flash of the Spirit* reads as if it were the source of some of Bambara's cultural markers. Here is Thompson on the riverain goddesses of the Yoruba:

> [There] is a retelling of a myth...the myth of conflict that threatens to destroy the world, and of the discovery of antidotes in mystic coolness.... Here, in the legend of Imoja and Ifa, a special rounded fan—like a giant soothing drop of water—restores peace and calm, associating itself with the images of Ifa's cool round house made of herbs and leaves. An indelible current of association links the roundness of habitations to the roundness of things pertaining to the riverain goddesses.[2]

It is not merely that Bambara's constant references to fans, cowries and things round (Hull uses several circular diagrams in her analysis of *Salt Eaters*) helps to link up commentary such as that of Thompson with her work;[3] it is that what Bambara creates is an African atmosphere in a New World space.

On a more important level, however, Bambara's work links her Afrocentric womanism to more global gynocentrism, since much of the work that has pushed a strong view of women as culture bearers is rooted in an analysis of the mythography of "traditional societies." From Gimbutas, Eisler and even Dinnerstein, we have come to understand that the further we push into the general human past, the more the reverence for things female comes to the fore, and the clearer it becomes that the rise of the patriarchy is related to the moves toward early settled agriculture. In other words, what Bambara accomplishes in her work is just another version of an investigation into the past in the Turkish seaboard area, in Greece itself, or for that matter in Northern Europe. In each area, artifacts from the Willendorf Venus to much later figures indicate that the rise and predominance of patriarchy is a fairly recent human invention, probably not more than several thousand years old. In speaking to an ancient African past, Bambara speaks to us all.

---

    1   *The Salt Eaters* is rich in such references. Rather than using specific orishas or deities, Bambara uses a general cultural base to refer to African-derived goddesses and gods.
    2   Thompson, *Flash*, 73.
    3   *Ibid.*, 73–74.

She also speaks to another, more controversial issue. According to the psychoanalytically-minded theorists, childrearing patterns around the world—obviously with local variation—have a great deal to do with the continued preeminence of patriarchal values. Although the West African societies themselves are more matrilineal and matrifocal, it is not clear that some of the analysis fails to apply to them. Theorists such as Chodorow and Dinnerstein urge us to think of the "reproduction of mothering"—forced heterosexuality means that the connectedness of women is subverted and turned to other purposes. It appears that this is what Bambara would like us to think happened to Velma Henry.

A sample of the standard sort of theorizing that asks us to think of ancient pasts is to be found in Dorothy Dinnerstein's *The Mermaid and the Minotaur*:

> This meaning of woman, as representative of the body principle in all of us that must be pushed down when we embark on any significant enterprise, clearly underlies many of the rituals surveyed [by anthropologists]. People under the most diverse cultural traditions seem to feel an opposition, an antagonism, between what is humanly noble, durable, strenuous, and the insistent rule of flesh.... Anti-female measures are prominent among these body-defying rituals....[4]

Here Dinnerstein explicates the near-globality of antagonism toward certain bodily functions, particularly those associated with the female, as having a great deal to do with the general opposition the genders/sexes feel toward each other, especially in adulthood. Although these sorts of tensions do markedly differ from culture to culture, some points are very strongly held: anything having to do with childbirth, lactation, menstruation and so on is usually marked off from other human functions, and thus ancient reverence for the "goddess" turns into patriarchal contempt. (To be fair, simply to contrast religious systems, one can demarcate, for example, the systems of Asia from what appear to be the more patriarchal Western systems, such as Judaism, Islam and Christianity.)

Bambara resuscitates thought having to do with the female as wholistic and healing for us all, but it is the black culture with which she is concerned, and it is the salvation of specific black souls that moves her writing. Hence Velma, after having worked too hard in the Civil Rights demonstrations that are described early in the book, must undergo a healing ritual with Minnie Ransom, whose spirit guide is aptly named "Old Wife." As Dinnerstein goes on to say, "the ordinary human female has been excluded from the kind of enterprise for which the flesh must be formally defied."[5] But if that kind of ritual includes the type of political movement that means men receive all the credit, while women do the dirty work but are denied access to "theory"—or to glory—Bambara, for one is determined to let it be known that such enterprises are unhealthy and toxic. The cure is a deep and profound gynocentrism.

Thus it is by no means impossible to draw links between Bambara and some other sorts of feminism, and, to be fair, with her consistent use of cross-cultural tropes in works such as *The Salt Eaters*, it is clear that the larger message of the book is that

---

4 Dinnerstein, Dorothy (1977), *The Mermaid and the Minotaur*, New York: Harper, 126.

5 *Ibid.*, 127.

salvation is something that every living being on the planet needs. Nevertheless, Bambara's view is womanism—it is the black feminism that she sees as being at the heart of what her community needs, and as being denied by hegemonic forces. Unlike some, Bambara would not hesitate to place the black male—particularly with respect to his own community—in the place of culprit, at least on the somewhat rare occasion.

The metaphors that tie us all to our ancient mothers and ritual-filled pasts are African for Bambara. Although we may all be able to travel to Turkey, for example, to view sites that presumably represented less patriarchal cultures for the Greeks, Bambara is concerned about a matrilineal past for those of African ancestry.

If the psychoanalytic gender theory has any merit, a number of cultures around the world that still exhibit traces of the more matrifocal views should also exhibit other hallmarks that we would recognize. Different practices of childrearing (although these certainly would not necessarily be consonant with what Western feminists might deem to be important) should yield different social structures—among important differences, one might find, for example, respect for elders of both sexes as one demarcator. Whether or not West African societies make reasonable instantiations of the sorts of distinctions that drive the work of Chodorow and Dinnerstein, it is obvious that such societies exhibit significantly different social structures, and that in many ways gender does not divide in the same sort of way.[6]

Bambara seems to envision changes in our industrialized society that might cut across in similar ways. Greater equality between the sexes might translate into childrearing practices that allow for less objectification and longer times of bonding. In the long run, we would expect these changes themselves to result in a culture with significantly different gender roles.

Bambara seems to hope for or to envision a society in which the true meaning of cowrie shells is not unknown. How this society will come about is unclear—but it does seem to be the case that it cannot come about without significant and profound alteration in the society we now possess.

Criticisms

In a sense, Bambara is her own best critic. Much of what she has written in *Deep Sightings* speaks to the same points that she makes in her fiction. In the eponymous essay in *Deep Sightings*, Bambara writes:

> I say something like "consciousness requires a backlog of certain experiences." Vera ain't going for it. From day one, she says, there's enough evidence around to peep the game and resist. "So it's a decision to be like that," she says. "And it takes a lot of energy to deny what's obvious." Denialists don't want to see, don't want to belong, don't want to struggle, she says, putting a pin in it.[7]

---

6   Again, Oyewumi (*Invention*) is a thinker who has done a great deal of work on this.
7   Bambara, "Deep Sightings and Rescue Missions," in *Deep*, 157.

Although Vera is an actual person with whom Bambara has had conversations, she could very well be the fictional Velma. Part of deeply feminist (or, in this case, womanist) work requires that a commitment be made to seeing things as they are, stating that the emperor has no clothes, and then beginning the healing process that should occur, even if it needs a push.

Bambara sees this process as part and parcel of the community's own identity, so that the very issues that she raises in her critical essays are, in fact, the issues that inform her fiction in general and *Salt Eaters* in particular. How can a community heal? What are the steps? How can power mongers be brought to account for their mistakes?

Womanist writing, Bambara claims at a number of points, seems to require that these issues be addressed. And in that sense, she has many other black women writers behind her, since similar statements have been made by June Jordan, Barbara Christian and others.

If it is the case that Bambara's own essays push a certain kind of stance—a "tell it like it is," truth-to-power black stand—we can see how Bambara takes herself to be engaging in an historical enterprise when we look at black women's voices over time. In a recent compilation titled *Africans in America*, Charles Johnson and Patricia Smith traced the historical openings of slavery in what is now the United States through the records of the Jamestown colony. Interestingly enough, they were able to find traces of what appears to be the first black American family—or at least the first of which we have record—in the colony's logs. Because Jamestown started out as an exercise replete with indentured servitude, the first distinctions had to do with class and religion, not race. As Johnson and Smith say:

> "[A]ntonio a Negro" is listed as a "servant" in the 1625 census.
> "Mary a Negro woman" had sailed to the New World aboard the *Margrett and John*. Soon she became Antonio's wife.... Over the course of a lifetime, he and Mary bought their way out of servitude, raised four children, and struggled to claim a slice of the stubborn new world as their own.... Anthony and Mary had no reason not to believe in a system that certainly seemed to be working for them, a system that equated ownership with achievement.[8]

Bambara is in a sense the voice of this African woman from the seventeenth-century American colonies, for a change soon came to Jamestown. We cannot be sure that Mary lived to see this change, or that she would immediately have understood the ramifications of it, but as Johnson and Smith note, in 1640, a difference in punishments assigned to escaped servants is observable—one based on race—and "Over time, powerful Virginia landowners began to realize that enslaving Africans made good economic sense."[9] We can only wonder what reaction either Mary or Antonio had, if they understood the implications of what was beginning to transpire around them.

---

8   Johnson, Charles and Patricia Smith, (eds.) (1998), *Africans in America*. New York: Harcourt Brace and Co., 38–39.

9   *Ibid.*, 41.

Giving voice to the voiceless is what drives Bambara's work and when we read her own essays we can see what her aim is, in plain and simple terms. Her essay "Language and the Writer" opens with the following lines:

> I want to talk about language, form, and changing the world. The question that faces billions of people at this moment, one decade shy of the twenty-first century, is: Can the planet be rescued from the psychopaths?... And the challenge that the cultural worker faces, myself for example, as a writer and as a media activist, is that the tools of my trade are colonized.[10]

So Bambara lets us know that a crucial component of her project is to decolonize the tools—the words, metaphors, literary forms and so forth must be altered to reflect the experience of the African-derived community.

Bambara has more than mastered these tasks. From Minnie's conversations with Old Wife, to Peaches' concern about her uncle's change-ups, and beyond, everything that Bambara has written speaks in the voice of the disempowered and articulates their concerns in a way that is sufficiently genuine as to be incomprehensible to some. But this, of course, is what Bambara wants. If her writing did not take us to that other place, it would not have succeeded, by her lights.

An illustration of Bambara's gifts in this regard is to be found in another short story in *Gorilla*, "Playin with Punjab."[11] The opening of the story—as is the case with so much of what Bambara writes—gets us in the mood right away. What she manages to accomplish in a few short lines is to set the stage, create a black vernacular voice, and have that voice at least speak minimally to women's concerns, all at once. Here is a selection from the opening of "Punjab":

> First of all, you don't play with Punjab. The man's got no sense of humor.... So when Jackson from the projects put it this way: "Punjab, baby, I got this chick in a trick, and her mother's got my ass in a bind and I gots to live—" Punjab peeled four or five bills off the top with a dry finger (which is his way, dry) and told Jackson what the rates was. Now, you gotta figure Jackson for a dumb dude.... So like I said, this boy Jackson never did have his proper share of sense.[12]

This is the voice of the streets, and it is a voice that, while articulated in a variety of venues in contemporary society, is seldom articulated with the feel and compassion that Bambara employs. When this voice becomes radicalized or politicized, as it does in *Salt Eaters*, a powerful view emerges, one that is all the more remarkable because it encompasses a wealth of experience that is normally omitted from the politicized voice.

Black feminist critics have long claimed that the genuine womanist black voice belongs to the unacknowledged workers who have struggled to retain their dignity and identity. As Collins says, one study found that "the domestic workers...refused to let their employers push them around."[13] The struggle to maintain identity in the

---

10 Bambara, "Language," in *Deep*, 139–140.
11 Bambara, "Playin with Punjab," in *Gorilla*, 69–75.
12 *Ibid.*, 69.
13 Collins, *Feminist*, 97.

face of overwhelming oppression is one that black women domestics have faced daily, and it is spelled out in a good deal of fiction, from Ann Petry's *The Street*, to Jamaica Kincaid's *Lucky*, to the nonfiction of John Edgar Wideman in *Brothers and Keepers*.

But part of the struggle is for the race, and this is what has always driven womanism. It is the reason that Paula Giddings' *When and Where I Enter* takes its title from the remark of Anna Julia Cooper in the 1890s, "When and where I enter, the whole race enters with me."[14] The black woman opened doors for herself, her men and her children. It is this community-oriented spirit that lends womanism its drive and poignancy and sharply separates it from the privilege of white feminism. Because white women tend to feel oppressed only by gender categorization, it has not been easy for them to move in other directions. Since it is clear that hegemonic power belongs to the Euro-derived male population, there is no need whatsoever for white women to think in terms of "saving" the white male.

But the black man was never the enemy for the black woman. Driven by the more immediate concerns of race, the black woman has had to forge a path that pushes her in the direction of creating a safe space for living beings. And that large vision is what Bambara tries to articulate in *The Salt Eaters*—it is a vision that sees the globe as in need of repair, and sees that women of color may be its natural repairers. While many have tried to create a similar space, Bambara is the acknowledged master of it.

Bodily Matters

Bambara's work, as we have seen, incorporates a view of women that is powerfully tied to the West African cultures, but by no means devoid of an intersection with the degradation of women in America today. In *The Salt Eaters*, Bambara moves back and forth between these two modes, testing the reader's ability to focus on how women's concerns might affect an Afrocentric view of black women in the United States. Although Bambara's novel contains passages descriptive of sex, it is other passages, in the main, that achieve something that might be along the lines of the *écriture* that we have examined for other authors. From the menstrual blood that Velma noticed on the march, to Doc Serge's stance on women and "players," Bambara brings a womanism into her work at every turn. Here is Doc Serge on pimping:

> "A woman in the hands of an undisciplined player is very nearly as dangerous a situation to all concerned as atomic energy in the hands of capitalists, as any kind of power in the hands of the psychically immature, spiritually impoverished and intellectually undisciplined....
>
> "If you're going to be a player and not just some mooching miscreant and misuser of women and women's knowledges, you've got to study the principles that govern the game."[15]

---

14 Cooper, Anna Julia (1998), *A Voice from the South*, New York: Oxford University Press.

15 Bambara, *Salt Eaters*, 133.

Doc Serge, in the worlds-within-worlds tradition that Bambara so frequently invokes, is the director of the Southwest Community Infirmary (where Velma is undergoing her healing) at the same time that he, as Hull puts it, is a "questionable character" who can "manage smoothly anything from a 'stable' of prostitutes to a [clinic]."[16] But what a character. Contra what we would expect from a pimp or street hustler, Doc Serge seems focused on women's energy. In fact, in a very odd sort of way, he seems himself to be a feminist/womanist, at least insofar as he understands that women have "knowledges," that there is a "principle" that "governs the game," and that women possess a dangerous "energy".[17]

This is a genuine instantiation of Bambara's skill at something resembling the *écriture*, even if the uninitiated reader has some difficulty recognizing it. Black women's energy comes from their bodies and from the long history of cultural associations (in West African cultures) with their special knowledge—from the Jungian collective unconscious of the "mud mothers" to the powerful mothers who pushed black culture forward during slavery times, to the cowrie shells themselves. This is why, as Hull claims repeatedly in her essay, women's collective knowledge has a psychic pull that can heal in and of itself. As Hull says of the Seven Sisters Collective, who come and go throughout the novel with their multicultural associations and outlooks, "[T]through them, too, we apprehend the truth of the street exhorter's cry: 'The dream is real, my friends. The failure to make it work is the unreality.'"[18]

There is, then, a genuine sense in which much of what Bambara does in anything resembling *écriture* is more along the lines of an epistemological approach, given that Bambara clearly wants to forward West African knowledge views, and that these views would mesh beautifully with what we already have as a womanism. But it is precisely this sort of concern that leads one back to some of the African views in the first place, particularly as propounded by contemporary philosophers. Does it make sense to say that some of these views are empirical? Wiredu and others have claimed that it does. Forwarding these views—along with the New World African Diaspora views that channel them—is part of Bambara's project.

Along with Akasha Hull, Elliott Butler-Evans stands out as one of those critics who has done the most to articulate Bambara's stance, and who does so within a range of both contemporary critical theory and historiography.[19] Although his main concern is to try to provide a critique of the work of three major black women writers within the framework of contemporary literary criticism, he does a masterful job of signaling what is feminist/womanist in Bambara's work, and of detailing the "semiotic." It is, in fact, this semiotic that helps to forward the notion that Bambara participates, at least minimally, in *écriture féminine*, and Butler-Evans provides a

---

16 Hull, "What it Is," 136.
17 Bambara, *Salt Eaters, loc. cit.*
18 Hull, "What it Is," 137.
19 Butler-Evans' work stands out in the still relatively small corpus of Bambara criticism. See Elliott Butler-Evans, *Race, Gender and Desire*, Philadelphia: Temple University Press, 1989. In this work, two of the chapters are either completely or partially on Bambara's short stories and her novel.

strong articulation of what this semiotic means. Here is his analysis of a passage from "Gorilla", one in which Peaches/Hazel describes how her mama would go to the school to complain if she thought her daughter was being mistreated:

> What is striking here is the exclusive deployment of an alternative code, one that attempts to reproduce the nuances of Black urban speech and diverges significantly from the linguistic forms of the dominant culture; at the same time, however, the substance is accessible to those who are familiar with the culture and to those who are not.... The references to playing the dozens, semantic constructions such as "talk that talk" and "be comin undone," the use of the term "bad" as a synonym for good, and the mother's physical statement as a semiotics of the body all contribute to the symbolic construction of a Black community and emphasize Hazel's role as that of an authentic self-ethnographer.[20]

It is interesting to note—and furthers Butler-Evans' main points—that part of the passage in question from "Gorilla" uses the following phrasing: "She stalk in with her hat pulled down bad and that Persian lamb coat draped back over one hip on account of she got her fist planted there..."[21] This is, indeed, a semiotics of the body, and constitutes, in its own way, an *écriture*. For it is not so much overt sexuality that is at stake in Bambara's work, but a coding, some of which is physical, some of which is verbal, and all of which is powerfully Afrocentric. As Elliott Butler-Evans also says, "The stories in *Gorilla* clearly locate the collection in the broad context of Black nationalist fiction of the 1960s."[22] And Bambara is nothing if not a strong nationalist, one whose primary concern is to emphasize race and race-bonding before all else. In this, she proved herself to be a contemporary race-woman of the 1990s.

In the West African cultures, with their reliance on oral tradition and spontaneous communication, storytelling, folk tales and the like become important locators of community-bonding. Despite recent research, funded partially by Henry Louis Gates of Harvard and several corporations, that seems to show the use of literacy based on Arabic, or actually in Arabic, in the Mali-Mauritania area, it is still the case that the vast majority of slaves transported to the New World came from regions without written languages. Bambara excels at capturing all of the important forms of oral communication without which a sense of "Blackness" cannot meaningfully exist, and she also excels at placing them at strategic points in her stories and in *The Salt Eaters*. As both Hull and Butler-Evans show, it takes a lengthy, full-scale analysis to do any justice to one of Bambara's creations.

For purposes of comparison, it might help to pit Bambara against another black woman writer from roughly the same time period so that semiotics can be foregrounded. Rather than making the standard comparisons with Toni Morrison or someone else equally well-known, one could compare passages from Bambara with, for example, work from Sherley Anne Williams. Williams is a moderately renowned author whose *Dessa Rose* is often taught; nevertheless, it would be fair to say that she is probably slightly less known than Bambara herself. What both authors have in

---

20 Butler-Evans, *Race*, 95.
21 Bambara, "Gorilla," 17. (Cited in Butler-Evans, 94–95.)
22 *Ibid.*, 93.

common is a deep desire to present the black culture—where they differ is in their mode of presentation.

In *Dessa Rose*, Williams has many passages that suggest a stream-of-consciousness from the black viewpoint. The plot has Dessa, a slave in 1840s Alabama, as part of a group of runaways who eventually end up, unusually, on the farm of a somewhat sympathetic white woman. The jacket blurbs from the Quill edition have the critics calling the tale "Extraordinary," and "Emotionally affecting and totally unforgettable."[23] In a frequently cited scene in the novel, Dessa awakes from the trauma of childbirth to find herself ensconced in a bed that obviously, from its texture and style, belongs to white people. Williams writes:

> Dessa watched the white woman. She knew she had lain like this before, body rigid, heart hammering against her ribs.... A white woman moving quietly around her bed—*bed*? (Feel like it feather, too! Dessa barely stifled a laugh. Lightheaded in a feather bed.)[24]

In comparison to the interior monologue of Peaches in "Gorilla," or Velma in *Salt Eaters*, Dessa's voice simply is not as strong or as clearly articulated. And that, in a sense, makes Bambara the expert at writing the body.

Theorizing Bambara

One of the reasons that Butler-Evans spends as much time as he does on Bambara in his work *Race, Gender and Desire* is simply that Bambara's writing lends itself to a great deal of theoretical analysis. Borrowing from both Jameson and Lacan, Butler-Evans notes, with respect to *The Salt Eaters*:

> Although I have used the term schizophrenia to denote the collision of two ideological discourses—the racially grounded one and one informed by gender politics—such an understanding only partially addresses the narrative's complexities. Frederic Jameson's appropriation of Lacan to read "schizophrenia" as one of the "basic features of postmodernism" can provide a useful framework in which to rethink the basic concept of a schizophrenic text.[25]

Butler-Evans sees the schizophrenia of the text—what we have termed its location in sacred space and time, and its Afrocentricity—as an "ideological position marked by concern for the social and political disintegration of an organic Black community" manifesting itself in "a seeming disintegration of the narrative."[26] But even if we think of this particular use of the term "schizophrenia" as highly theoretical, and also highly metaphorical, this analysis is probably on to something. For all of the ills of which Bambara writes are, in fact, the ills of contemporary society. And Bambara knows that these ills affect everyone on the planet, the black community no less than everyone else.

---

23 Williams, Sherley Anne (1986), *Dessa Rose*, New York: Quill of William Morrow.
24 *Ibid.*, 82.
25 Butler-Evans, *Race*, 176.
26 *Ibid., ibid.*

What Butler-Evans terms the text's anomie is manifested not only in Velma's breakdown, but in the dysfunctionality of almost all of the other characters within the work.[27] Most of the male characters in the book—as Doc Serge notes—seem to have problems with the women in their lives, and many of the institutions are either falling apart literally or non-workable. As Butler-Evans also says, in contrast to the relatively stable black communities presented in Bambara's short stories—and their recognizable cultural features—the visions of *Salt Eaters* are far from functional. As he writes:

> *Gorilla*...because of its commitment to an ideological discourse of cultural nationalism, largely assume[s] a narrative mode that is wedded to classic realism and characterized by monologue. The focus is on an organic, somewhat non-problematic black community. Hence, the stories appear to be unified, coherent discourse engaged in either celebrating that community, or representing its conflicts with a hostile Other. By contrast, in the *Salt Eaters* that community is the site of uncertainty and disintegration where heterogeneous, as well as dissonant and contradictory, desires surface.[28]

In a sense, then, Bambara reproduces some of the concerns that Henry has labeled "existentialist" in his essay on the importance of Rastafarianism. If existence fills us with dread, when in a thoughtful mode, then the black individual's existence manifests much of that dread in its response to the most overtly oppressive force—the dominant white community. This is precisely why Jan and Ruby wish that they could get back to the "honky-nigger" rhetoric—at least it is comparatively non-problematized.

In the Introduction to his work, *Existence in Black*, Gordon makes it clear that many European thinkers (such as Sartre) recognized a specific site for the location of existential dilemmas writ in full in the black community. It is as if the human dilemma is exposed more fully in such a situation of overt brutality and degradation. As Gordon says, the fundamental question of existence may be rendered as "Why go on?" But the black population feels this question more fully, and differently, since it manifests itself in the plain hatred of Europeans toward things African and the descendents of Africans. Thus to live in black skin requires a commitment, and the commitment must be made on some level even if it is not made consciously. This is, as Gordon notes, another version of the question, originally formulated by Du Bois, "What is to be understood by black suffering?"[29]

Bambara takes this notion of black suffering and makes an unusual move in *Salt Easters*. Although it is clear that much of the suffering is racial, Bambara dares to push larger, ecological and grand-scale political issues, even though there is little in her stories that would lead us to think that she would move in this direction. The larger moves are what make the novel so remarkable—although some nationalist rhetoric might militate against taking these causes seriously, Bambara ultimately refuses to get caught up in that sort of strategy. She understands that, as she says, some communities are the locales for more "dumping" than others, and that all of

---

27 *Ibid., ibid.*
28 *Ibid.,* 177.
29 Gordon, "Introduction," in *Existence*, 1.

these issues are related. Thus the despair of *Salt Eaters* is, at a fundamental level, more than black despair. It is the despair of all humankind, and Bambara is willing to try to articulate it. Although there are other works that may address these issues to some extent (such as Wright's), *Salt Eaters* is remarkable in this regard.

Finally, a sort of existentialist view of organized religion allows Bambara to mix what essentially are Afrocentric healing rites with the religious tropes of black American culture, many of which are, of course, fundamentally Christian. The importance of some sort of religious view here cannot be overstated; in a line of argument that might be paralleled to a good deal of what goes on in *Salt Eaters*, Paget Henry says:

> [For] the Rastafarian, the affirmation of the self-God relation is the foundation of his/her identity. It is more important to self-affirmation that any specific Judeo-Christian belief. Because of it, the Rastafarian feels endowed with religious knowledge that is hidden from the socially powerful—particularly the divinity of Haile Selassie.[30]

Here the political radicalism of someone like Velma melds with access to some other sort of spiritual orientation, whether we claim that it be at base Yoruba, or linked to some other region of West Africa. This larger orientation is empowering in ways that bourgeois religions cannot be, because it is linked to "hidden" knowledge. Employing more of his strategy of locating a "schizophrenia" in the text, Butler-Evans melds the black bourgeois reliance on the routine preacher with Velma's radicalism, and, implicitly, with the new religious attitude of *Salt Eaters*. As he says, one of the most important passages in the novel is that which finds Velma in a public toilet stall at the end of her disastrous march. Noting that "the speaker" is described in this section by first making reference to King, and then to several other black male personalities of the 1960s, Butler-Evans notes:

> In direct contrast, "the speaker" arrives escorted by "eye-stinging shiny, black sleek limousines" and proceeds to perform.... The male body is presented by an aggregate of signifiers that suggest superficiality rather than substance.[31]

Although this set of linkages is designed more to show the lack of substance of some alleged or purported political views, the linking to King also suggests that attacks on standard black religion may be at work. Thus there is a reading of Bambara that is very similar to that which Henry employs to do work on Rastafarianism: in order to escape dread a new commitment has to be made. For Bambara, that new commitment is the female-centered view of the cowrie shells and the Seven Sisters. It is a world of healing and of ancient rituals, and, as has been said before, it can be argued that many of these rituals simply parallel modes of functioning used the world over in pre-literate societies. Following along the lines of analysis that have been given to us by many researchers, these modes are deeply gynocentric and profoundly goddess-linked. They also help to heal the "schizophrenia" and the distortions of the society in which Bambara's characters find themselves.

---

30 Henry, "Rastafarianism," in Gordon (ed.), 161.
31 Butler-Evans, *Race*, 179.

In a world of analysis led by Lacan and Kristeva, we have no difficulty finding the semiotic in Bambara's writing. But, as indicated before, much of what we can label or demarcate as within the realm of the semiotic actually shows up in her short stories. It is in "Punjab" and in "Gorilla"—it is the everyday speech and body patterns of the black community.

The Knower and the Known

It would be easy to say that Bambara forwards something that can lend itself to a feminist epistemological analysis, especially insofar as a sort of group knowledge is concerned. Because almost all of what has been done under the rubric "feminist epistemology" has been written from a white or Eurocentric perspective, it is not clear that this is the case. In examining Patricia Hill Collins' Afrocentric feminist epistemology, we could see certain effects that might be related to group features, such as notions of storytelling and the generational verbal transmission of knowledge.

If anything, Bambara's work focuses on a sort of epistemic approach that is more solidly related to what we know about at least some of the West African cultures. As indicated before, Kwasi Wiredu, for one, has argued that most of the constructs of West African metaphysics and epistemology (he uses the Akan as his primary example) are essentially empirically-based. By this Wiredu means that it is empirical questions and concepts that drive the formation of the apparatus. Any traditional West African society will have as its primary concerns the growing of food, rotation of crops, gathering of some other foods, finding of water, and so forth that are central to all traditional and non-industrialized societies the globe round. Thus although the spiritual constructs might strike a Westerner as having little to do with empiricism, they are the result of careful observations of natural phenomena over a period of time.

In a sense, Bambara achieves something similar in *Salt Eaters*. Velma is like a traditional West African in a village society in that she has noticed a number of ills around her, and has come to the conclusion that things are out of balance. Her initial response is simply to break down—but the work of Minnie Ransom and others is designed to help restore the notions of balance, based on observations of nature.

A citation from Wiredu might help us to see some of the differences between West African and European thought, and to come to grips with why it is—as Wiredu frequently suggests—that we can think of West African thought as driven by empirical concerns. Here is a remark of his apropos the distinction between the European concept of "nothing" or "nothingness," and the difficulty of formulating a similar concept among the Akan:

> It might be of some interest, however, to expatiate a little on the reasons for the incoherence of the notion of creation out of nothing within the Akan conceptual framework. It is incoherent therein not only on account of the meanings of some [Akan terms] but also because of the comparable empirical orientation of the Akan account of nothingness. Significantly, there is no abstract noun in Akan for this concept. The only available

translations are in terms of a gerund in some such formulation as "the circumstances of there not being something *there*…"[32]

The universe is full, and "nothing" can occur, Wiredu seems to be saying, only under specific circumstances—as if one were to look in a place where one expected to find something, and then found nothing.

In a sense the feminist knowledge that Bambara tries to impart in her novel is an interesting amalgamation of both Wiredu and aspects of Hill Collins. Like the Akan, the residents of Claybourne are observers—they do not like what they see around them, and they need to find out how to rectify the situation. Where they feel that they should see health, they see illness. Where there should be social justice, there is injustice. Finding out that little makes the sense that it is supposed to make, they take matters into their own hands. Here we can see where the ties between the articulation of the more traditional views, such as those espoused by Wiredu, and the view articulated by Hill Collins, will come in. The work of Patricia Hill Collins is concerned to articulate a broad general black feminist view, achieved here in the New World. We might think of it as a cultural response to the observations of many about the very disparities concerning which Bambara writes. Patricia Hill Collins writes of "lived experience as a criterion of meaning." She says:

> "My aunt used to say, 'A heap see, but a few know,'" remembers Carolyn Chase, a 31-year-old inner-city Black woman. This saying depicts two types of knowing—knowledge and wisdom—and taps the first dimension of Black feminist epistemology. Living life as Black women requires wisdom and because knowledge about the dynamics of intersecting oppressions has been essential to U.S. Black women's survival, African-American women give such wisdom high credence in assessing knowledge.[33]

The combination of an empirical orientation and the necessity for knowledge tropes to be handed down generationally is a powerful mix, and Bambara's characters embody it.

It might naively be inquired by some why it is that an orientation that, according to Wiredu, is more empirical than some have claimed ultimately yields, for most societies in West Africa, a belief set that includes a strong adherence to non-embodied entities. But those who would ask such a question are forgetting the trajectory of what is usually referred to as "Western" science and epistemology. Almost all of these areas of endeavor are outgrowths of what were originally openly philosophical areas, and in the tradition of antiquity—the Greek tradition—the original modes of inquiry have now more or less passed into myth. Thus such historians of philosophy as Kirk and Raven remind us that we consider, in Western terms, the origins of true philosophical inquiry (the sort that will eventually lead to the sciences) to lie with such thinkers as Thales, who wrote of "first principles."[34] But a bigger question—and one that might be thought to partake of the postmodern—is what it is that represents the demarcation between myth and discussion of first principles.

---

32 Wiredu, "Tradition," in *Philosophical Forum*, 45.
33 Hill Collins, *Feminist*, 257.
34 Kirk and Raven, *The Pre-Socratics*.

In some of the myths that we traditionally think of as being the heart and core of both the Greek and Latin traditions, there is some discussion of causality, albeit in a somewhat disguised way. The myth of Phaeton and his chariot attempts to account for the obvious differences—seen by the ancients—between various peoples, their lands, and so forth. The point is that this sort of thinking is what also characterizes, according to some, West African cultures, and yet the main difference here is simply that, at point of encounter or discovery, the cultures from the coasts of Africa had not made precisely the same type of turn toward "first principles" thinking that the Greeks (by their lights) later made.

The Eurocentrism of our account here is obvious, but the greater point should be apparent: almost all cultures have posited non-material entities as causal agents to account for various phenomena at some point in time. To fail to see this is to fail to inquire into the "origins" of our own Western thought patterns. In any case, insofar as the black American cultures are concerned, retention of some of the beliefs in, for example, Legba or Damballah, or retention of the story-telling mode as being a central focus for cultural expression should not blind us to the ubiquity of similar constructs, or to the plain importance of these constructs in the African-derived cultures in the New World.

Thus, to recapitulate, Bambara should be applauded for the very real effort she makes to pull together a number of progressive issues with the resonant voices of the African cultures. Her characters may not know the names or terminology of all of the constructs to which they point, but they do engage in the very oral tradition practices that both Wiredu and Hill Collins would no doubt claim are important cultural indicators. All societies originally started out as "oral tradition" societies, and even the beginnings of literacy do not go back more than a few thousand years. If it is the case, as linguists and anthropologists maintain, that literacy alters thought patterns, what we can say with respect to the attainment of literacy in the New World by individuals of African ancestry is that these eighteenth and nineteenth century persons—and Bambara and others of their descendants—found literacy, acquired it, and used it to forward their own cultural ends. This has to count as a powerful kind of knowledge.

Looking Forward

What is it that allows us to think that Bambara might have more to offer for future readers than some other authors? All of the moves that we have noticed, particularly with respect to *Salt Eaters*—those moves that allow for the construction of a global view, those that ask for a feminism that transcends boundaries—are precisely those that make Bambara relevant for looking ahead.

It is a series of moves that Bambara herself made as an author, at least according to some of her critics. Butler-Evans notices this when he claims that some actually see Bambara's motion as retrograde: "Focusing on the language and the ideological issues related to black cultural nationalism in *The Salt Eaters*, Ruth Elizabeth Burks sees the work as inferior to Bambara's short stories, as a significant failure in language and a loss of political vision."[35] The work could be categorized as a loss of political vision, presumably, only if one was wedded to the notion that the entirety of political views expressed by blacks should fall in the resoundingly nationalist vein.

But one would like to be able to make the claim that an author is capable of growth, and with Bambara this claim is sustained. Not only is *Salt Eaters* richer, longer and more complex than any of the short stories, it is precisely the change in vision that allows for us to see it in a different way. The nationalist vision of the short stories propels a certain kind of consciousness, but does not make the point that Peaches—or Punjab—is caught up in a larger society where others may, indeed, be oppressed. In *Salt Eaters* Bambara exchanges that rather limited view for something altogether more profound.

In "The Education of a Storyteller," in *Deep Sightings*, Bambara writes:

> Back in the days when I wore braids and just knew I knew or would soon come to know everything onna counna I had this grandmother who was in fact no kin to me, but we liked each other.
> And she had this saying designed expressly for me, it seemed, for moments when I my brain ground to a halt and I couldn't seem to think my way out of a paper bag—in other words, when I would dahh you know play like I wasn't intelligent.
> She'd say "What are you pretending not to know today, Sweetheart? Colored gal on planet earth? Hmph know everything there is to know...."[36]

This knowledge, of course, is the knowledge that is available to the multiply oppressed—the wretched of the earth. And because the black woman has always had to live with the extensive practical knowledge of how to get things done—for herself, and for a multitude of others—she is the possessor of wells of wisdom that are hard to articulate. She knows how to do for her own, and how to do for others. She knows all of Missy Ann's business, all of her own business, and all of the Man's business. She can theorize when necessary, cook with one hand, straighten out the school principal with a look and teach a small child to count while simultaneously cleaning an entire room. It is this type of knowledge and wisdom of which Bambara writes.

Salt Eaters, then, picks up on this sort of wisdom, merges it with the traditional wisdom of African societies, and also throws in other sorts of knowledge derived from the lives of other oppressed people. This is why the notion of the Seven Sisters is such a valuable one—this troupe has knowledge to burn from a wide variety of women's perspectives. The "borders" metaphors now associated with the work of Anzaldúa and some other Latina feminists are already present in *Salt Eaters*, because not only do the sisters borrow from each other and inform each other, each of them is her own border crosser. (And, as it happens, a twist on this metaphor is created early on in Velma's reminiscing while seated on the healing stool.)

---

35 Butler-Evans, *Race*, 173.
36 Bambara, "The Education," in *Deep*, 246–247.

Patricia Hill Collins remarks that:

> U.S. Black women's experiences as othermothers provide a foundation for conceptualizing Black women's political activism. Experiences both of being nurtured as children and being held responsible for siblings and fictive kin within the networks can stimulate a more generalized ethic of caring and personal accountability among African-American women.[37]

This is an academic way of making the point that Bambara makes in her work. If we are to have a future on this planet, all of us must become caretakers, and all of us must be held personally accountable. The future of ecological destruction, nuclear proliferation and increasing horror that seems to fill part of *Salt Eaters* is but an apocalyptic vision of what may come to pass if there is no change in values. Bambara seems to feel that we can educate ourselves toward that change by looking to the past, and trying to find the fit between ancient wisdom and contemporary life. If she seems to feel that persons of color (especially the black population) can lead in this task, it may be because she sees them as already more in touch with this wisdom to begin with.

The Education of an Audience

The aim of acquainting others with the issues of the black community—and, at a later point, of the world—is one that shines through almost all of what Bambara has written. If the original task for black women writers was to let others know of the double oppression faced by black women, that task has been somewhat surmounted by the plethora of written pieces turned out by black women in the past three decades or so.

Because of the status that now seems to accrue to the rubric "black woman writer," it does not make a great deal of sense to say that the works of such authors are unknown or underappreciated. But Bambara moves on to a larger stage in her later work. In fact, although Bambara passed away before the phrase "globalization" reached its current level of use, one can make the claim that globalization is what she is targeting. She is on the spot when she remarks, as we saw in the previous section, that young black filmmakers should have access to the works of other filmmakers around the world, or that they need to be aware of a wide variety of issues. What makes her work unique is her insistence on developing awareness of these issues in the black voice.

Just as Peaches sees grown-ups as constantly doing "change-ups" in "Gorilla," Bambara sees capitalist global expansion as a change-up on everyone around. Destruction of the environment, damage to indigenous cultures, and the general degradation of women (much of which has been increased by globalization) signal to Bambara that the awake and alert person, from whatever community, must be aware of these issues.

---

37 Collins, *Feminist*, 189.

In *Salt Eaters*, the characters not only discuss the issues, but have the issues come to them, so to speak, in the form of revelations. A typical passage displaying Bambara's virtuosity occurs in the middle of the book, while Velma is still undergoing the healing:

> Panic. Pan. Pan-Africanism. All of us. Every. God. Pan. All nature. Pan. Everywhere. She was grinning, as she always grinned when she was able to dig below the barriers organized religion erected in its push toward a bogus civilization. "I'd welcome panic," she said aloud, certain of it. That said, that done, and nothing forthcoming, she was waiting no longer. She was drifting, her gaze skimming the grasses, drifting to the far side of the marshes...[38]

Bambara's neat twist on the nationalist phrase "Pan-Africanism" signals to us that she is making a powerful move. Pan-Africanism refers, of course, to all things black, and allows for the sorts of cultural moves that many whites do not understand—the importance, for example, of Haile Selassie and Ethiopian tropes for individuals living in Jamaica and the Caribbean who are descendants of West African slaves. But Bambara's "pan" is greater. "Pan" is the Greek demi-god of frenzy, the spirit of nature naturing. And that spirit is global. "Panic" is the sense that the Apollonian is breaking down, and that the results of that breakdown are upon us. Velma has already experienced such a breakdown; her personal foibles and the stress of overwork for the community have precipitated it. The same Bambara who composed the extremely progressive essays of *Deep Sightings* is at work here. Being "Pan-African" is not enough. One has to employ one's energies to try to come to grips with all of the problems on the planet, and this Bambara wants us to do.

---

38 Bambara, *Salt Eaters*, 170.

Chapter Ten

El Mundo de Poniatowska

Elena Poniatowska, author of novels, reportorial essays, and extended flights of fantasy, has yet to receive the attention that is her due in the United States, despite the current wave of interest in Latin American authors. This may be due to her political stance—long celebrated in many regions for her extensive reporting on right-wing government moves within Mexico, she may be seen more as a politicized essayist than as a novelist. But Poniatowska's work is infused both with a strong feminism and a solid political stance, and it certainly merits a great deal more attention than it has received.

One of the virtues of her work is her ability to translate the plight of the poor into both fictional and non-fictional forms. Using a variety of modes of expression—from the epistolary novella to straight narration—Poniatowska engages the imagination by creating alternative worlds to help the reader along. *Dear Diego*, for example, is an epistolary effort that might be thought of as an extended story or short novel.[1] Here the life of Diego Rivera during his somewhat underexamined time in France (where he honed the skills that later made him Mexico's best-known painter) is set out in imaginative detail, with a relationship posited between Diego and a woman who has given birth to his child. The Diego of Frida's writings and international fame we know; Poniatowska imagines another life for Diego. And yet this writer of fantasy is the same individual who did the now famous journalistic efforts on the massacre at the Plaza de las Tres Culturas in Mexico City in 1968, a tragedy made all the more memorable as it took place during the year of international student protest. Here is Poniatowska on the victims of this government repression:

> Why? The story of what happened at Tlatelolco is puzzling and full of contradictions. The one fact that is certain is that many died.... All the people in the plaza—casual bystanders and active participants alike—were forced to take shelter from the gunfire; many fell wounded.[2]

It takes a special sort of talent to move from the world of brute fact to the imagined ontologies that we have examined throughout this work, but it is clear that Poniatowska has this talent. A political philosophy, as was argued in one of the opening chapters, may best be presented in the form of a utopia. Poniatowska does not move toward the easily imagined utopia, but in presenting the dystopic version

---

1 Poniatowska, Elena (1986), *Dear Diego*, trans. Katherine Silver, New York: Pantheon Books.

2 Poniatowska, Elena (1991), "Voices from Tlateloloco," in Castro-Klarén, Sara, Sylvia Molloy and Beatriz Sarlo (eds.), *Women's Writings from Latin America*, Boulder, CO: Westview Press, 308–314.

of reality that constituted an oppressive Mexican regime in the 1960s, she paved the way for something greater in the imagination.

Latin American writing, we are told, is suffused with "magical realism," but this particular label does not seem to do justice to Poniatowska's work. Rather, this author, working from within the extremely patriarchal male Mexican tradition, expresses the voices of the very women who have always been the unacknowledged backbone of Mexico. The government's official stance on the *mestizaje* almost never does justice to the lives of the women who gave birth to it.

One of Poniatowska's longest and most complex works, *Hasta no verte, Jesus mío*, has only recently been translated into English (*Here's to You, Jesusa!*).[3] This work, like *Dear Diego*, is a fictionalized version of an actual life, and like *Dear Diego* it contains many elements that might almost be dubbed a philosophy of the *mestizaje*. The history of Mexico is one of colonial conquest, the mixing of Spaniards and the indigenous, and the resulting offspring. Until the middle of the nineteenth century, Mexico retained much of the flavor of colonial Spain: the nation was run by individuals of European ancestry, and indigenous people and those of mixed ancestry were decidedly at the bottom. But the enormous numbers of persons of mixed ancestry—because of Catholicism, perhaps, much greater than in an Anglo-dominated society such as the United States—began to exert their understandable pull on the country as Europe started to industrialize, and by the time of Porfirio Díaz at the end of the nineteenth century, the rise of the *mestizaje* and their prominence was part of the official myth of Mexico.

Like a contemporary *adelita*, Elena Poniatowska gives a feminist twist to the story of Mexico, while infusing it with the holdovers of indigenous elements and customs that can readily be seen throughout the nation. *Here's to You, Jesusa!* is the imagined life (based on tapes) of a woman who actually served as a *soldadera* in the Revolution of 1910. Afraid of nothing, and armed to the teeth, such women nursed babies while tending the dead and wounded, and shot anyone who looked like he might prove to be a danger. Of their lives, the novelist writes in the introduction to the American edition:

> [I]n 1914, between January and September, at Fort Bliss and then Fort Wingate, 3,359 officers and soldiers were incarcerated, as well as 1,256 *soldaderas* and 554 children. The *soldaderas* were called that because they welcomed the soldiers, took care of them, never hesitated to take up a rifle and shoot when their man was eating or taking care of business…. They gave birth on the road and kept on walking. They fought in the trenches.[4]

A woman's eye view of such matters is redolent, in some ways, of the types of concerns that Bambara expressed—cultural factors that are omitted from many recountings, but that drive most of what is going on. But the world created by Poniatowska in *Jesusa* has an added layer of complexity, because by ancestry that world is semi-European, and caught between the history of the indigenous and the

---

3 Poniatowska, Elena (2001), *Here's to You, Jesusa!*, trans. Deanna Heikkinen, New York: Farrar, Straus & Girous.

4 Poniatowska, "Introduction," in *Jesusa!*, xvi.

colonial efforts of Spain and even of Portugal. It is a world of Catholicism blended with the beliefs of the Native Americans, and it is a macho world in which women carve a space at their own risk. It is, indeed, the same world that will later give rise to the massacre at the Plaza de las Tres Culturas, but it is important to be able to draw a line between these spheres. It is at this sort of demarcation that Poniatowska excels.

The world of the Mexican woman is a natural world, even within the confines of a slum in Mexico City. Chickens and dogs, water and tamales, the earth and the sky—these are the confines of the lives sketched in *Jesusa*. Social class barriers mean that those who live like Jesusa will never be understood completely by the bourgeoisie, but Poniatowska recreates this world with an eye toward its spiritual concomitants, and a verve for capturing all of the available cultural constructs.

Interviews with Poniatowska—many of which are available only in Spanish—help us to understand how this daughter of immigrants eventually was able to "become Mexican," and how fully her life has been informed by pleas for justice.[5] Esteban Ascensio has spoken extensively with her about the events of 1968, and it is clear that Elena was involved from the first. As soon as she heard from visitors that tanks had broken up the student movement on the night of October 2, 1968, she went to see for herself.[6] As Ascensio writes, she went to see "si había manchas de sangre in todas partes..."[7] As she says, she was looking to see if there was blood everywhere, blood of the students who had been demonstrating against the Mexican government in particular, and, like students worldwide in 1968, against general conditions. In few nations was the response as vicious as in Mexico, and Poniatowska was one of the first courageous chroniclers during an era of extensive repression.

From her work on the Tlateloloco massacre to *Jesusa!* and her imaginative work on Diego, Poniatowska uses available cultural tropes to create alternate worlds descriptive of the Mexican culture. What makes her work remarkable is both its range and scope—few journalists become novelists, and still fewer novelists can claim to have written penetrating sociopolitical essays that actually detail conditions among the lower classes. Relying on the *curanderismo* of the Mexican masses, Poniatowska delineates a worldview that has seldom received an evocative voice. Those few from that world who managed to penetrate middle-class Mexican society at an earlier point in time inevitably felt themselves to be clashing with the government and the larger social structure. Here Poniatowska shines as an author, since it is their take on things that receives her fullest attention.

The *Mestizo* Imaginary

Jesusa! opens with an extended narration in which the protagonist—a somewhat fictionalized version of a very much older woman whom Poniatowska had actually

---

5   One of the best available interviews—and easily accessible to those with only a moderate knowledge of Spanish—in Esteban Ascensio (1997), *Me lo dijo Elena Poniatowska*, Mexico, DF: Ediciones del Milenio. It contains extensive material on her concern for social justice.

6   *Ibid.*, 40–41.

7   *Ibid.*

met in the slums of Lecumberri—describes how she has led her previous lifetimes and why she is being reincarnated on Earth. As the author notes in her Introduction, this kind of spiritualism, although frowned on by official Catholicism, is not at all uncommon throughout Mexico. Jesusa has had revelations about her previous lives, and she is at pains to make the author understand that, as she phrases it, "I must have been very bad...[which is why I have been left here] so long, to purge myself of corrupting, harmful influences."[8]

Functioning with a sort of homegrown metaphysics at least partially derived from the indigenous cultures, Jesusa inhabits a space that is partly in the material here and now and partly a creation of her spiritualist teachings. Her material poverty, which Poniatowska is at pains to describe in the Introduction, seems to be accepted by her with only the smallest reservations. Like many poverty-stricken Mexicans, she lives on the edge of the capital with enough animals that, were a reader not familiar with the lives of city dwellers in Latin America, one would have the impression that she lived on a farm or ranch. Her day consists of work at a local printshop (much of which is cleaning up after the printers), caring for animals, and allowing herself a smoke in the evening. Into this world the author comes, and the result of numerous conversations with the older woman is a recounting of the life of a *soldadera*, one of the women of the Revolution.

The partly indigenous, partly Catholic ontological space created by the *mestizos* is one that lends itself to a number of non-standard beliefs. A less charitable commentator could simply refer to these concepts as folk beliefs, but Poniatowska's gift for storytelling and narration is such that she makes us feel that Jesusa genuinely holds all of these beliefs herself. For example, Jesusa, who as a child worked in and around Mexican prisons, tells the following story about a woman prisoner who was "freed" and by some miracle traveled form Oaxaca to Zacatecas, a distance of hundreds of kilometers, in one day:

> She [the prisoner] fell to her knees [in a church to which she had been able to walk], began to cry, and asked the child to forgive her sins. When the people outside heard her crying with such sorrow, they wanted to know where she was from.
> –I got out of the prison at Tehuantepec at two this afternoon.
> –Which Tehuantepec?
> –Tehuantepec, in the state of Oaxaca.
> –That's not possible, it's very far away, very far.
> –Really, it was two this afternoon and I just arrived.
> They all came closer and crossed themselves. It was one of the Niño's miracles....[9]

The relative simplicity of the narration indicates that the story that Jesusa had heard was real for her, and that she did not question it. The power of the Niño de Atocha (an image of the Christ child), miracles, voyages on foot of hundreds of kilometers in one day—these things are part of the worldview of the indigenous and *mestizo* people who constitute the overwhelming majority of Mexico's population.

---

8 Poniatowska, *Jesusa!*, 4.
9 *Ibid.*, 37.

In this view—as was also the case with the Afrocentric views used by Bambara—the world of the spirit comes first. Much of what Jesusa has to say is straight narration of a life of poverty and hard work; from the time she is a young girl, she grinds, cooks, cleans and washes for others, often without pay, or with only one or two meals a day. She frequently has no more than one change of clothes. But although Jesusa is not particularly religious in the traditional sense, it is clear that she envisions another sort of life from early childhood, and that that life of the mind and the spirit is, in a sense, more real for her than the life she is leading.

What is remarkable about Poniatowska's writing is that the political ramifications of what she describes are always close to the surface. The same author who was one of the first to arrive and report on the massacre of October 2 is also the one who sees into Jesusa's world. When the Revolution does come, the hope for something better—and the belief in the spirit-filled world that to some extent drives it—is one that Poniatowska is easily able to depict.

Spaniards, *criollos*, *mestizos* and the indigenous all played roles in the history of Mexico, resulting in the nation we know today. We can trace the formation of at least some of the beliefs through the application of basic concepts of syncretism: we know, for example, that many of the various versions of the Virgin manifested themselves, most famously, of course, the Virgin of Guadalupe. But although a belief in miracles and their possibility is by no means foreign to traditional Catholicism, when combined with the worldview of the indigenous it yields a strongly non-materialistic stance.

That these Catholic realities drive the culture of Mexico writ large is an undeniable fact, and one that has not been lost on most commentators. Although colonial times saw the establishment of a Mexican culture, particularly in the capital, that had strong European roots, the sheer infusion of blood over a period of time insured that ultimately the *mestizaje* would triumph. Poniatowska is a particularly poignant observer of the culture since she is herself originally a French citizen, and European. But the extent to which a work such as *Jesusa!* attempts to incorporate the relevant views is articulated, for example, by Maria Medeiros-Lichem:

> The affiliation of women with the periphery is essential to Poniatowska's ideology as her narrative is constructed on the *voice of the oppressed* and of those excluded from the mainstream.... Poniatowska writes that Mexican women's oppression is twofold since submission was introduced by the Conquest and Christianity, and because women are also oppressed due to their gender.... In this context, Jesusa Palancares, the protagonist of *Hasta no verte Jesus mío* emerges as a new character type in Latina American fiction. Jesusa is a "desmitificadora" as she portrays an unseen side of reality.... [Emphasis in original.][10]

The "unseen side of reality" is, of course, Jesusa's poverty, and since the work originally appeared in 1969 there is no doubt that the claim that this voice was unheard at that time is beyond dispute. But more importantly, in a double sense, unseen reality manifests itself in Jesusa's worldview, which is somewhat representative of the

---

10 Medeiros-Lichem, Maria Teresa (2002), *Reading the Feminine Voice in Latin American Women's Fiction*, New York: Peter Lang, 53–54.

oppressed the world over. The faith that sustains the poverty-stricken is, of course, a faith based on things unseen, and Jesusa's combination of a sort of Catholicism and strong folk belief is exemplary of much of the Mexican belief system, especially insofar as we may claim its ties to the indigenous. As Medeiros-Lichem goes on to say, Jesusa's worldview is "an essential emotional support."[11]

The well-educated of the world can afford a scientific worldview that tends not to posit the existence of "spirits," and that focuses on the here and now, whether the question revolves around the existence of life on other planets, the search for a cure for AIDS, or debates about amelioration of the status of women. But the poor and semi- or illiterate have no such luxury. The world of empirical concerns is one that has always been foreign and hostile to them, and that scarcely allows for enough aid and succor to keep life going. Thus Jesusa envisions a better world, which is as real to her as travel along a Mexican road. If this invisible world sometimes allows for miraculous journeys of many miles in a single day, all the better. At least it provides a way out of the very sort of existence that has always been her lot.

It is Poniatowska's gift that she renders this world in such a way that we do not forget it. We, too, become enmeshed in Jesusa's concerns and her way of seeing, and we find ourselves believing in the possibility of a miraculous journey. One thing that can certainly be said is that, in creating Jesusa, Poniatowska has already taken the reader on a voyage of discovery that, for most, is an initial journey.

The Critical Poniatowska

Although there is a paucity of criticism on Poniatowska available in English, a number of works dealing with Latin American women authors do address her work to some extent. As her work continues to be translated—*Jesusa!*, despite being published in Mexico in the late 1960s, has only recently been translated—more criticism will continue to emerge. What is remarkable is the comparative unanimity of a great deal of what has already been done. A leading theme has been that Poniatowska is the voice of the oppressed; this assertion is easy to make and one that can obviously be borne out by close analysis of the text. So far there has not been as much attention given to other aspects of her work.

Using *Dear Diego* as the text, with its imaginations regarding the affair between Angelina Beloff and Diego Rivera, Raysa Gomez-Quintero and Mireya Pérez Bustillo argue that the extraordinary streak in Poniatowska's work is her extrapolation of the woman's point of view. Although *Dear Diego* is a fictional version of the relationship, Bertram Wolfe and others had enough documentation of Beloff's letters to Diego Rivera to provide a starting point.[12] As the authors write:

---

11 *Ibid.*, 135.

12 Amador Gomez-Quintero, Raysa E. and Mireya Pérez Bustillo (2002), *The Female Body: Perspectives of Latin American Artists*, Greenwood Publishing Group, 14. The authors are citing Poniatowska's own postscript to *Dear Diego*, in which she acknowledges that much of it is based on the information taken from Wolfe.

In the novel *Dear Diego*, there is a complicity between Poniatowska and Quiela, which hooks the reader at the same time that it challenges the mythic image of Diego Rivera.... Poniatowska reveals [in another source] a Diego Rivera 'that can be seen as a contradictory figure whose political ideas and hopes for the *pueblo*'s future liberation are framed by an oppressive patriarchal discourse and *machista* posturing.'[13]

In other words, in this series of celebrated lives (Diego Rivera and his various wives, mistresses and muses, among whom, of course, was Frida Kahlo) the voices of the women have heretofore been left out. Gómez-Quintero and Pérez Bustillo see the articulation of these voices as a must, and Poniatowska's rendering of at least one of them as a new step forward in *écriture* for Latin American women.

But appealing as it is to make this commentary, it does not seem to do justice to the complexity of Poniatowska's overview. Even in *Diego*, although one is impressed by the rendering of the woman's voice, it is the imagined world that captures the reader's attention. To be sure, the imaginings here do not possess the same sort of ontological force that is achieved in *Jesusa!*. Because Angelina (Quiela in the novel) was a European woman, it is not a worldview or an alternate reality that is achieved, but nevertheless a complex articulation of the life of a Russian emigré woman in Paris in the early part of the twentieth century is given. This is indeed Poniatowska's strong suit—one comes to be enmeshed in this view so thoroughly that it is difficult to believe that what the author has given us are not the actual letters from Beloff to Rivera themselves. Details are provided that startle—not only does Poniatowska offer minute descriptions of Parisian life, but she is able to imagine a smaller world composed of Russian émigrés who intermingle and see each other on regular occasions. Their fondness for Russian delicacies, their homesickness for a certain sort of cooking—all this is captured by Poniatowska in such a way that the reader comes to feel that she is hearing Beloff's actual voice.

The peculiar strength of Poniatowska's that allows her to achieve this effect is a strong version of internal monologue with the addition of numerous tiny details to support that monologue. This general trope of capturing the "voice" is an important one for Elena Poniatowska, and is a mode that is all the more important in *Jesusa!*.

Criticism has tended to focus on *Jesusa!* as her most important work for the obvious reason that, by length and scope (not to mention subject matter), it was a breakthrough in its time. Never before had the life of a woman from Mexico's bottom been captured in such a way by a Mexican author. Aligning herself with the general notion that voice is crucial, Maria Medeiros-Lichem uses the Bakhtinian notion of dialogism to analyze *Jesusa!*, and she, too, emphasizes the worldviews explicit in the text and its refusal of patriarchy. Medeiros-Lichem sees the genuine dialogism here as that between the author and Jesusa; she interprets the author as placing the text in such a way as to create this effect. Her points are insisted upon when she writes:

> The text of *Hasta no verte Jesus mio* is an encounter of two minds, two fragments of Mexican culture. There is a double authorship in this fictional piece, as the voice is genuinely Jesusa's and it is the writer, who edits her oral report. Poniatowska recognizes

---

13 Thompson, *Flash*, 73.

her debt in appropriating Jesusa's historical record, and claims to have invented characters and events to give the text a fictional form, but she insists that the voice of the narrator is Jesusa's.[14]

Some points are, of course, obvious—we experience no difficulty in assenting to the notion that Poniatowska has made the text cohere in a way that, for example, the oral transcription probably did not. But other areas having to do with the assertion of "double authorship" are more subtle—it may be, for instance, that some of what we interpret as the anti-hegemonic and anti-patriarchal stance of Jesusa's is more attributable to Poniatowska herself. This, obviously, sustains the notion of dialogism.

In any case, there is no question that, dialogism or no, a great deal of the sense of anti-authority that seems to suffuse poverty-stricken Mexico may be pulled from this text. Medeiros-Lichem notices that Jesusa both confronts gender roles and, in her own way, reappropriates at least some of them. Medeiros claims that she "confronts *macho* behavior and succeeds in her feminine roles."[15] In addition, Medeiros also underscores the importance of Jesusa's spiritist community, *Obra Espiritual*—it is clear, she claims, that this metaphysical twist in her life is not only sincerely assented to by her, but is a source of her own personal strength in her fight against poverty. As Medeiros phrases it,

> Traumatized in her childhood, and also through the turmoil of the Mexican Revolution, Jesusa finds in the *Obra* a source of power in helping other marginalized people with alternative medicine. In the *Obra Espiritual* Jesusa has the faculty to cure not only as "curandera" or shamanistic healer with medicinal herbs, but also with spiritual powers transmitted by her supernatural "protectors."[16]

Poniatowska succeeds in giving us the life of a *soldadera* in all of its difficulties and hardships, and at the same time is able to present the ways in which that woman struggles against the oppression around her. Some of the struggle is escape into another world—some of it is literal struggle, as when she repeatedly fights with the men in her life, often giving just as good as she gets. There is little in Jesusa's life that meets any sort of middle-class standard, but that is precisely the point of attempting to capture her voice. Here Poniatowska presents the sort of life that was previously the province of Oscar Lewis.

If Poniatowska has a gift for delineating the various sorts of oppression that one woman can encounter during her lifetime, she also makes known to us the "many Mexicos." Although this phrase has become a staple and a cliché of the literature, it is an important one, in that many North American readers will be sufficiently unfamiliar with Mexican culture to be aware of its vast regional variations. Jesusa is a woman originally from the isthmus of Tehuantepec; over a period of time she moves around the country, first with Carrancistas, then with the Zapatistas, until she winds up in Mexico City. She is not only from Mexico's bottom in the socioeconomic

---

14 Medeiros-Lichem, *Reading*, 141.
15 *Ibid.*, 136.
16 *Ibid.*, 135.

sense, but as so often happens to Mexicans (especially now) she winds up in a far away place, nowhere near her region of origin.

Maureen Shea notices this strength of Poniatowska's when she comments:

> At the time of the narration, Jesusa is also an outsider in the physical sense because she is not in her native province of Tehuantepec and she feels uncomfortable with her surroundings in Mexico City. She refers with nostalgia to the green and blue pastures of rural Mexico, with its fresh air, in contrast to filth-laden skies of Mexico City. Jesusa equates this filth to the decadence and hypocrisy of life in the Mexican capital.[17]

Poniatowska captures one woman in her near totality, and in a sense that woman becomes emblematic of many. For the thousands of *soldaderas* whose stories were unheard, she serves as a voice that links the nation to its revolutionary past. The green fields of Jesusa's childhood may exist no longer, but they live in what Poniatowska has written.

Feminisms and their Other Categories

Medeiros-Lichem wants to write of the Bakhtinian dialogism present in Poniatowska; Raysa Gomez-Quintero and her co-author are concerned about "inscribing the body." All comers seem to agree that the only reasonable way in which to interpret Poniatowska is to give her a feminist reading.

But to give Poniatowska this reading is related to the very points that we have made in the previous section; it is not merely that Poniatowska is susceptible to such a reading, but that her work seems to demand it simply because it is among the earliest work done in Mexico that allows for the now ubiquitous "women's voices" to be heard. In other words, trying to force the line of feminism here is somewhat unnecessary; it comes up naturally simply because a work like *Here's to You, Jesusa!*, although already having counterparts in English-language writing, was a completely original item when published in the 1960s.

Poniatowska's greatest strength—especially insofar as *Jesusa!* and *Dear Diego* are concerned—may well be the interior monologue. Each work has extended sections that are nothing but such monologue; indeed, aside from introductions and postscripts, that is probably an accurate description of each work. Although *Dear Diego* is a fictionalized version of an affair that Diego Rivera had in Paris, Poniatowska imagines Beloff's world, and has no difficulty placing herself in it. Interior monologues used to be the property of male narrators, or at least of female narrators of a certain class. Jesusa's monologue is certainly a mine of invention.

The importance of Jesusa's story—and her mode of telling it—is more than simply the appropriation or articulation of a woman's voice. Jesusa is not simply any woman; manifestly, she is not a middle-class woman, and she refuses to mouth any middle-class verities about a woman's place in life, even if these staples might be thought to be completely consistent with the Mexican cultural framework in general. Rather, if anything, she undercuts the traditional notions with a string of curses, a

---

17 Shea, Maureen (1993), *Women as Outsiders*, San Francisco: Austin & Winfield, 29.

round condemnation of the abuse that she has suffered at the hands of men (both her relatives and lovers), and a general series of imprecations against the government and those around her. Jesusa does not, of course, make any utterances from the standpoint of theory—rather, she simply reflects on her life (which she interprets, from the standpoint of the *Obra Espiritual*, as a punishment for previous sins) and says what comes to her mind. It is this aspect of the work that made it remarkable in its time, and gives it a sort of permanent feminist flavor that is beyond any one sort of theory. As Shea says,

> Jesusa exemplifies the teller-character and first-person narrator who constantly reminds us of her presence. She offers innumerable comments and opinions, hence marking a distance between the moment of enunciation (the present) and the events she is relating.[18]

Although Poniatowska edited and shaped the text, the care that she takes to let Jesusa's story constitute a coherent narrative indicates that we are getting something like a factually accurate version of the life of this *soldadera* of Revolutionary times.

If it has been difficult, especially in so-called developing nations, to capture the voices of women not of the middle-class, it is also difficult to navigate between what must appear to be an acceptance of the sexism surrounding such women in the general culture and their moments of refusal of it. Jesusa is seldom directly critical of such cultural factors as the necessity of women doing all of the cooking and food preparation—this seems to be taken for granted, and the outspoken Jesusa would no doubt have some choice words for a man who ventured to participate in such activities. But Jesusa is much less accepting of the appalling level of violence that seemed to accompany her and the other women whose lives she described on a near daily basis. In this sense, Jesusa develops her own kind of feminism, and her own kind of awareness of the possession of her body. She has little respect for her husband because of his treatment of her, although many might claim that such treatment is a more-or-less mandated feature of life for her social class.

Nor does Jesusa replicate, in traditional ways, the emphasis on the role of the mother that also seems to be a feature of Mexican life, indeed of Latin American life in general. As Medeiros-Lichem says, "In the case of Jesusa Palancares her 'reproduction' of mothering is the result of social circumstances of extreme necessity."[19] Jesusa may not exhibit the care that we associate with a maternal figure, but she seldom received such care in her own life, and she has never been in a situation of caring for her own children; rather, any "mothering" situation has been forced on her. When discussing children, Jesusa does not exemplify what, according to Mexican cultural patterns, should be the thoughts of the maternal caregiver. In that sense, she more than breaks set.

There are, of course, a number of ways of presenting women's voices. A careful narrative might simply present such voices in the third person, or might attempt something in the way of a social sciences approach (albeit a literary one). What makes Poniatowska's work special is probably best captured in some remarks by

---

18 *Ibid.*, 31.
19 Medeiros-Lichem, *Reading*, 137.

the feminist critic Josephine Donovan, although her conception of the arts is more driven by the status of the visual arts:

> The objectifying perspective sees matter or nature as dead; it is not perceived to have interests or indeed to have an existence apart from the subject whose mathematizing gaze is seen as redemptive. This allows the subject—whether it be artist or scientist—to manipulate matter or nature without retaining an empathy with or ethical respect for its independent existence. And it allows the subject to extract "significant" matter—that which corresponds to the subject's ideal conception—and elevate it, set it above the "trivial" matter of everyday life.[20]

Poniatowska tries to enter the spirit and voice of the woman whose story she is telling; this is a completely different mode from the mode of objectification, even were such mode to be placed in feminist hands. The "existence apart" that Jesusa has is there for all to see—rather than Jesusa being reduced, she is enlivened and brought to the fore. This is no small accomplishment, given not only gender issues but the clear and ramifying social class issues that exist in most societies, particularly developing nations. (And that in Mexico have always been associated with the divisions between those of European ancestry and the *mestizaje*/indigenous.)

Interestingly, much the same thing is said of Poniatowska's writing in *Dear Diego*, even though it is clear that the voice of Quiela is greatly fictionalized, and does not bear the same straightforward resemblance to Beloff that Jesusa does to Josefina (Jesusa) Bórquez. The critics Gomez-Quintero and Pérez Bustillo note that:

> Poniatowska, as an intermediary for Quiela, constructs her for the reader, making her the core of the narrative. The letters evidence the emergence of a triumphant Quiela, for she tells the reader that from very early in life she has been self-sufficient, both economically and emotionally. Quiela reaffirms her self-worth as a woman.[21]

Again, this is further evidence of the "empathy" and "ethical respect" of which Donovan writes. Although this respect—and this vocalization, or perhaps we should say ventriloquism—could in fact be practiced by any writer, we have come to associate this sort of attention to women's issues with a decidedly feminist slant that has, itself, been practiced overwhelmingly by women authors. As indicated in the critical reception to her work on the events of Tlatelolco, Poniatowska has impressed one and all with her ability to capture the lives of the marginalized and to render them significant and even central. If, as Enrique Krauze seems to say, the story of Mexico is one of "biography of power," Poniatowska gives us the biographies of the powerless.[22] Krauze is one of Mexico's leading male intellectuals. Perhaps it is no accident that we may categorize Poniatowska as one of Mexico's foremost female thinkers.

---

20 Donovan, Josephine (1993), "Everyday Uses and Moments of Being: Toward a Nondominant Aesthetic," in Hein, Hilde and Caroline Korsmeyer (eds.), *Aesthetics in Feminist Perspective*, Indianapolis: Indiana University Press, 53–67.

21 Gomez-Quintero et al., Body, 16.

22 Krauze, Enrique (1997), *Mexico: Biography of Power*, New York: Harper Collins.

Continentalizing

At an earlier point, we had alluded to the work of Helene Cixous. Writing in one of the introductory sections in his anthology *The Continental Aesthetics Reader*, Clive Cazeaux has said:

> On the one hand, Cixous' account of painting is somewhat idealized or romanticized.... On the other hand, Cixous' essay is an expression of the desire for fulfillment which an artist of one background feels in response to the work of an artist from another. It is the hope or promise that an artist sees in another way of working that intrigues her.[23]

Cixous' fascination with the difference between the written word and the visual arts is a distinction that leaps at someone familiar with Poniatowska's work, for as it happens Mexican culture in general is suffused with the visual, and in the arts it is safe to say that Mexican painting stands preeminent. So a comparison that, in a sense, is only metaphorical for Cixous becomes more literal within the cultural context in which Poniatowska finds herself.

Moving in the direction suggested by Cixous, what would a painting or mural telling of Jesusa's life look like? We do not have to struggle unduly with this question, because we already have quite a bit of evidence from the visual arts that helps to answer it. We can think of the murals of Rivera, Orozco or Siqueiros for an answer—and they come readily to mind. Perhaps most noteworthy (and somewhat underappreciated) is the work of Siqueiros, in some ways the most militant of the three painters and the painter whose attacks on the bourgeoisie became the most pronounced. In his *Portrait of the Bourgeoisie*, found in the Sindicato Mexicano de Electricistas in Mexico City, a furious rifleman stares out at the viewer. The slashing paintstrokes are a mix of surrealism and futurism, and the revolutionary intent of the work is palpable.[24]

In a sense, this painting tells us a great deal about the violence and anger that filled the early part of Jesusa's life, as she lived through the continued assaults and advances of the opposing forces of Carrancistas, Zapatistas and others. But although the *adelitas* are renowned in Mexican history—and this is a decidedly male-oriented culture—there is perhaps no one visual work that gives prominent place to them. Poniatowska's work is a portrait of an *adelita*, anger, resistance and all. Beaten, humiliated, violated and furious, Jesusa pushes back against the forces around her, even as she is pummeled by them. Here Cixous speaks on the visual arts:

> Seeing the world as it is demands strengths, virtues. Which ones? Patience and courage.
> The patience one has to have to approach the nonostensible, the minute, the insignificant, to discover the worm as a star without luster. To discover the grasshopper's worth.[25]

---

23 Cazeaux, *Reader*, 503.

24 Folgarait, Leonard (1998), *Mexican Mural Painting and Social Revolution in Mexico, 1920–1940: Art of the New Order*, Cambridge: Cambridge University Press, Plates XIV–XVII.

25 Cixous, Helene, "The Last Painting or the Portrait of God," in Cazeaux (ed.), 583–597.

Here Cixous imagines the painter or artist in a visual medium as able to express that which cannot be expressed in words. But Cixous exaggerates for effect, of course, much as Cazeaux admits. Not only does the poet frequently capture the "grasshopper's worth"—think of "Lines Composed Above Tintern Abbey," or "Intimations of Immortality"—but other writers can go far toward capturing at least some of what drove Cixous.

Hasta no Verte Jesus Mio captures the life of a woman of the Revolution, and in the sort of detail that Cixous demands. Wonderful moments of women's lived lives are to be found throughout the text—and not merely moments of tragedy. In the midst of stress and strife, the continued attempts of older women to teach Jesusa how to prepare meals, to work with a *metate*, to stack items in the order that custom demands, speak volumes about the place of women in Mexico, and, indeed, the place of the *soldadera* in the Revolution. Jesusa's continued gratitude toward them (even if they fail almost every middle-class test of "stepmotherliness") signals to us in a powerful way what parenting, if the expression may be employed, consisted of during Jesusa's childhood and early adulthood.

Écriture may consist of a mélange of the stated, the implied, and the inarticulable. Poniatowska has a gift for detail, and the detail in combination with the direct interior narration places us squarely in Jesusa's life. Indeed, for most readers the difficulty will be that our perplexity at the jumble of events, the level of violence and the plain disheartening nature of much of Jesusa's life becomes overwhelming, and the desire will be to put the book down in order to try to gain some perspective. It is this that makes her work remarkable—her pulling together of the tale is so real that the reader is likely to feel undone.

Jesusa may lack some insight into what she has experienced—at least in the terms that the privileged and educated normally employ—and this also gives the work a certain resonant poignancy. Her husband Pedro treats her very badly, and yet life with him is a form of attention. To be able to articulate a view for Jesusa is already an accomplishment, since she does not manifest the sort of worldview that a middle-class woman might employ when subjected to the same abuse (even a middle-class woman of her time). Poniatowska is able to weave her story together.

Thus we can claim a form of *écriture* for Poniatowska, but we can also claim that at least some other Continental thinkers have theorized in a fashion that is relevant. The social and racial formation of Mexico, although in general lacking much input from African societies, is seen in European terms as an equivalent, since the Native American portion of the society is strong enough to give Mexico as a whole a sort of "otherness." Famously, Sartre referred to American blacks as "untouchables":

> These untouchables, you cross them in the street at all hours of the day, but you do not return their stares. Or if by chance their eyes meet yours, it seems to you that they do not see you and it is better for them and you that you pretend not to notice them. They serve you at the table....[26]

But Jesusa and others from her group are in a sense the untouchables of Mexico. Not quite, to be sure; beneath them is the group of the actually indigenous, of which

---

26 Sartre, Jean-Paul, "Return from the United States," *Existence*, in Gordon (ed.), 83–89.

Mexico had at the time (and still possesses) many millions. But Mexico has always had a certain number of individuals at the top of society, of purely European—or, at the most, slightly mixed—ancestry. Manifestly, Jesusa does not belong to this group, and neither do the thousands of *soldaderas* fighting in the Revolution. The social forces of objectification that allow the blacks of America, as categorized by Sartre, to become "unnoticed," even when plainly present, are at work in Mexico in another way. Indigenous and *mestizo* alike are invisible to the *criollos* and those actually born in Spain who dominate the upper social strata of Mexican society.

Perhaps part of Poniatowska's gift for entering the lives of the "others" comes from being a sort of "other" herself—born in Europe, Poniatowska struggled to become "Mexican" as an adult, and she also undertook the rather shocking activity of earning her living by writing at a time in Latin America—the 1950s—when one could scarcely think of women being employed. As she says in her interviews with Esteban Ascencio, "Cuando en 1953 empezé a trabajar en Excelsior mi familia no se acostumbrada al hecho de que una mujer fuera una reportera."[27] ("When I began to work for *Excelsior* in 1953, my family didn't believe that a woman could be a reporter.") New Mexican, employed woman, French-speaking child—Elena Poniatowska has to carve out a place for herself in Latin American society, and the social structure of the time will be anything but friendly to her efforts.

Although it may seem a stretch, Poniatowska and Jesusa have something in common—they are both outsiders. Poniatowska has to understand the past of Mexico if she is to become fully a part of it, and few parts of its past are more celebrated than the Revolution of 1910. At the time that she began *Hasta no Verte*, the generation that would have been old enough to participate in the fighting was already approaching 75 or 80. Thus Poniatowska performed an enormous service in attempting to recreate Jesusa's life, even if her efforts did not initially meet with encouragement from Jesusa herself. In that sense, she engages in a genuinely female writing, as she tells and recaptures the life of a woman from Mexico's bottom.

Philosophical or Not

Whether or not Poniatowska's work could be thought of as having philosophical content depends largely on how individuals are seen to construct their own worldviews. We have to ask the difficult question of whether or not deeply-held beliefs—even in pre-literate, or largely non-literate, societies—count as implicit philosophical views. It would seem that the answer must be in the affirmative; after all, many of the African societies that are cited in *Flash of the Spirit*, for example, were originally societies that functioned in the oral tradition. We count the views of the Yoruba, Igbo or Ashanti as being ontological or cosmological because they attempted to answer questions of basic import to humans, with or without advertence to written languages and frames of thought.

In the case of the indigenous of Mexico and Central America, a similar line of argument can be brought to bear. We experience no qualms, for example, in attributing

---

[27] Ascencio, *Dijo*, 30.

philosophical views to the Maya or the Mixtec, and, to be fair, these social systems did at least have the beginnings of a script and a system of enumeration. But the world of the nineteenth and twentieth century *mestizaje* of Mexico is a world functioning largely in oral tradition, albeit that the language of transmission is Spanish. There is, then, a bit of a conundrum—with written Spanish widely available, even in the Mexico of the Revolutionary period, it could be argued that it makes little sense to attribute Jesusa's homegrown beliefs to any kind of metaphysical quest, given that she could have acquired the ability to read and write in Spanish, and given that a new world would then have become open to her.

But this is precisely the point. The protagonist of *Dear Diego*, for instance, has a European worldview, and hence her views do not push us in any new and largely unexplored directions.[28] Jesusa, however, is a *mestiza* who has adopted, as was and is so common, many of the folk beliefs of the indigenous without herself identifying as an indigenous person. Commentators on the Mexican scene from Paz to Krauze seem to want to claim that much of the Native American influence in the culture is manifest in food choice, or possibly architecture; a comparatively unexplored phenomenon is the syncretism of the folk beliefs of the indigenous with the Catholicism that was forced on them by Spain's priests. Jesusa has her own syncretism, so to speak. Her beliefs in the *Obra* certainly do not square with taught Catholicism—she is very aware of that. But what she may not be completely aware of is the extent to which the spirit world that she comes to believe in mirrors indigenous spirit worlds; indeed, her story early in *Jesusa!* about the voyage of hundreds of kilometers in a single day recapitulates an essentially native view of the world.

So it does not seem wrong to attribute an ontology to Jesusa, and it is clear that what is attributed to her is one that is intensely dualistic. As is so common with dualistic worldviews, the life of the spirit seems more real, in many ways, and certainly more genuinely evocative of human capacities, than the life of the body. So Jesusa rejects any sort of material view that would be in accord with the facts taught in schools, partly because it does not bring emotional relief, and partly because (we may assume) she finds such reductionism demeaning.

In addition it is obvious that much of what Jesusa believes simply reflects an amalgam of beliefs familiar from the *mestizaje* and the indigenous, and referred to, at length, by Octavio Paz in his *The Labyrinth of Solitude*.[29] Famously, in that work Paz makes it clear that what he regards as being at the center of Mexican culture is a sense of violation. He sees this sense reflected in the everyday referencing of Mexicans to themselves as "hijos de la chingada" (a polite translation would be "children of the violated.") Historically speaking, this sense is a carryover from the knowledge held by every Mexican that the nation was formed from the rape and violation of Indian women by Spaniards and other Europeans. A sort of fatalism seems to drive much of Mexican culture, at least according to Paz—and we can see this atmosphere played out in Jesusa's belief systems, which rely heavily on the notion that she is doing penance for some other life. As Paz writes:

---

28 As indicated earlier, Poniatowska is at pains to create a believable Russian protagonist for Dear Diego, since the character is based on Beloff.

29 Paz, Octavio (1961), *The Labyrinth of Solitude*, New York: Grove Press.

When we shout, "Viva Mexico, hijos de la chingada!" we express our desire to live closed off from the outside world and, above all, from the past. In this shout we condemn our origins and deny our hybridism. The strange permanence of Cortés and La Malinche in the Mexican's imagination and sensibilities reveals that they are something more than historical figures: they are symbols of a secret conflict that we have still not resolved. When he repudiates La Malinche—the Mexican Eve, as she was represented in the mural by José Clemente Orozco in his mural at the National Preparatory School—the Mexican breaks his ties with the past, renounces his origins and lives in isolation and solitude.[30]

Plainly, what is also being said here is that the effect of racism on the formation of the Mexican culture is such that European ontology construction is held out as some kind of an ideal, and European racial goals (if they may be called that) have a sort of transcendental power.

Todo en Todo

Much of the force of Poniatowska's work derives, as we have seen, from a combination of her care with the voices of those who have been voiceless, and a nascent concern for the overviews of the indigenous and the *mestizaje*, even if these are groups with which Poniatowska herself can scarcely be said to be conversant. It might very well be the case that the most helpful line of critical theory in attempting to do justice to Poniatowska's work is postcolonial thought, since it seems to enable the reader to get a very good grip on her set of cares and concerns. When we remember Mexico's origins as one of the first colonial societies in the New World, the relevance of this line of theory is manifest.

In an essay titled "Columbus and the Cannibals," Peter Hulme reminds us that almost everything we think we know about the New World and its formation is itself a transcription of after-the-fact notes (and in some cases not even that). Alluding to the original series of voyages and the commentary on them by Bartolomeo de las Casas, he writes:

> For a start the actual text on which we presume Columbus to have inscribed [the word for "cannibals"] disappeared, along with its only known copy, in the middle of the sixteenth century. The only version we have...is a handwritten abstract made by Bartolome de las Casas, probably in 1552, and probably from the copy of Columbus' original then held in the monastery of San Pablo in Seville.[31]

Read metaphorically, as Hulme intends, it is not merely Columbus and his pronouncements on cannibals (he was very worried about them) that is at issue here. Rather, as the author is at pains to point out, virtually everything that has come down to us from that period reflects the same kind of second-, third-, and fourth-hand reporting that we have of the actual voyage itself, and, given the social structure of the New World, much of it represents European encounters with the indigenous.

---

30 *Ibid.*, 86–87.
31 Hulme, Peter (1995), "Columbus and the Cannibals," in *The Post-colonial Studies Reader*, Ashcroft, Bill, Gareth Griffiths and Helen Tiffin (eds.), New York: Routledge, 365–369.

In a sense, what Poniatowska tries to achieve in a work such as *Jesusa!* is a rectification of this kind of displacement and Othering. Although Jesusa frequently refers to persons in her story as "Indians," she clearly does this as a reflection of the cultural patterns imposed on her from above. As a *mestiza*, she might very well appear to be *muy India* to a European-ancestored woman in Mexico City. Just as the testimony of the voyages and the initial encounters is all an encoding that the colonizers put together in order to frame their point of view, so Poniatowska tells us—by having Jesusa speak in her own voice—that previous efforts to depict the *los de abajo* segment of the Mexican population, however well-intended, ultimately were part of the process that started when de las Casas tried to put together smatterings from the original voyages.

Neither las Casas nor anyone else, however sympathetic, was in a position to let the indigenous speak for themselves, but Poniatowska, as a writer of the twentieth century, can break new ground. When Jesusa says, "My husband had the luck of a street dog with women. They followed him all over the place…",[32] we can hear an authentic voice of pain and betrayal. We can also note the use of the vernacular and we can assume that this is something close to Jesusa's actual phrasing. (We can also hear it in Jesusa's remarks to Poniatowska herself in the Introduction when she says—of the author's handwritten notes—"So many years in school to end up with that scribble-scrabble!")[33]

This care with the speech of one who is powerless is a hallmark of Poniatowska's work, and insofar as the metaphysical overview presented derives from the force of the indigenous, she has more than succeeded in her goal of getting the reader to feel a certain point of view. In an essay similar in spirit to Hulme's, Terry Goldie writes that there are "a few basic moves which the indigenous pawn has been allowed to make."[34] Even novels of only a decade or two earlier, were they to attempt to address issues not essentially centered in Mexico's European class, would most likely have used the very moves to which Goldie refers. What makes Poniatowska's work decisively different is that one is tempted to say that these issues simply do not come up in the context of her writing—it is as if a quantum leap has been made.

---

32 Poniatowska, *Jesusa!*, 102.
33 *Ibid.*, xi.
34 Goldie, Terry, "The Representation of the Indigene," in Ashcroft et al. (eds.), *Post-Colonial*, 232–236.

Chapter Eleven

Las Mujeres de Mexico

If the feminist commentary on Poniatowska has tended to focus on her use of voice, a new move in such commentary was made with the publication of the first major book-length work on the author available in English, Beth Jorgensen's *The Writing of Elena Poniatowska: Engaging Dialogues.*[1] Jorgensen attempts to examine all of Poniatowska's available works, and the point is to try to make a case for the dialogic nature of her texts. Although it is clear that Medeiros-Lichem, among others, has already tackled this topic in a small way, Jorgensen's work is some one hundred fifty pages long and represents a major attempt to come to grips with the author and her work.

The focus on *Jesusa!*, for instance, has tended to be on the extent to which Jesusa (Josefina) Palancares is an actual *soldadera*, a survivor of the Revolution, and, as was said in the last chapter, one of that group of *mestiza* women whose work created contemporary Mexico, but who are seldom acknowledged. But it was acknowledged by Medeiros-Lichem in her emphasis on the Bakhtinian that Jesusa is, of course, a creation—a creation of Elena Poniatowska. Jorgensen begins her chapter on *Jesusa!* with the following:

> ...*Hasta no verte Jesus mío* has generated the most intense interest among "professional" readers. Why? Because it is surrounded by a forcefield of confusion. Confusion over how it was written; confusion over the distinction between Jesusa Palancares (character) and Josefina Bórquez ("real life" reference); confusion over the book's genre (novel? testimony? testimonial novel?); confusion over its ideological value and its aesthetic effects: this is rich fare for the academic consumer.[2]

Here we have a clear presentation of what is really at stake in Poniatowska's writing; the same author who gave us *Voices from Tlatelolco* has also given us *Tinísima*, *Dear Diego* and *Jesusa!*. The latter three works, although clearly fictionalized, represent stories of Mexican women (or women with strong connections to Mexican culture)—but then the question is where precisely the fiction ends and begins.

Fortunately, as Jorgensen has said, these sorts of questions, now familiar from the range of post- theorizing with which most philosophers and literary critics have grappled, are never ending and provide genuinely insightful incursions into the writer's work. That Poniatowska is able, especially for *Jesusa!*, to give us a creation whose antecedents remain murky, but whose overall authenticity is beyond dispute, is testament to her power as a writer. As Jorgensen has written, we are left with

---

1 Jorgensen, Beth (1994), *The Writing of Elena Poniatowska: Engaging Dialogues*, Austin: University of Texas Press.
2 *Ibid.*, 28.

a set of "crisscrossing threads which weave a marvelous net, both instrument of entrapment and elusive object of our contemplation."[3]

Although a plethora of narrative styles might be evoked if one were to try to construct a taxonomy, the narrative styles of the nineteenth century, for example, might be regarded as more straightforward. In this respect, we expect a novel—or any lengthy fiction work—to perhaps alternate somewhat in voices of narration, but to adhere, in most cases, to a third-person structure that would give a chronological (and hence easy to follow) delineation of the plot.

Although *Jesusa!* is a product of the 1960s, and could easily be the sort of work that would be categorized as "postmodern," it is not really that sort of concern that drives Jorgensen's criticism (or, indeed, that of Medeiros-Lichem). Rather, what both critics find interesting about *Jesusa!* is what they take to be the narrator's own meanderings—but this, of course, means that Poniatowska placed those meanderings in the text. In other words, Jesusa herself jumps forward and backward in the narrative, providing a story of her life over time, but bringing us into the text as readers of a piece of journalism, so to speak, by alluding to her then-current life in Mexico City on occasion. Medeiros-Lichem calls these moves "Bakhtinian"; Jorgensen takes a still stronger stand. As she writes:

> The shifting relationship between narrator and protagonist to which I have alluded is, in part, simply a consequence of the variable time interval that separates the single present moment of narrating from the many different past moments of the story.... The narrator expresses a striking ambivalence or unease toward her past actions and toward her own survival which I read as a function of the novel's portrayal of Jesusa Palancares as both a dominated subject and a contestatory agent in Mexican society.[4]

In other words, the split that Jorgensen finds so interesting is not the split between Poniatowska and Jesusa, but Jesusa's various stands and, bluntly, personalities. Sometimes a caretaker, sometimes heedless, sometimes political, sometimes not; Jesusa is all of these things, and the ultimate survivor. The extent to which she is a creation of Poniatowska is, of course, also up for grabs. In the sort of episode that the reader is unlikely to forget, the long-suffering (but indomitable) Jesusa, still a teenager at this point in the text, recounts one of her husband's infidelities:

> When he was in the 77th regiment, he took up with someone else. I knew she was his mistress, but I didn't say anything; it was her husband who demanded to know what right Pedro had to be involved with his wife. [Her husband is taken to jail after a fight, and then the mistress goes to see him.] She'd just gone in when I got there with a basket of food. She was lying against the bars, and he was leaning against the other side, the two of them real happy there.
> –What a nice picture these two pieces of shit make! Too bad the cock is penned up in another cage![5]

---

3   *Ibid.*, 29.
4   *Ibid.*, 36.
5   Poniatowska, *Jesusa!*, 102.

In a short set of a few lines, we go from feeling sorry for Jesusa as victim, to cheering her on—and possibly being somewhat appalled at her unfailing repertoire of curses and foul language.

But the point is, of course, that Jesusa could not have survived had she not had the rage to keep going—and that rage fueled her tactics not only against her husband, but against all of those who took advantage of her. Poniatowska is gifted at being able to place all of these shifts in a relatively short and abrupt sequence; one of the features of the text that makes it so remarkable is that Jesusa scarcely stays in the same place (literally or metaphorically) for any length of time. It is this part of the text that Jorgensen finds remarkable, for a text could have been constructed that would have attempted to render Jesusa a more consistent person. Presumably it would not have been true to the person herself.

In *Dear Diego*, a similar level of switching is accomplished, although this highly fictionalized tale—based only on second- and third-hand evidence about the individual in question—centers around another sort of woman entirely. But again what makes Diego noteworthy is the extent to which Poniatowska has created a life for the protagonist, Quiela. In a sort of *écriture* all its own, Poniatowska gives Quiela a range of sensations and emotions that carries the reader into her interior. It is difficult not to believe that this story was not told by Angelina Beloff to the author, much as Jesusa's tale was at least partially taped. Quiela tells us of her history as an artist, her work in Paris, her meetings with other artists, and then in a tour de force of evoked internality, of her desire that Diego return:

> Only a miracle could make you emerge from that throng of people with their heads bent, dark and faceless figures, and come over to me with your head up.... And the next afternoon, there I was in front of my round market table, in between the Spaniard who, like me, was always looking out into the street, and the Turk...both of them unaware of my desperation, of the cup trembling in my hands, of my eyes devouring the grey and anonymous multitude that passed by and out of which you would emerge and walk towards me.[6]

Poniatowska achieves, then, a multiplicity of voices, but it is important to realize that this multiplicity is itself subject to many ramifications: in *Diego* and *Jesusa!*, it is the result of the author's interactions with her protagonists (real and imagined), and then, especially in Jesusa's case, the character's interactions with her selves over a period of time. This highly alembicated rendering of women's "voices" is characteristic of Poniatowska's work.

Another Round of Criticism

Beth Jorgensen's work focuses, as we have indicated, on the multiplicity of voices in Poniatowska's work, and highlights the extent to which this technique dominates *Jesusa!*. But there are many ways of interpreting this very "multiplicity." It is not merely a differentiation of time and place, or a narrator's distancing herself from

---

6 Poniatowska, *Diego*, 49, 52.

her past; nor is it Poniatowska's subtle insertion of herself in the text. *Jesusa!* also interrogates gender roles, and to an extent unusual in Latin American writing of the 1960s. On the topic of Jesusa's rejection of feminine values, Jorgensen writes:

> As a child, Jesusa is a typical tomboy, and she unquestioningly adopts boyish pastimes and even masculine forms of violence. The death of her mother and her dependence on her father and older brother mean that her role models are predominantly male, a situation that she apparently accepts as natural. Her later criticism of machista values, including violence against the weak, results from many years of personal experience and does not apply to the young protagonist.[7]

Indeed, Jesusa gives as good as she gets. But the strands woven by Poniatowska in an effort to get us to see all of Jesusa's facets are indicators of the extent to which her writing manifests dialogism, and this is a line of criticism that is undertaken by Jorgensen and Medeiros-Lichem.

In a work on women and modernity, especially in the visual realm, the Australian theorist Liz Conor states that she wants to "[P]ropose *appearing* as an alternative term, and to investigate the impact of visual representations of women on the production of a new modern feminine subjectivity, *the appearing woman*." [Emphasis in original.][8] Conor could not have been thinking of women in Latin America, obviously, much less of the Mexican *mestiza*, but as a general way of beginning an investigation of tropes of the woman during the twentieth century, Conor seems to be on to something. For there is, in fact, a visual image of what Jesusa accomplished as a young woman in the period 1910–1920, and that image is that of the *adelita*, the *soldadera*. Numerous photos from the time show a young woman—frequently wearing sashes of bullets and carrying a rifle—riding on a train, leading small children, or carrying food and water. These *machista* women were the ones who clearly accomplished a great deal of the work that was done by the Revolution, period. As an older woman still living in Mexico, Jesusa must have seen these images countless times, for they are among the most widely publicized of that historic era—perhaps even more so than the ubiquitous photos of Pancho Villa and Zapata. It is tempting to think that, in creating a number of voices that are captured by Poniatowska, Jesusa must have seen her "appearances" so to speak, and that they played back to her in ways that allowed her to articulate a given stance.

In a sense, Elena Poniatowska herself appears to be teasing out these appearances in her text, for Jesusa moves back and forth between past and present, *machista* and adherent of *curanderismo*, *soldadera* and homemaker with rapidity.

Poniatowska tells us what she takes herself to be doing in a widely-cited essay written in the early 1980s. In a piece titled "Literature and Women in Latin America," she says:

> The voice of the oppressed in Latin America includes literature by women. I believe this so deeply that I'm willing to make it a leitmotif, a ritornello, an ideology.... The cause for

---

7 Jorgensen, Writing, 41.
8 Conor, Liz (2004), *The Spectacular Modern Woman: Feminine Visibility in the 1920s*. Bloomington: Indiana University Press, 3.

this literature is a painful and outrageous experience. We want to bear testimony of this here and now....[9]

A simple method of bearing testimony, especially in the case of someone like Jesusa, would have been for the author to write a literal transcription of her words, or to keep the editing down to such a minimum that what emerged was more-or-less chronological reporting. But although there are strokes of this in *Massacre in Mexico*, for example, Poniatowska has the capacity to do more.[10] *Jesusa!* is thus often categorized as a sort of novel, but something more than a novel: Castro-Klarén calls it a "cross between fieldwork and fiction...[it is] a collective autobiography."[11]

Why Poniatowska has taken this route is addressed at least partially by the nature of Mexican society itself. Although Spanish has a rich literary heritage, and although Mexico (along with Argentina) is one of the publishing giants of South and Central America, this literate tradition has had difficulty reaching the masses. Lourdes Arizpe has noted that "History has imposed a greater silence on peasant women than on any other social group."[12] Insofar as that silence is broken, it is likely to be broken within the mode of the oral tradition; Mexico contains millions of indigenous who do not even know Spanish, and millions more who can speak Spanish but are not literate in it.

Thus Poniatowska has created a world that mimics Mexico's oral tradition, and expands upon it. By weaving a narrative of disparate chronology, changes in identity, and moments of close to authorial interruption (one of which is the Introduction, placing *Jesusa!* in context), the author parallels Jesusa's storytelling without being so flat and unimaginative as to give us a literal transcription of it. If Poniatowska can now say, "Yo sí pertenezco," it is because she has become, like the dozens of women she has interviewed, a Mexican who sees the world through the eyes of Mexican history.[13] This is indeed what Jorgensen is writing about when she notes "The shifting relationship between narrator and protagonist...."[14]

Once again we have to look to Mexico's past to understand the peculiar role of the *mestiza* woman. She is herself one of the offspring of La Malinche and the *conquistadores*; she can be labeled an *hija de la chingada*. She is silent not only because she has never been given a voice, but at least partially out of shame. The violation that is at the core of Mexico and forms its roots is not a cause for celebration; it is that same violation that led Octavio Paz to title his work, in English,

---

9 Poniatowska, Elena (1997), "Literature and Women in Latin America," in Castro-Klarén, Sara, Sylvia Molloy, and Beatriz Sarlo (eds.), *Women's Writing in Latin America*, Boulder, CO: Westview Press, 81.

10 One of the most widely cited excerpts from this work in its English translation is, in fact, the piece reprinted in Castro-Klarén et al. (eds.), "Voices from Tlatelolco," 308–314. This particular excision contains much direct quoting from eyewitnesses to the government violence.

11 *Ibid.*, 80.

12 Arizpe, Lourdes, "Peasant Women and Silence." In Castro-Klarén et al. (eds.), *Writing*, 333–338.

13 A good translation of this phrase would be "I belong, too."

14 Jorgensen, *Writing*, 36.

The Labyrinth of Solitude. If the Mexican goes through life with a fatalistic feeling that death is close at hand and that life has little to offer him (which can be seen in the elaborate ceremonies of Mexico's Day of the Dead, one of the widely-observed such ceremonies), how much more shame devolves upon the woman, who is already a secondary creature at best. As Paz says, she is the descendant of a confluence of forces best described as "symbols of a secret conflict that we have still not resolved."[15]

More light is shed on this topic by still other work by Paz, including a little-known essay that served as the introduction to a compilation published in the 1950s titled *Anthology of Mexican Poetry*.[16] In this essay, written for an English-only audience at a time when the work of Mexican intellectuals was still comparatively unknown in the United States, Paz is at pains to describe how the history of the Mexican literary scene first paralleled that of Spain, and then took on a life of its own. This growth, of course, reflects the rising growth in power of the *mestizaje* and concomitant loss of power of the *criollos* or Spaniards. It is important to get clear on this trajectory for the simple reason that Poniatowska reflects an important move along its path, especially with the publication of *Jesusa!*. Looking back, Paz writes:

> The poetry of the Colonial period, like all derivative art, tends to exaggerate what it copies. In this tendency to go to extremes it is not difficult to detect a desire for singularity. But this exaggerated "Spanishness" was one way of expressing our diffidence in the presence of Spanish art, itself trenchant and given to excess.... The nascent literature of Mexico gained ground at times as a curb on "Spanishness", at others as an intensification of it. In either case it represented the diffidence of a national genius not yet venturing to be itself, oscillating between two extremes.[17]

Although Paz is specifically discussing poetry, his remarks could be applied to the Mexican intellectual world in general, and certainly have an overall applicability to Mexican writing. How does the "nascent literature" gain ground? The gain begins when the voices of the Spaniards are no longer heard in anything like their former degree of predominance. In post-war Mexico, Poniatowska is one of those who succeeded in making the crucial moves to enable a certain plateauing to take place.

Inscribed Bodies

In the works examined here, there is little that is overtly sexual in the way that we have come to expect of writing that might fall under the *écriture* category. But because the "Other" on the colonial view simply is the body, there is a sense in which (as was the case for Bambara) an *écriture* in the standard sense is unnecessary and even superfluous.

The marks of colonization are all over Jesusa's life: her body, her habitations, her food and her very mode of being. In physical appearance she is darker than

---

15 Paz, *Labyrinth*, 86–87.

16 Paz, Octavio (ed.) (1958), *Anthology of Mexican Poetry*, trans. Samuel Beckett, Bloomington: Indiana University Press.

17 Paz, Octavio, "Introduction to the History of Mexican Poetry," in Paz (ed.), *Anthology*, 23–44.

Europeans, which already makes her an "Other" on the colonial scene (although like many of mixed ancestry, she is careful to distinguish herself from the Indians). The violence of her life is a direct result not only of her overt poverty, but of the hyperrealized violent times through which she lived—times when the very group of individuals to whom she belonged decided to take what they had come to believe was rightfully theirs.

Jesusa is first abused by her father, and to some extent by a variety of "stepmothers" over whose choosing she has little or no say. Although some provide a sort of nurturing, substantial care is not experienced by Jesusa during her childhood or teenage years. Most markedly, she has the misfortune to suffer abuse at the hands of numerous lovers and would-be lovers, whose approach almost always has nothing to do with any behavior that is not an attempt at forced sex.

The general degradation of the *mestizaje*—expressed by themselves toward each other—is signaled in the following passage, where the horrors of war are brought home to Jesusa, in a fashion to become all too familiar in the twentieth century:

> [T]he Villistas had blown up a passenger train between Conchos and Chihuahua and killed all the guards. They made mincemeat of everyone. They were all civilians escorted by a few military men, and when someone yelled: "Down with the Carrancistas!" the Villistas wiped them out. Women, men, children, all naked with their eyes open so that the vultures could pick them out easier.[18]

The in-the-bodiness of these non-European individuals is signaled throughout the text (in the Introduction, Jesusa/Josefina tells Poniatowska that "It's obvious that you're high-class and useless"[19]), but contrasts readily with the life depicted for Quiela/Angelina in *Dear Diego*. There the "savage" is Diego himself; an indigenous exotic in France, Diego can never, in a sense, be more than an alluring attraction for French women. Angelina, however, is a European, albeit a displaced one. Poniatowska's Quiela writes toward the end, as she remembers the beginning of their affair:

> I met you at La Rotonde, Diego, and it was love at first sight. I was interested in you the minute I saw you enter, so tall, with your wide-brimmed hat, your fiery eyes and friendly smile. I heard Zadkin say, "Here comes the Mexican cowboy," and some others chimed in, "Voila l'exotique."[20]

Angelina's love is romanticized, idealized—even when it involves the body, it is beyond the body ("I see my swollen belly you lingered over dotingly"[21]) and hence not the sort of thing that the vultures will ever go after.

Writing about general colonial attitudes, Trinh Minh-ha has articulated the notion that the indigenous, or whatever passes for the indigenous in a given set of cultural tropes, must be kept from the persons who would be contaminated by their presence. Speaking more specifically, this sort of maneuver varies from region to region. In

---

18 Poniatowska, *Jesusa!*, 126.
19 *Ibid.*, x.
20 *Ibid.*, 28.
21 *Ibid.*, 75–76.

South Africa it took the form of overt apartheid; in other places and times, it is spelled out differently. But the idea is that there are those who are purer, those who are less pure, and finally a class who are irredeemably impure. In pre-Revolutionary Mexico—and certainly in Jesusa's early years—the *mestiza* was one whose presence would have been avoided by the upper classes. As Minh-ha writes, "With a kind of perverted logic, they work toward your erasure while urging you to keep your way of life and ethnic values *within the borders of your homelands*."[22] [Emphasis in original.] The point of the Revolution was to move beyond the "homelands": Mexicans wanted a way in their own nation. Jesusa represents this spirit; it is the same spirit, when convoluted, that allows Quiela to focus lovingly on Diego's foreignness. However successful a painter he may have been in Paris, he was not even a Spaniard.

There is a certain aspect to Mexican culture that yields notions of the "bi-" variety, even within the culture. These notions need not be taken in a limited, pedestrian way, as is so often done when speaking, for example, of bilinguals (although Mexico has many more Spanish-indigenous bilinguals than some would believe). What is inscribed in Mexican culture—and on the bodies of the *mestizaje*—is the biracial, bicultural mix that their nation has produced, one that is also manifest in social class distinctions. Some of the best known Mexican writing of the twentieth century, no matter how celebrated, is still lacking when it comes to an authoritative voice with respect to this particular mix. Vasconcelos, for example, who formulated the concept of the "*raza cósmica*" and was responsible for the massive output of mural paintings in post-Revolutionary Mexico, was not as much a champion of the indigenous, or even the persons of mixed ancestry, as might be thought. He retained a great and undaunted admiration for European culture, and some of his theorizing about Mexico's future sounds a bit forced.

Poniatowska, on the other hand, is truly bilingual. That is to say that despite her privileged upbringing, she has become comfortable among the downtrodden, and can translate at ease. And although Jesusa herself is not precisely "bi-" in the sense that she has a comfortable familiarity with Mexico's ruling group, she is at least aware of their leanings, and Poniatowska manages to display this in her writing. The importance of these notions of a sort of two-foldness within the depiction of a culture is articulated smoothly in a recent work by Doris Sommer, who has written at length on the multicultural. In *Bilingual Aesthetics*, she writes:

> Bilinguals can get caught between bad fits of thrilling and risky borders.... Arguments for the social and psychological advantages of fluent—as opposed to limited—bilingualism underestimate, I believe, the added value of even faulty familiarity with an added language.[23]

Although in this particular passage Sommer is referring to actual bilingualism—mastery of two languages, as opposed to the metaphorical constructions that might

---

22 Minh-ha, Trinh T., "Writing Postcoloniality and Feminism," in Ashcroft et al. (eds.), *Post-colonial*, 264–268.

23 Sommer, Doris (2004), *Bilingual Aesthetics*, Durham, NC: Duke University Press, 41.

be placed on the term—her point is applicable to the range of "bi-" constructions that are now part of cultural analysis. Displacement between works such as *Diego* and *Jesusa!*, for example, shows a bimodal familiarity on the part of Poniatowska with the world of European privilege (even if a touch Mexicanized) and the world of the *mestiza*. In Quiela's world, it is Diego's body that is inscribed, even though, as a male, Diego plays the dominant role, and one that clearly leaves Quiela reeling. In Jesusa's world, she has the marked body—and her body becomes, in postmodern parlance, the site of contested realities (and given the violence of what she endures, this usage is more than metaphorical). Poniatowska is equally adept at depicting both worlds, and both worlds are part of contemporary Mexico. Sommer herself alludes to Poniatowska as one who "learned Spanish from the maids and envied their authentic Mexicanness."[24] It seems that both the author and her characters have become bilingual, and in that sense they all enjoy risks.

Poniatowska's risk-taking lends itself to multiple lines of analysis, and for this reason her work has been cited in a number of contexts. Her European background alone seems to propel much of the commentary toward a contemporary Continental slant.

Post Notes

In part of the essay normally translated with the title "What is Literature?," Sartre tries to make a distinction between the type of literature that does not rely on signs alone—that might be thought to have a greater resemblance to the visual arts (poetry, for example)—and that other sort of literature with which he, as a philosopher, is ultimately concerned. As he says at the opening of Cazeaux's excision from the essay:

> But today it's the thing to 'talk painting' in the jargon of the musician or literary man and to 'talk literature' in the jargon of the painter. As if at bottom there were only one art which expressed itself indifferently in one or the other of these languages, like the Spinozistic substance which is adequately reflected by each of its attributes.[25]

What Sartre specifically wants to inveigh against here, other than for exceptional cases, is the notion that one can "talk literature" in the jargon of the painter. As he later goes on to say, "The writer can guide you and, if he describes a hovel, make it seem the symbol of social injustice and provoke your indignation."[26]

In a sense, Poniatowska's writing is precisely that sort of "committed writing" that pushed Sartre into his analysis in the first place. (One of the opening questions had been whether there could be "committed painting" or "committed sculpture.") But although there is no doubt that part of what Sartre wants to get across here is ensconced in Poniatowska's work, it is not nearly so simple as that.

---

24 *Ibid.*, 42.
25 Sartre, Jean-Paul, "What is Writing?," in Cazeaux (ed.), 102–116.
26 *Ibid.*, 103.

Elena Poniatowska commits herself first in the reportorial sense (in her early work for *Excelsior*, and in the work on the Tlatelolco massacre) and then goes on to develop the semi-fictionalized work from it. But the semi-fictionalized work is not merely committed; in a sense, it would have been easier to make up a novel out of the whole cloth, provide it with fictional Jesusas, and get on with the job. What makes her work so remarkable is that it is a weave of the reportorial and the fictional, and that it is done so skillfully that there are very few obvious points of digression. Jesusa (Josefina Bórquez) said some words into a tape recorder; Poniatowska took them down. In between tapings, she tried to help Jesusa feed her animals, showed herself (on multiple occasions, apparently) to be a "useless" rich girl, and listened to Jesusa talk about her past lives. But the result is indeed a *mélange*, and it is this aspect of the work that leads more than one of her critics to focus on Bakhtinian dialogism.

Why should the writer be "committed," if this is indeed a worthy goal for authors in general? Poniatowska is a writer with first-world, European connections, living and working in what is still a developing country. She has multiple options. There is absolutely no reason for an individual from her social class to take an interest in the lives of the poor, and yet she has done so. (Today, for example, she writes for the left-wing paper *La Jornada*.)

She has made her commitment in the name of humanity, and, as she specifically says, in the name of women. That this is difficult to do within the framework of writing as constructed in a "developing" nation is manifest in much of the feminist criticism on this and related topics. Gayatri Spivak has written:

> It seems particularly unfortunate [that] the emergent perspective of feminist criticism reproduces the axioms of imperialism. A basically isolationist admiration for the literature of the female subject in Europe and Anglo-America establishes the high feminist norm. It is supported and operated by an information-retrieval approach to 'Third World' literature which often employs a deliberately 'nontheoretical' methodology with self-conscious rectitude.[27]

But what is the woman author of color herself to do about these matters? Why is the "basically isolationist" admiration so often supported by individuals in the very cultures and nations in question?

Part of the answer has to be that so often women from the upper classes—who obviously would constitute the overwhelming majority of those in a position to write in "colonial" areas—continue to identify with Eurocentric norms, even if this is not done so on a conscious level. Indeed, identification with such norms is often a path toward social mobility in previously colonized areas. Poniatowska herself may have started out in such a way—the young reporter in the well-dressed corridors and offices of *Excelsior* might not have taken an interest in any story similar to those that she later chose. But there frequently is a break-through moment; an epiphany, perhaps. In Poniatowska's case we cannot cite one single example, but as Doris Sommer seems to imply, some of Poniatowska's literal "bilingualism" (French/

---

[27] Chakravorty Spivak, Gayatri, "Three Women's Texts and a Critique of Imperialism," in Ashcroft et al. (eds.), *Post-colonial*, 269–272.

Spanish) and some of her sensation of "otherness" (European or more-European woman in the *mestiza* world) may have propelled her toward examining the others in her own society.

In a chapter in her work called "Irritate the State," Sommer claims that "Provocation describes an inside-outside maneuverability (or aesthetics) between particularism and universalism, slaps and embraces, which uncouple culture from politics so that they can interact in restless dynamic ways."[28] It is difficult to say whether Poniatowska was provoked or the provoker, but it may very well be the case that this scenario probably starts with a provocation felt by the author. Listening to the maids speak Spanish may well have impressed a sensitive child with the disparity of the upstairs/downstairs dichotomy in a wealthy home. Being a woman reporter in a nation where it was virtually unheard of for women to work outside the home (especially women of her social class) no doubt also helped. Whatever the causal relationships, there is no question that Poniatowska finally became herself a committed writer, and in that sense Sartre's comments about commitment, writing and the arts are more than relevant (and can be contrasted with Cixous' earlier remarks about painting and writing).

The pull in Poniatowska's life and work is perhaps best exemplified, as mentioned earlier, by the disparity between the voice of *Dear Diego* and the voice of *Jesusa!*. Angelina Beloff is a woman entranced by the exotic—exemplified by the "sauvage" Diego in France—but she is not herself an exotic. Jesusa is precisely the sort of woman who would fall into that category for a European. (One thinks, for example, of Gauguin's well-known predilection for young Polynesian girls as companions after he moved to Tahiti and then the Marquesas.)

Poniatowska is doing what Sommer describes—she is, in a sense, code-switching. Not just simply in the literal mode, between languages (although that does happen in *Dear Diego*), but between class contexts. In a society such as Mexico, this is an extremely important move. In the following passage, Sommer is writing of the challenges for a legal system, and for a state, of multiculturalism. But in a sense, it is parallel to the social challenges in general, and as Sommer also says, the bilingual, the bicultural and the biracial "punctuate the democratic signs of cultural difference."[29]

> So it is thanks to the multiplicity of national cultures within one polity that (cultural) affiliation can be distinguished from (constitutional) law. The two codes of belonging are often parallel and mutually interfering. It is time we envision them as codependent....[30]

In order for there to be a Euro- and moneyed class in Mexico, the classes beneath this group must be demarcated, and in any society it seems to be helpful as a demarcator if the lower socioeconomic groups come coded in differing skin pigments. In Mexico, largely devoid of individuals of African ancestry (except for some coastal regions) the skin pigmentation problem is neatly solved by the Indian and mixed groups, who are overwhelmingly substantially darker than the Spanish-ancestored class. This particular situation is the class concomitant of the situation

---

28 Sommer, *Bilingual*, 85. The chapter in question is 71–114.
29 *Ibid.*, 73.
30 *Ibid.*, 83.

described by Sommer above. Interestingly, she later cites Vasconcelos on the formation of the *mestizaje*, since Mexico features so predominantly in Latin America as a whole.[31] Poniatowska is not content, however, with a simple investigation into various lives. Her in-depth look at Jesusa also opens up epistemological issues.

Yo Sé y lo Conozco

Jesusa's particular ontology is a strong enough construction that it affords her not only a glimpse of the eternal, as she herself believes, but a glimpse of how to get there, so to speak. She is completely unimpressed with formal learning, and indeed seems to hold it against her husband (along with his propensity for abuse) that he liked to read books in the evening, no doubt a somewhat unusual activity for a 1920 Revolutionary.

Jesusa is determined to hold onto the notion that she has special access into a spiritual world, and, more importantly, manifestations of this attitude show up in her even during her early years (before she joined the *Obra*). If life in the corn-growing Mexican countryside seems to demand a certain naturalistic bent—and a strong empiricism—much of Jesusa's interior life does not run along these paths. The belief in spirits, the certainty that there is another realm beyond that accessible to the five senses, the force of the syncretistic Catholicism around her—all of these catalysts reinforce her notion that she can know a great deal that is not available through sensory stimuli. Part of Poniatowska's gift as an author is to make this special mode accessible to the reader, and it shows up on a regular basis in Jesusa's memory world, not only in her recounting of her childhood, but also in her telling of her adult experiences.

The special insight that Jesusa takes herself to possess is a frequent feature of the Indian-derived Mexican culture, and it is something that, although somewhat foreign to Poniatowska, is appreciated by her. As she writes in the Introduction with respect to Jesusa's ultimate commitment to the *Obra*:

> Their [members of the *Obra*] cultural roots have been disturbed by the television and the radio, and for them, spiritualism is more satisfying than Catholicism: the emotions are stronger, and they are treated like "people." Spiritualism makes men and women feel like they are chosen by God from among all the whirling souls on Earth.[32]

Poniatowska, as a sympathetic observer, can see the force behind Jesusa's beliefs. But there are a number of ways of articulating the ontological, epistemic and even ethical and aesthetic commitments that run through variations on the theme of the *mestizaje* throughout Mexican culture. A more naturalized account of knowing is also available, and one would have to contend that this sort of account—foregrounded, for example, by Lourdes Arizpe—is one that drives life in the countryside on a daily basis. It is a remarkable facet of Jesusa's testimony that she seems, to some extent, to have participated in both. Because so much of her story revolves around the fighting of the Revolution, she has comparatively little to say about the growing of crops,

---

31 *Ibid.*, 99.
32 Poniatowska, "Introduction," *Jesusa!*, xxviii.

the harvesting of corn, and so forth. But it is intriguing that she regards her various "stepmothers'" tellings of these things as a form of genuine parenting, and even in her tiny apartment in Mexico City at the end of her life she exhibits a concern for her animals. With respect to daily life in the countryside, Arizpe has written:

> It is not that they [peasant women] have not spoken, only that their words have not been recognized. Because their words are discomforting when they denounce exploitation; disturbing when they display a deep understanding of the world not shared by their city sisters;...and because, being women's words, they are not important to androcentric history.... Within the wide range of integrating philosophies of the peasants, "being" is not restricted to humans. Each element derives its existence from its relationship to the whole.[33]

Here, in Arizpe's characterization, we find the tie-in between a naturalized epistemology that might be thought to be representative of peasant life on the whole, especially for women, and the kind of unusual cosmology that the indigenous-flavored views gives rise to. The corn is not only a crop to be harvested; because it is traditionally one of the great sustainers of life for those in the countryside, spirits may be associated with it, it may need to be placated, or some other special set of circumstances may surround it. The original syncretism of Juan Diego's seeing of the Virgen at the site of Tonantzín becomes more comprehensible; the effect of the vision of the Virgin was simply to integrate the importance of corn with other sorts of worship.

This strain is, of course, somewhat gynocentric, but the importance of this type of thinking for traditional and indigenous cultures has never been denied. Indeed, it has a great deal to do with why it is that, globally, cultures that precede early settled agriculture are almost uniformly driven by respect for the feminine principle, and the artifacts of these cultures typically exhibit a great deal of recognition of this fact. Cycles are important to those who grow food, and the female cycle merely recapitulates a great deal of what is to be found in nature in other forms.

This strain of advertence to the natural and naturalization is what drives a great deal of contemporary feminist epistemology, and in that sense this part of the set of beliefs and attitudes that Poniatowska attempts to set out in *Jesusa!* is indeed a sort of feminist epistemology. A number of lines of argument can be adduced here: contemporary naturalized epistemology has a decidedly empiricist flavor, with allusion being made both to individual knowers qua epistemic agents and to collectivities. Although, again, Jesusa herself says little about village life insofar as actual farming and ranching are concerned, she would have had to have known about these activities because of her childhood. The village woman—the indigenous woman or *mestiza* of central and southern Mexico—is a cognizer who uses the five senses to find her way, literally, around a maze of obstacles everyday. Where is the water? How is it possible to prepare the corn if the *metate* has been damaged? Who is currently caring for the animals? Although the constructed ontology that we have referred to previously may possibly be of some help, it is most likely that

---

33 Arizpe, Lourdes, "Peasant Women and Silence," in Castro-Klarén et al. (eds.), *Women's Writing in Latin America*, 334, 338.

the epistemic takes on these sorts of activities by the women in question will be empiricist, and they seem to fall under the rubric of the collective knowledge that so many contemporary feminist epistemologists have alluded to.[34]

Kathleen Lennon and Margaret Whitford, in the Introduction to their *Knowing the Difference: Feminist Perspectives in Epistemology*, make the following set of assertions:

> Feminism's most compelling epistemological insight lies in the connections it has made between knowledge and power. This, not simply in the obvious sense that access to knowledge enables empowerment; but more controversially through the recognition that legitimation of knowledge claims is intimately tied to networks of domination and exclusion.[35]

Here we have a thesis that propels much of what Poniatowska does. The lives of women like Jesusa are routinely devalued not simply because they are women, brown and poverty-stricken, but also because any knowledge that they might be deemed to possess is routinely devalued. Herbal remedies? These are simply a part of folk wisdom. Knowledge of soil conditions and when to plant? Of possible interest, but such areas might better be investigated by a trained agronomist. Skill in birthing a foal or calf? Of use only on the farm, and not anything worthy of being part of a written record.

As Poniatowska says, it is no wonder that Jesusa and thousands like her are drawn to *Obra Espiritual*, fundamentalist Catholicism, *curanderismo* or some similar sort of movement: "they are treated like 'people.'"[36] And part of what is constitutive of the recognition of another human being's worth as a person—her or his personhood—is the recognition that the individual knows something, can make her or his way in the world, and has something to offer as a citizen. Indeed, many of the current tortured debates about the status of "persons," some of which are directly tied to the abortion debate, have at their core a denial of personhood to those who cannot make their way. But Jesusa is not one of those, and neither are her fellow *indias* and *mestizas*. It is simply the case that what they do, what they know, and who they are has never been recognized by the power structure. Poniatowska's work had the effect of bringing this to light.

La Futura

Jorgensen and other critics are impressed by the degree to which Poniatowska, by manipulating voices, has managed to achieve a mode of communication for the

---

34 So many citations can be made to this work that, for purposes of what we do here, we will confine ourselves to one. An important work in contemporary feminist epistemology with a naturalist bent is Nelson, Lynn Hankinson (1991), *Who Knows: From Quine to a Feminist Empiricism*, Philadelphia, PA: Temple University Press.

35 Lennon, Kathleen and Margaret Whitford, (1994), *Introduction to Knowing the Difference: Feminist Perspectives in Epistemology*, eds. Lennon and Whitford, New York: Routledge.

36 Poniatowska, *Jesusa!*, xxviii.

oppressed. It is, after all, remarkable that this woman who ordinarily would not have had contact with someone like Jesusa managed to tell her story. Citing Poniatowska's reading of Simone Weil, Jorgensen writes:

> Clearly, in spite of her admiration for Weil's philosophy of solidarity, Elena Poniatowska has made a different set of choices. Rather than abandon one world for another, Poniatowska lives between worlds, struggling to keep her balance between her witness to injustice and her own comfortable level of existence.[37]

But however praiseworthy Poniatowska's efforts, there is always the difficulty that the plain insertion of herself into the text wreaks havoc with the notion that a work such as *Jesusa!* is a testimonial. Indeed, part of Jorgensen's point is that it is not a testimonial in the standard sense—and that Poniatowska herself has been explicit about this.[38] Feminist critics of the notion that some sort of "essentializing" is going on in this type of writing have been very straightforward, however, about the deleterious effects. As Susan Strickland has written, "It is not the case that all we have to do is declare our limitedness and situatedness and leave space for others to offer their own equally limited and situated perspectives—I have my (white western middle-class, etc.) view of the world and you have yours."[39]

If privileged women who identify with the Eurocentric point of view are to make a difference in their writing, they must actually allow other voices to be heard, or so the argument goes. The point is that all too often the use of the other's voice falls into a pattern of co-optation, or of encapsulating what the other has to say in one's own point of view. There is no question that one might argue that Poniatowska is guilty of this—as Jorgensen says, the amount of change and alteration to what we can presume Josefina Bórquez to have said is presumably great; toward the end, Poniatowska did not even use a recorder or take notes in her informant's presence, because Bórquez objected to both as too intrusive. So, philosophical feminism can argue, what is the value of an enterprise such as the one that we find in *Here's to You, Jesusa!*?

Strickland herself may give part of the answer toward the end of her own essay. As has been contended by many, if we allow the notion of "difference" to do too much work, we cannot articulate any genuine sort of feminism—if the concept of global feminism means anything, presumably it has something to do with the difficulties of women all over the world. Focus on difference often has the palliative effect of keeping a genuine political stance from developing—if we focus too much, for example, on the cultural differences between a life such as Jesusa's and the life of a woman in Morocco or in the working-class south of the United States, we lose any impact, globally, that might be felt by creating alliances and forming views. Thus Strickland recommends that rather than conceptualizing these different strands as parts of a "conversation," we admit what is plainly the case: attempting to come to

---

37 Jorgensen, *Writing*, 57.
38 *Ibid.*, 50–53.
39 Strickland, Susan (1994), "Feminism, Postmodernism and Difference," in Lennon and Whitford (eds.), *Knowing the Difference*, 265–274.

grips with difference is painful, and may be far from pleasant. She closes her essay by stating:

> The process I have in mind is generally far more uncomfortable, a product of conflict and tension, more like an argument where you go away angry and hurt and defensive of your own point of view, but can't forget theirs, which you keep mulling over and in the process, gradually altering your own point of view, so that at the next encounter, it has changed in interaction with theirs and so on.[40]

Although Poniatowska's *Jesusa!* is admittedly not the type of conceptual or argumentative piece that Strickland has in mind (she is, after all, taking a directly philosophical stance), much of what she says can be placed against Jorgensen's analysis for aid and succor.

The Once and For All Telling

How any sort of politicized voice is articulated is now—and will certainly become—one of the key questions for literature as we move through the twenty-first century. The fact that writers overwhelmingly come from privileged classes in the developing nations (and, to some extent, even in the industrialized countries) means that they often have more difficulty in identifying with the subjects of their discourse than might ideally be desired.

But the fact remains that, on an overall analysis, it seems crucial that the stories of the dispossessed be told, even if we are not always happy with the telling. Poniatowska's work stands by itself, at least within the Mexican tradition, in that the split between her background and the backgrounds of her informants is even greater than might be the case with some other Mexican authors (few, for example, would have spent their early years in Europe), but her reach is also greater. She has moved much further into the lives of those whose stories she is telling than most writers who have essayed work in the same general direction.

We get a sense of the distinction between Poniatowska and even others well-known on the literary scene when we examine the interviews she gave to Esteban Ascencio. She said at one point, for example, "Tengo un gran entusiasmo for el movimiento de los zapitistas.... Los Zapatistas han creado una nueva imagen moral, un ejemplo moral."[41] That she would identify with this somewhat problematized radical movement speaks volumes, since it is essentially a movement among the indigenous, and has its origins in one of Mexico's poorest states, Chiapas. But this is all in keeping with the Poniatowska of *Jesusa!*, who managed to find a way to convey the *soldadera*'s sense of being at the bottom of society at the very time that she felt compelled to work for the cause of social justice.

---

40 *Ibid.*, p. 271.
41 Ascencio, *Dijo*, 57. Poniatowska says: "I have a lot of enthusiasm for the Zapatista movement, and for the struggle that they began.... The Zapatistas have created a new moral imagination, a new moral example."

In his postcolonial essay "Columbus and the Cannibals," already cited here, Peter Hulme makes the point that no record of the encounters of the Europeans with the New World can be taken at face value. As he says with respect to the journals of Columbus' voyage,

> To write about the text we call 'el diario de Colón'...is to take a leap of faith.... It would be perverse and unhelpful to presume that no such relationship exists [a relationship of some correspondence between the text and the actual voyages themselves], but credulous and unthinking to speak—a some have done—of the *Journal*'s 'frank words, genuine and unadorned.' Circumspection would certainly seem called for.[42]

Hulme's comments cut both ways with respect to work like Poniatowska's, but there is no question that his overall point is well-taken. We can posit a much greater correspondence between Poniatowska's *Jesusa!* and the set of events it purports or alleges to describe than much of the "Columbus" journals and their concomitant situations, simply because of the time period, modes of transcription, modernization of belief sets, and so forth. But just as the Columbus manuscripts can easily be problematized, so too can the type of fictionalizing in which Poniatowska engages, and this is precisely what Jorgensen, for one, has done.

The bottom line is that, unless the subaltern herself or himself is actually the author, there is inevitably a distancing and an "Othering" that takes place in the work. But the strong counterargument here is that without the reportorial work of someone like Poniatowska, little will be written that will speak to these issues.

---

42 *Ibid.*, 28.

PART IV
Closings

Chapter Twelve

Wrapping it Up

The ancient battle between the poets and the philosophers can never fully be resolved. Two different ways of approaching matters through literary output are involved, and these two different approaches are to some extent immiscible. If the one approach may be said to rely on argument, the other relies largely on the imagination. Arguments can be imaginative, and flights of fantasy can occasionally involve argument, but the straightforward approach of philosophy, especially in the Western tradition, is to some extent simply not consonant with matters literary. Part of our argument here has been that some authors are more philosophical than others, and that when these authors are women any explication of the work is made more complex.

What counts as philosophy also, itself, varies from period to period, not to say from culture to culture. The recent influx of feminist theory and several approaches that are at base Continental into the American philosophical scene means that an analysis of any one of the five authors we have chosen is now significantly different than it would have been at an earlier point in time. Although ontological themes are clearly present in Woolf's work, for example, only in the past thirty years or so has there been a great enough development in feminism for the philosophical approach to matters concerning gender to receive a full articulation.

In the Introduction to his anthology *Rhetoric and Philosophy*, Richard Cherwitz writes:

> Discerning the rhetorical forces at work in all varieties of conduct and inquiry underscores the habitual problem of locating certainties as a basis for action, and reminds us of the virtues of tolerance.[1]

This statement is particularly apt in a project like ours, since different genres of literature—the novel, the essay, the short story—lend themselves to different sorts of tasks, and since the employment of rhetoric within any given genre is itself reliant on other factors. In examining the work of Margaret Drabble, Virginia Woolf, Simone de Beauvoir, Toni Cade Bambara and Elena Poniatowska, the rhetorical forces employed rely not only on the genre, but on time, place and language, and on sociocultural forces that, in some instances, are scarcely susceptible of articulation.

If the New Historicism, as employed by Greenblatt and others, allows us to examine, for instance, *Measure for Measure* as a work much influenced by the recent accession of James I to the throne, any sort of contextualized view will allow us to look at *The Ice Age*, *The Voyage Out*, *The Woman Destroyed*, *Gorilla, My Love*, and *Jesusa!* in a similar sort of way. When we examine these works in context, and with

---

1   Cherwitz, *Rhetoric*, 3.

an eye toward themes that address ethics, ontology, or even epistemology, the works appear to us in a new way, and we are able to make full use of reader response. One might argue that this is what has always been done with literature, but previous rounds of criticism—especially with respect to Woolf and Beauvoir—indicate that not all readings are on a par with each other.

In an essay titled "English romanticism, American romanticism: What's the Difference?", J. Hillis Miller has argued that the main difference between these two modes of expression lies in the reading. In other words, it is what we find in the work that gives rise to some of the most prominent categorizations. As he says:

> The notion of an American difference in poetry or criticism is an example of the fallacy of misplaced concreteness. It is at once too general and too specific. It ascribes a unity and a reified existence to an entity (American romanticism) which is a fictitious creation of the critic, made by ignoring all sorts of differences from one text to the other.[2]

The same could be said of the notion of a "philosophical" novel. Because of the diversity of authors examined here, there is no question that, insofar as articulation of philosophical points is concerned, it could well be said that what has been created is a "reified entity." But then again, this speaks to the very point that Miller is ultimately making. Americanism—that spirit that pervades Whitman and Twain, for example, as opposed to Wordsworth and Dickens—is where one finds it. As Miller also claims, "The interpreter too is as much inextricably woven into…context as is the writer."[3]

Philosophy in a literary work is where one finds it. The differences between Virginia Woolf, Toni Cade Bambara and Elena Poniatowska are so great that one hardly knows where to begin—but there is a similarity, too. Each writer grapples with a set of themes and then, rather than backing off from addressing fundamental human questions, addresses them in a form that we can recognize as philosophical without a struggle. This not only sets these writers apart from the authors of much contemporary popular fiction, but it also sets them apart from other canonized authors of their period and place, in many instances.

Questions that have been deemed to be perennial are often those that are thought to be philosophical—we recognize immediately, of course, those that involve the profundities of human existence and how we came to be on this planet, but now, more latterly, we also recognize questions having to do with the social constructions of race, class and gender. The interplay between these various areas itself creates new philosophical questions and puzzles. For Bambara and Poniatowska, the perennial matters are cast in terms of women working within cultures of racial hierarchy; Bambara's black women function in a white society, and Poniatowska's *mestiza* protagonist is set up against the Euro-dominated class structure of Mexico as a nation. Timeless political questions about the nature of the just society take on a greater degree of poignancy for these authors, for their protagonists are very likely to find themselves at the bottom of any society.

---

2   Miller, *Theory*, 223.
3   *Ibid., ibid.*

The standard Eurocentric overview found in Drabble, Woolf and Beauvoir allows these authors to work with philosophical material in a more straightforwardly recognizable way. Because they may be thought to adhere more directly to the tenets of a tradition, it is easier (or at least seems to be easier) to pick out the relevant philosophical themes and to delineate their articulation within the work. Drabble's postmodern twists play against the tradition of the British novel, and Woolf writes almost completely within the framework of that tradition. Although Beauvoir's work is groundbreaking in the French realm, she adverts to a great deal of French cultural material in the course of her novel.

If we can discern the outlines of the traditional questions in the writings of these various authors, it also may be said that the responses vary from culture to culture, and from woman to woman. We began our inquiry with a dual set of questions: one set revolved around the conundrum of literature versus philosophy, and the second revolved around the notion of what, if anything, women would have to offer that would differ significantly from that of male authors, even if we could accept at face value a philosophical approach to literature.

It will strike many as being irretrievably essentialist to attempt to articulate an intersection for the work of five women from such disparate backgrounds. But it has also been asked—in a variety of contexts—why we are so quick to assume that something is wrong with essentialism. Here the old problem about formulating a voice to address oppression immediately rears its head: as has been argued in many places, and as we have said here, we cannot begin to address the global condition of women unless we assume at least some areas of commonality. We can begin with the easy intersection—we can probably find more areas of commonality between, for example, Bambara and Poniatowska, simply because circumstances force them to identify as women of color. (Some commentators have mistakenly thought that Poniatowska is a person of completely European ancestry; in fact, she is half Mexican.) It is obvious that we can find an intersection between Drabble and Woolf—in fact, Drabble may appear to some to be a descendant of Woolf. Perhaps the bridge between these two sets of authors is Simone de Beauvoir.

But in any case we need to address once more, in closing, the questions regarding women, philosophy and literature. To fail to do so is to fail to articulate a response to the original problem.

Women Again

A striking fact about the works of the authors we have examined here is that, in most cases, there is an implicit acceptance in the text of woman's secondary lot, and an implicit attempt to address questions that might arise from the recognition of it. Thus, although we have wanted to begin our analysis of each author with an overview of points that might be thought to be ontological—since, after all, such issues are quintessentially philosophical—issues having to do with feminism force themselves upon us as readers more quickly than one might have thought.

Bambara is perhaps the most striking case in point; many more politically motivated readings of black authors tend to foreground race over gender. As Butler-

Evans noted, Bambara weaves back and forth here, but there is no question that many of the issues most keenly felt by Velma are at bottom feminist issues. To take as our primary case the one author whose works might be deemed by many (at least initially) to be the least relevant to issues of gender helps to foreground the main line of argument.

As a black woman, Velma has had to carry the burden of race in a personal way—caring for the victims of race, so to speak—more than any male she knows. This is why she finds it difficult to take the men around her seriously. And this is why Bambara makes it clear in the text that a sort of knowing stems from Velma's encounter with the realities of her everyday life.

Feminist criticism—which has really come to the fore only in the last thirty years or so—is simply one of the modes of criticism available to us, but one that does help in answering our question "Why women?". If we have developed lines of criticism, ranging from Northrop Frye of the 1940s, to contemporary Marxist and poststructuralist criticism, then we can find room for feminist criticism as well. And it does not seem too naïve to state that feminist criticism has taken on the life that it has because it fulfills a great need for the reader. Of the range of criticism available to us in contemporary terms, J. Hillis Miller has written:

> [T]he range of viable alternatives in literary methodology has become bafflingly large. Il faut choisir. Along with the still powerful New Criticism, archetypal criticism, and positivistic literary history, there is…a new semiotic formalism…. There is a structuralist criticism derived from structural linguistics and structural anthropology.[4]

In this lengthy litany (which is only partially quoted here), Miller goes on and on. Oddly, he does not mention feminist criticism, but then he may either think that it has been subsumed under another mode, or he may be taking it for granted. In any case, feminist criticism, like all of the modes cited above, employs a new way of seeing. And that way of seeing foregrounds women's views and women's presence.

Thus philosophical questions can be recast in feminist terms. We are now, in most cases, completely comfortable with this recasting, and we can engage most philosophers in these terms—this, in fact, is the *raison d'être* of such lines of publication as the Pennsylvania State University Press series *Re-Reading the Canon*.

So a take on the intersection of philosophy and literature that valorizes the feminist is not only necessary, but one that would leave most feeling completely comfortable. Having said so much, however, there remains the question of how all of this intersects with the choice to read women authors in the endeavor to pinpoint interstices between philosophy and literature. It is too simplistic to think that the reading of a woman author will automatically yield a feminist construal of the question at hand. Indeed, we have seen that both Drabble and Woolf might be said to be a great deal more concerned (insofar as one can read them philosophically) with ontological questions or questions that can be cast in standard philosophical terms. So a careful reading of the author in question is demanded, and in some cases the reading will be less overtly feminist than might initially have been guessed.

---

4   Miller, *Theory*, 174.

Miller takes the trouble in the essay cited above to list a number of sorts of criticism for the obvious reason that authors as canonical as Shakespeare and Wordsworth can be read completely differently under different guises. (Indeed, Miller spends a great deal of time on Wordsworth in this particular essay.)[5] What we need to do, in order to get a clear picture of the importance of feminist criticism, is to oppose it to some other currently available method of criticism, and come to grips with the differences. We do not need to do this at length—a thought experiment will do. Stephen Greenblatt, for example, might help us with portions of *Hamlet* by reminding us of the notion of a king's progress during Tudor times. This might assist us in making sense of the concept that a king may "go a progress through a beggar." But a feminist reading might be a great deal more helpful for characters such as Ophelia or Gertrude, or in other aspects of the play.

In writing on a similar set of issues, Lilian Alweiss has recently noted:

> When it comes to questions of ethics we reach the limits of philosophy. Philosophy can do little to determine how we should conduct our lives. Guidelines, strategies or principles never seem to be sensitive to the specificity of our human predicament. Whereas philosophy seeks to establish objective truths, moral issues seem particular, subjective, context dependent and not open to generalizations.[6]

Part of Alweiss' larger argument is that literature has a special role to play, and that literature can do for us things that philosophy cannot. But if this is accurate, then surely one of the sorts of "specificities" to which we would like to be sensitive—and to which philosophy has failed to be sensitive in the past—in that of women's lives. If literature can assist us, and if literature in general has something to offer that philosophy does not, literature by women may (although certainly not in all cases) shed light on these complexities and particularities, and point us in new directions.

Last, but by no means least, all of the foregoing can assist us with a somewhat different project, but one that many have found valuable. That is the attempt to uncover the androcentric foundations of philosophy, a line of endeavor that might be thought to be irretrievably theoretical, but that can use some assistance from other sources. The argument made by feminists has been that a great deal of the androcentrism of philosophy does not consist in something as flat-footed as mere exclusion, but rests more on a sort of style. The Complete Accounts style, as it is sometimes called, resulted in former times in a sort of grand systematizing, and in the late nineteenth and twentieth centuries, seems to have resulted in attempts to make logic do the work of previous systems.

Whatever the merits or demerits of such trials, all sorts of particularities have routinely been overlooked by philosophers, and require development. It is here that literature comes in, and literature by women—so often in tune with a variety of lives, and not simply female lives—can do a great deal to fill in the blanks. Drabble, Woolf, Beauvoir, Bambara and Poniatowska may have little in common, but they

---

5 Miller, "On Edge: the Crossways of Contemporary Criticism," in Miller, 171–200. 176ff are devoted to a close reading of Wordsworth's "A Slumber Did My Spirit Seal."

6 Alweiss, Lilian (2003), "On Moral Dilemmas: Winch, Kant, and Billy Budd," in *Philosophy*, 78, 205–218.

are women authors writing in such a way that a number of sorts of different lives are touched upon. In *To the Lighthouse*, Woolf shows us, in the "Time Passes" section, that not only was the Ramsay family held together by Mrs. Ramsay, but by women like Mrs. McNabb, whose presence was scarcely acknowledged. She is the one who attempts to undo the damage done by time and tide, albeit with comparatively little success. But Woolf knew through her own observations that her class and that immediately above it could not survive without the tireless effort of the domestics and servants who kept things at bay.

Literature opens us to the imagined worlds about which philosophers sometimes write, but all too frequently in a less specific vein than we could have wished. Those imagined worlds are the very stuff of which philosophical theory is made, and it is important to acknowledge attempts to set them out in detail. Literature by women, already in a secondary position simply by virtue of birth, opens doors to the voices of the oppressed from multiple walks of life. Jesusa, Mrs. McNabb, the Indian women of Guatemala and others whom we have discussed here must have someone to serve as a voice.

Dystopias and Utopias

There is a great deal about fiction that yields worldviews, even in cases where none may be intended. We now hear champions for the work of, for example, Anne Rice and Walter Mosley as of philosophical import, even if it is difficult to discern how a case for either author could be made. But from the naïve point of view, one would suppose that it would be much easier to try to argue for a theoretical or worldview-laden content for Woolf or Drabble, because we know these authors already to be "difficult" enough that we have some hesitation in recommending them for leisurely reading.

Although the naïve take set out above might be thought by some to be simply too naïve, a great deal of the commentary on the intersection of philosophy and literature makes this very point. Dutton and Hagberg note, in their commentary on the twenty-fifth anniversary of *Philosophy and Literature*, "Would-be peacemakers will be disappointed to see fresh hostilities breaking out just when they thought differences were at last being reconciled."[7] In other words, there is nothing easy about the ancient battle—discerning the intersection between philosophy and literature will always require effort, and there will doubtless be times when the effort is not repaid.

Writing about the philosophical content of Jack London's work, Per Petersen comments "In his preface to *Jack London*, [Earle] Labor notes that, in his efforts to avoid exaggerating the worth of his subject, he might actually have underestimated 'the full magnitude of London's achievement.'"[8] The same might be said, at least to some extent, of any of the authors we have examined here. Drabble and Woolf seem to be valued primarily as stylists; we noted several times the extent to which no delineation of Modernism seems complete without an examination of Woolf,

---

7   Dutton and Hagberg (2002), "War of the Worldviews."
8   Peterson, Per, "Jack London," in *Philosophy and Literature*, xx (xx) 43–56.

and yet there is much more to *To the Lighthouse* than its breakthrough in style and narration. Beauvoir is still seen by many as too heavy-handed, and yet somehow insufficiently philosophical. There seems to be very little middle ground, despite the fact that close scrutiny of her work has been going on for some time. Bambara is still insufficiently appreciated, although we are often told that there is a "rage" for black women writers. And Poniatowska has yet to receive her due in English-speaking circles, a fact that is obvious from the very recent timing of the translations of her major works, such as *Jesusa!* and *Tinisima*.

What is it, then, that allows us to see the philosophical vein in these authors? With Woolf and Drabble both, the focus on interior narration allows the reader to discern a new world, one largely of the protagonist's making. Dystopic though it may be (and in Woolf's case, it is clear that understanding Rachel Vinrace, for example, is not made much easier by the distancing and world-creating that her dissociative states allow), this new realm is often of philosophical interest. And the intersection between these perceptions and material reality—as set out for us by the narration—is often of major philosophical interest. Thus Mrs. Ramsay, Lily, Cam and other characters in *Lighthouse* struggle with their own perceptions, which they know to be at odds with the material world around them.

Another sort of philosophical take allows us to glean political stances from the author's attempts to deal with gender, race and class. Beauvoir's most interesting passages in *Mandarins* may well be those where Anne and the Nelson Algren stand-in visit Mexico. In these passages, Anne's discomfort with poverty and oppression are made manifestly clear, and a certain political view comes across immediately.

Those who favor the view that the old and hoary debate between the philosophers and the poets pits them against each other in a way that is irretrievable may be surprised to learn that much contemporary commentary on thinkers from the classical period is already implicitly literary. In other words, dystopias and utopias are a product of both the literary and philosophical imaginations, and there is more intermingling here than might immediately be apparent. For example, contemporary work by David Sedley on Zeno—not the sort of thinker that one would be tempted, ordinarily, to categorize as literary—reveals such a bent, and moreover, the orientation is taken for granted. Sedley writes:

> His [Zeno's] first studies are said to have been with the Cynic Crates, and Cynic ethics remained a dominant influence on Stoic thought.... The most provocative of Zeno's own twenty-seven recorded works—reported also to be his earliest, and very possibly written at this time—was a utopian political tract, the *Republic*.... What was presumably not yet in evidence, but was to become the key to Zeno's mature philosophy, was his attempt to rescue an ethical role for conventional values.[9]

Here, too, it is easy to show the meshing of philosophy and literature, even in areas where we least expect it. There is, then, a multitude of ways to conceptualize the utopian imagination, and works that are more straightforwardly philosophical

---

9 Sedley, David (2003), "The School, from Zeno to Arius Didymus," in *The Cambridge Companion to the Stoics*, Cambridge: Cambridge University Press, 7–32.

and more straightforwardly literary are not necessarily as easily separated in this regard as one might have thought.

The Cosmological Imaginary

On the old view, metaphysical issues themselves divided into two parts: traditionally, metaphysics was comprised of cosmology and ontology. As is the case with so much that once passed as core philosophy, cosmology is now a head that finds itself thrown in with the natural sciences, and it does not have much of a place in contemporary philosophical thought, except perhaps where that thought is engaged with science.

One might think, then, that cosmological issues would have little place in an examination of the intersection of literature and philosophy, but then it must be remembered that most former attempts at the construction of a cosmology were non-materialist. When we consider the religious issues involved in a god's-eye view of nature in the seventeenth and eighteenth centuries, we can see that—particularly for Europeans—to grow up in a society with at least the rudiments of an educational system in those times was to be exposed to a particular strand of cosmological thinking.

All of the ontological issues that we have dealt with in our perusal of the novels by our five writers themselves intersect with a cosmology. How did we, as humans, come to be? How was our world formed? What are its origins? These implicit issues—to be sure, in some cases actually spelled out—guide the thinking of a number of the lead characters in the works under examination.

A certain sort of Christian view underlies a good deal of the work done by Drabble, Woolf and Beauvoir. In other words, some EuroChristian ontology is presupposed by the characters, and hence cosmological explanations would be subsumed under this rubric. None of this is as unimportant to aesthetics and philosophy in general as some might be tempted to argue, because, even without an explicit adumbration of a metaphysical stance, there is also the notion—examined at length by various critics—that tragedy itself demands a sort of cosmology.

Eagleton, in his most recent work, *Sweet Violence*, begins with an overview of current attempts at dealing with the concept of tragedy, but is quick to point out that almost all of them find it hard to accept that the tragic could be accidental. In other words, a theistic or deistic cosmology is a work on some conception of the tragic, even if this is more understood than articulated. As he says with respect to some less-than-successful definitions encountered in a perusal of the literature:

> [One view of tragedy demands that] the suffering be largely unmerited, preordained, non-contingently caused, inflicted on a preeminent figure,....revelatory of divine order.... Someone who clung to the normative sense of the word could always exclaim 'I don't regard *that* as tragic!' no matter how much blood was being spilt and torment inflicted.[10]

---

10 Eagleton, Terry (2003), *Sweet Violence: the Idea of the Tragic*, Malden, MA: Blackwell Publishers, 8.

In other words, tragedy demands a certain sort of worldview, a type of predestination. So the implicit cosmology of at least Woolf is consonant with what it is that Eagleton wants to demarcate, and hence in that sense Woolf is a bit more of a standard narrator than one might have thought (and probably more of an implicit philosopher). But Drabble's ironic detachment almost pushes us in the other direction—one senses that part of the difficulty is that the world is now devoid of tragedy, precisely because the postmodern era has deprived it of its master narrative and hence of any meaning.

For Beauvoir, Bambara and Poniatowska things are a bit stickier. Beauvoir, also, functions in a world devoid of coherent narratives, so it is difficult to see Anne (or Paula) as a tragic figure—unless there is something tragic about being a woman. Here the cosmology strikes one as being entirely accidental. Something similar might be said of both Bambara's characters and Poniatowska's—the sadness in their lives is more a feature of human and social construction, and certainly, as we have maintained, more a feature of real-world oppression. Is Jesusa's life tragic? It is a bit more like a car accident—and the accident here is the Revolution itself.

Explanation, cosmological or otherwise, is, then, an important feature of the work of these writers. A focus on interiors, such as we have certainly employed by Woolf, tends to miss this element of the writing, but it is present nonetheless. Rachel is a haunted figure, and it is obvious that Woolf sees her, an intellectual and an artist in a sordid and vulgar world, as a tragic figure indeed. Perhaps the message here is that all intellectuals are tormented, and even doomed.

Literary Strategies

It might be thought that some literary strategies would lend themselves to philosophical articulation more readily than others. For example, the standard omniscient narrator is now on the decline, and use of such a device makes it somewhat difficult to construct the interior life that, as we have seen—for Drabble and Woolf in particular—is such a crucial part of their endeavors.

Drabble's postmodern irony, if we may term it such, alternates narrative strategies, and at the same time gives a certain sort of distance to events transcribed, leading critics to insist that Drabble is trying to tell us something about history. This argument may well go through, but much of what makes Drabble's work so unusual is not only her alternation of narratives styles, but her range of characters. In both *The Ice Age* and *The Peppered Moth*, as we have seen, characters who might be identified with England's historically ascendant group are paired off against characters from other sorts of backgrounds, and the result is a *mélange* that moves the reader down a path leading toward "today's Britain."

When investigating Woolf, we noticed that critics had often focused on such devices as her punctuation, sectioning, and so forth—perhaps because the works were originally published by Hogarth Press, this was deemed to be important. But what makes Woolf's work remarkable in the philosophical way that we have delineated here is, again, not only the interior voice, but the interior voice as it suffers from the anxiety, depression and, indeed, dissociation that we might think of as characteristic of Woolf's own life. We have seen how it could be argued that this interiority carries its own philosophical charge with it.

Both Bambara and Poniatowska use the vernacular to make points that, insofar as they mesh with ideas about race and gender, are ultimately philosophical points. Bambara's narrators in *Gorilla, My Love* not only speak in the black vernacular—they assume that the reader does, too. This use of the black vernacular gives a power to the notion of the black community that is seldom found in any other contemporary black author. Poniatowska's Jesusa, although her words have been translated to some extent by Poniatowska, also gives us the day-to-day life of a woman caught up in the Revolution—and there is no question that the violence and sheer scope of the Revolution are part of her everyday life. Some of Beauvoir's strategies are, as has been noted, almost too literally philosophical. She has characters at the opening of *She Came to Stay* engage in philosophical speculation in a way that seems pointed and almost off-putting—but at a later point, such as *The Mandarins* and *The Woman Destroyed*, the questioning and the quest are woven into the text, and there is little difficulty in proceeding with the reading. Hers may be the most overtly philosophical of the groups of writings that we have encountered, but that is the case only if one construes the adjective "philosophical" in a certain sort of way.

Terry Eagleton's work on tragedy, which has been cited at more than one point here, makes it clear from the outset that the apparent transparency of a notion such as tragedy is just that, apparent. One could argue that the same might be said about a "philosophical" text. Perhaps our favorite mystery or crime novelist, P.D. James or Walter Mosley, is in some sense philosophical. After all, solving a mystery, it could be argued, might be seen as a metaphor for working on difficulties of other kinds. But we can also claim, with some sense of being judicious, that there are demonstrable literary strategies by the women authors we have examined that help to forward philosophical theses within their work.

Tersely, we can delineate three or four separate such strategies, depending on how one would like to make the cuts. We have already taken a close look at two: the use of interior voice, a use that we have associated particularly with Drabble and Woolf, is one that allows a female-centered concern for the establishment of the real to emerge. The use of the vernacular, where it helps to create the demarcations of social class and status that are a part of gender issues, resonates especially in the work of Bambara and Poniatowska and is what gives Bambara's work, in particular, its urgency. The use of social class alone as a demarcator is perhaps most noticeable here in Drabble's writing, but we have to remember that she as an author is faced with the problem of trying to make distinctions among characters' viewpoints while writing within the timeframe and cultural view of one European society. Finally, of course, there is the most obvious sort of strategy of all—Beauvoir simply inserts philosophical issues into her text, in some cases without a great deal of subtlety, and then tries to show, primarily through use of interior voice and dyadic conversation, how those issues intersect with lived lives. It might be said, on a charitable view, that this sort of device is constitutive of a great deal of the difficulty of *She Came to Stay* as a novel.

But if strategies of the women novelists under examination here might be said, in some sense, to simply replicate a repertoire of general literary devices, there is one resounding fact about the writing of Drabble, Woolf, Beauvoir, Bambara and Poniatowska that needs to be foregrounded. Each of them has as central characters not simply a woman, but more than one woman. And the combination of female authorship, feminist concerns, philosophical modes and concerns for social issues makes for a powerfully gynocentric writing. A number of writers might be thought to attempt to address women's issues, including some of the most celebrated male novelists of the nineteenth century. One can scarcely name a novel that gives a more accurate depiction of crucial issues facing bourgeois women in European societies than *Anna Karenina*, for example, and despite Flaubert's famous claim that Mme. Bovary represented his own views, a similar stand could be taken with respect to that novel.

But however gifted Tolstoy and Flaubert may have been, they were not women. Indeed, we are struck by their attempt to articulate problems facing women for that very reason—in a sense, we do not expect it. From a woman writer—particularly one working at a later point in time—we might justifiably expect more, and with this quintet we are completely justified in our expectations. Modernist or postmodernist, ironic or straightforward, we would hazard a guess that the rarity of women's writing and the history of exclusion would make a female author extraordinarily sensitive to women's issues, and the combination of this sensitivity with any sort of bent for the conceptual yields what we have tried to depict, writing that is simultaneously philosophical and in spirit feminist.

Finally, it might prove intriguing to examine our project in the light not merely of philosophical issues or literary criticism, but from the standpoint of more grounded and straightforward feminist theory. Although bodied relations has been one of the main foci of the commentary here, it is clear that there is a long strand of deeply feminist thought that has not yet made its way into much alembicated theory. To allude to this thought constitutes, in and of itself, a sort of path toward the gynocentric, and it may indeed be an unconscious motive in the work of at least some of our authors.

Although the sophisticated and superficially Eurocentric styles of Drabble, Woolf and Beauvoir may not always lend themselves to the most obvious sort of feminist concerns, in Bambara and Poniatowska both we can discern a sort of respect for—as current feminist thought has it—the Goddess and all things related to her. Contemporary work from Eliade to Gimbutas to Sjoo reminds us that early societies were overwhelmingly matrifocal, and, as we have seen, respect for and cognizance of this matrifocality is part of what drives Bambara and, to a certain extent, Poniatowska.[11] Bambara's Minnie, in her healing of Velma, shifts our focus from the world of patriarchy to the world of the mud mothers, and she does so in a way that raises crucial notions of race, gender and social structure. Monica Sjoo adverts to the centrality of these issues when she writes:

> What...modern researchers are now "discovering" is something ancient women always knew. The warring dualisms of "matter vs. spirit," the hostile antagonisms of "sexual

---

11 For an account that ties together a number of strands of such thought, see Sjoo, Monica (1991), *The Great Cosmic Mother: Rediscovering the Religion of the Earth*, New York: Harper Collins.

body" versus "religious truth," are recent patriarchal inventions, destructively forced on the world and the soul.... [T]he first religion, originated by women, was a sexual-spiritual religion, the celebration of cosmic ecstasy.[12]

It would be too facile to say that this sort of infusion drives the work of the writers under examination here, but it would not be an exaggeration to say that shades of it can be found at least in Bambara and Poniatowska, and very occasionally in the others in the forms of certain characters or situations. Ultimately, when we inquire into the intersection of women writers and philosophical thought, we come back, in circular mode, to the questions with which we began. We experience little difficulty in finding the intersection of philosophy and literature, for questions surrounding these issues form the core of disagreements in the ancient battle originally under examination. But what women have to offer that might be constitutive in some sense of differing philosophies or philosophical styles is, seen in the traditional way, something of a question-begging enterprise. Allusion to core areas of feminist theory helps us to remember what it is that constitutes a woman's worldview. And if it is the case, as Eagleton has written, that "Classical antiquity did not share the modern conception of the human personality," then it may also be stated that the classical world was perhaps more in touch with the significance of gender divisions than any modernist would be.[13] Such divisions have not only to do with philosophy, worldviews and matters literary; they form the backdrop of human existence in every culture. That is why an inquiry into women, philosophy and literature opens up crucial material with respect to our existence on the planet, and with respect to our place in any cosmology.

---

12 *Ibid.*, 54.
13 Eagleton, *Sweet Violence*, 77.

Index

Fictional characters are indicated by an asterisk after the name e.g. Velma*. Where surnames for characters have been used in this book, characters are filed under their surname. If surnames are not given, characters are filed under their first name.

A

Abel, Elizabeth 77, 80, 81
abjection 82–4
African ontologies 135–8
Africans in America (Johnson and Smith) 154
afrocentric womanism 141–4, 151–3
Age of Discretion, The (de Beauvoir) 119–21
altered states 73–4, 96–7, 120, 124
Alweiss, Lilian 211
Ambrose, Helen* 63
Approaching Abjection (Kristeva) 8
arts
    emotions and irrational behaviour 7
    and philosophy 6–10
Ascencio, Esteban 171
authorial distance 18

B

Bakhtinian dialogism 175–6
Bambara, Toni Cade
    afrocentric womanism 141–4, 151–3
    black feminism in 144–5
    black mindset and world view 141
    black women and existential concerns 147
    and black women's voices 154–6
    compared to Sherley Anne Wiliams 158–9
    compared to Woolf 135
    conceptions of space and time 137–8
    conceptual changes required of reader 134
    and contemporary American culture 147–8
    and continental thinking 144–7
    criticism of 138–41
    and the écriture feminine 156–9
    and ego boundaries 134
    existential takes on blackness 145–7
    existentialist view of organized religion 161
    and the female body 143, 152, 156–9
    feminist issues in work 209–10
    feminist knowledge in work 162–4
    global gynocentrism 151–2
    globalization as target 166–7
    issues other than race 160–1
    mode of presentation 138
    mud mothers 135, 143
    myth and first principles 163–4
    and the mythography of traditional societies 151
    oral communication 158, 164
    reality in fiction of 133
    relevance for the future 164–6
    respect for the Goddess 217–18
    safe spaces for black women 134–5
    salvation of black souls 152
    self criticism by 153–5
    short stories compared to *Salt Eaters* 164–5
    theories regarding work of 159–62
    and tragedy 214–15
    use of the black vernacular 216
    voice of the disempowered 155
    West African metaphors 151
    writing for a black audience 148–9
    see also Deep Sightings and Rescue Missions; Education of a Storyteller; Gorilla, My Love; Language and the Writer; Playing with Punjab; Salt Eaters, The
Barnes, Hazel 101–2, 111
Barren, Bessie* 26–7

Bawtry, Bessie* 31–2, 36, 38
Beauchamp, Gorman 11
Beauvoir, Simone de
  altered states 96–7, 120, 124
  compared to Camus 129
  compared to Drabble and Woolf 95, 102, 129
  compared to Sartre 113, 121–3, 129
  contemporary social relevance 126–8
  criticism of work 100–3
  denial of the body 114–15, 117
  depiction of fear of death 120–1
  depiction of the bourgeoisie 127–8
  dialogue in novels 95, 96
  enclosure-in-the-body as a theme 107–8
  EuroChristian ontology 214
  female characters, development of 113–14
  female narrators 100–1
  feminist influence of 115–18
  feminist themes 102–5, 113–15
  as a figure of many camps 97
  and knowing 124–6
  lack of families in work 117
  literary merit of novels 102–3
  literary strategies 216
  masculinist view of the world 114–15
  objectification 121
  personal relationships 114–15
  philosophical aspects of work 95–7, 128–9, 213
  philosophy in the novels of 107
  political philosophy in work of 108–10
  politics as a focus of the novels 102
  rationality 114–15
  self and the other 97–100, 101–2, 106–7, 108, 110–11, 121–3, 127
  sexual descriptions 118–21
  and tragedy 214–15
  see also Age of Discretion, The; Mandarins, The; Monologue, The; She Came to Stay; Very Easy Death, A; Woman Destroyed, The
Between the Acts (Woolf) 13
Bilingual Aesthetics (Sommer) 194
Black Feminism: Liberation Limbos and Existence in Gray (James) 144
Black Feminist Criticism (Christian) 138–9
Black Feminist Thought (Collins) 139, 141
black literature, commentary on 135
Bloom, Harold 13
bodies 46–51, 107–8, 114–15, 117, 143, 152, 156–9, 192–5
Booth, Wayne 12, 18–19
Bradshaw, David 91
Brazil 136
Briscoe, Lily* 62, 69–70, 84
Burks, Ruth Elizabeth 164–5
Butler-Evans, Elliott 157–8, 159–60, 164, 209–10
Byatt, A.S. 4–5, 26

C
Cazeaux, Clive 35, 47–8, 85, 180
Changing Times in Utopia (Beauchamp) 11
Chapman, Abraham 135
Cherwitz, Richard 207
Christian, Barbara 138–9
Cixous, Helene 45, 180–1
Collins, Patricia Hill 134, 137, 139, 142–3, 144, 155–6, 163, 166
colonial attitudes 192–4
Columbus ad the Cannibals (Hulme) 184, 203
Conor, Liz 190
Continental Aesthetics Reader, The (Cazeaux) 180
continental thinking 144–7, 180–2
Cooper, Anna Julia 156
cosmology 214–15
Creighton, Joanne 43

D
De Salvo, Louise 74
Dear Diego (Poniatowska) 169, 174–5, 179, 189, 193
Dedalus, Stephen* 12
Deep Sightings and Rescue Missions (Bambara) 148, 153, 165
Dessa Rose (Williams) 158–9
dialogism 175–6
Dinnerstein, Dorothy 33, 116, 142
Doc Serge* 156–7
Donovan, Josephine 179
Drabble, Margaret
  awareness of self as author 28, 36
  characters 39
  compared to Virginia Woolf 70
  complexity and development of characters 44–5
  concern for women intellectuals 38
  and contemporary Britain 54–6

critics' views of 28–31
debris of everyday life 48
écriture feminine 45–9, 56
epiphanies of characters 13, 27
and epistemic issues 52–4
EuroChristian ontology 214
existential themes 57
female body and sexuality 46–51
female protagonists 31–3
female tropes and images 41–3, 46
feminism 31–4, 38, 41–3
history as a chain of culture 29–30
interiority of voice 23, 31, 39
lack of closure 30
libidinal body 50
literature and the emotions 37–8
male characters 33–4, 51
notion of connectedness 33
philosophical aspects 37–9, 56–7, 213
popularity with readers and critics 25
post-modern irony 215
post-modern notion of history 25–7, 39
range of characters 215
real life mirrored by characters 24–5
shift in time sequences 25
subversion of history, chronology and narration 29–31, 35–7, 40
symbolism 36
as a traditional novelist 23, 40
and tragedy 214–15
use of authorial voice 27
use of time 4–5
women and the arts 32–3
worlds created by 24
see also Ice Age, The; Jerusalem the Golden; Millstone, The; Peppered Moth, The; Summer Bird-Cage, A; Waterfall, The
Dubreuilh, Anne* 96, 98–9, 101, 104, 105, 110, 114, 118, 119, 125
Dutton, D. 5–6, 56–7
dystopias and utopias 212–14

E
Eagleton, Terry 5, 8, 59, 214
écriture feminine 45–9, 156–9, 181
see also bodies
Education of a Storyteller (Bambara) 165
emotions 7–8, 10, 20, 37–8
Epicurus 7
Evans, Mary 114–15, 116–17

Existence in Black (Gordon) 144, 160

F
Fallaize, Elizabeth 100–1, 119, 120, 124
fantasy and philosophy 10–14
feminism
  black 144–5
  Elena Poniatowska 170–1, 198–200
  Margaret Drabble 31–4, 38, 41–3
  and philosophy 17
  Simone de Beauvoir 102–5, 113–15, 115–18
  Toni Cade Bambara 162–4, 209–10
  Virginia Woolf 61, 67–70, 77, 78–9, 79–82, 91–2, 93, 212
  see also women
feminist criticism 210–12
Fetterley, Judith 13–14
Flash of the Spirit (Thompson) 151, 182
Foucault, Michel 27–8, 34, 35
Foucault and Feminism (McNay) 49
Fox-Genovese, Elizabeth 46
Fox Keller, Evelyn 81
Francoise* 99–100, 107–8, 111, 114
Freud, Sigmund 81
Fullbrooks, Edward and Kate 123, 126

G
Gaulden, Chrissie and Nick* 34, 49, 50, 51
Gaulden, Faro* 23, 24–5, 35–6, 37, 39, 44–5, 51, 54–6
gender and literature and philosophy 14–18, 217–18
Genius (Bloom) 13
Giddings, Paula 156
Gilbert, Sandra 16, 17, 19–20
Gilligan, Carol 33, 81–2, 116
Gimbutas, Marija 142
Goddess, respect for 217–18
Goldie, Terry 185
Gomez-Quintero, Raysa 174–5, 179
Gordon, Lewis 144, 160
Gordon, Lyndall 66, 78
Gorilla, My Love (Bambara) 140, 158
Granite and Rainbow (Leaska) 64
Gray, Jane* 31, 33, 37, 39, 41–3, 49, 50, 51, 52–3, 54
Gubar, Susan 16, 17, 19–20

H
Hagberg, Garry 5–6, 56–7

Han, Beatrice 26
Hannay, John 39
Hansen, Elaine Tuttle 28–9
Hasta no verte, Jesus mio see *Here's to You, Jesusa!*
Hayes, Floyd 147, 148
Heath, Jane 101, 103
Henry, Paget 145–6, 146–7, 160, 161
Henry, Velma* 134, 137–8, 146, 147, 161, 210
Here's to You, Jesusa! 170–4, 175–9, 181–2, 185, 187–9, 189–90, 191
Hewet, Terence* 83, 84, 86, 90
Hull, Gloria 139–40, 140–41, 142, 157
Hulme, Peter 184, 203
Hyde, Michael 57

I
Ice Age, The (Drabble) 23–4, 26, 33–4, 36–7, 38–9, 40
imagination and philosophy 10–11
In a Different Voice (Gilligan) 81–2
In-Between of Writing, The (Skoller) 23
interior voice 12, 23, 31, 39, 175, 177–9, 215, 216
Irigaray, Luce 46–7, 83–4
Irigaray Reader (Whitford) 84
ironic detachment 12–13, 18
irrational behaviour 7–8
Irvine, Lorna 30

J
James, Joy 144
Jane Eyre (Brontë) 14
Jerusalem the Golden (Drabble) 30
Jesusa! see *Here's to You, Jesusa!*
Jesusa* 172, 177–9, 183, 185, 187, 188–9, 190, 192–3, 198–9
Johnson, Charles 154
Jorgensen, Beth 187–8, 189–90, 201
Jouve, Nicole Ward 71, 73
Jowett, B. 7
Joyce, James 12–13, 18

K
Keating, Anthony* 33–4, 38–9, 48
Kirby, Maureen* 36, 40
Klaw, Barbara 118–19
Klein, Melanie 79–80

Knowing the Difference: Feminist Perspectives in Epistemology (Lennon and Whitford) 200
Kristeva, Julia 8, 82–4

L
Labyrinth of Solitude, The (Paz) 183, 191–2
Lacan, Jacques 85
Language and the Writer (Bambara) 148, 155
Las Meñinas 27
Leaska, Mitchell 63, 64–6
Lennon, Kathleen 200
libidinal body 49–50
  see also bodies
literary strategies 215–18
literary theory and philosophy 5
Literary Theory (Eagleton) 5
literature
  and the emotions 37–8
  philosophical, reader's reaction to 13–14
  philosophical content of 20
  and philosophy 3–6, 10, 207–9
  and poetry 9
Literature and Women in Latin America (Poniatowska) 190–1
Literature of Their Own, A (Showalter) 14–15, 25, 32, 40
Lizzie* 121–2
Lodge, Rupert 9–10
Lolita (Nabokov) 19
Love and Sex in Plato's Epistemology (Fox Keller) 81

M
male writers 19–20
Mandarins, The (de Beauvoir) 96, 98–9, 101, 102, 104, 105, 108–10, 114, 117, 118–19, 120, 124–5, 126, 127–8, 128
Marcus, Laura 75
Margaret Drabble: Puritanism and Permissiveness (Myer) 31
Marks, Elaine 115–16
McNay, Lois 34, 49
Medeiros-Lichem, Maria 173–4, 175–6
Merleau-Ponty, Maurice 105–6
Mexico
  biracial and bicultural mix 194
  and colonial attitudes 194

effect of racism on culture of 183–4
history of 170
literacy in 191
literary scene 192
mestiza woman 191–2
non-standard beliefs in 172–4
and otherness 181–2
regional variations of 176–7
see also Poniatowska, Elena
Miller, J. Hillis 4, 210, 211
Millstone, The (Drabble) 44
Minh-ha, Trinh 193
modernism 90
Momaday, N. Scott 138
Monologue, The (de Beauvoir) 122–3
Moore, G.E. 63
mother-infant relationship 84–5
mud mothers 135, 143
Murielle 122
Murray, Alison* 23, 29, 31, 38
Myer, Valerie Grosvenor 29–30, 31, 32–3
myth and Western thought 9

N
Nabokov, Vladimir 19
Nadine* 119
No Exit (Sartre) 106–7
Notebook for an Ethics (Sartre) 123
Novels of Simone de Beauvoir, The (Fallaize) 119
Nussbaum, Nartha 6–7, 7, 9, 10

O
object relations theory 115–17
objectification 86, 121
Oliver, Kelly 86–7
ontologies, literary 18–20
Ophir, Anne 104–5
Otford, James* 41–2, 49, 54
otherness 123, 181–2, 182
   see also self and the other
Outsider, The (Wright) 147

P
Palancares, Jesusa* *see* Jesusa*
Paula 117
Paz, Octavio 183–4, 191–2
Peppered Moth, The (Drabble) 23, 24–5, 26–7, 31–2, 34, 35–6, 37, 44–5, 48–9, 54–6
Pérez Bustillo, Mireya 174–5, 179

philosophy
   and the arts 6–10
   battle with poetry 8
   and fantasy 10–14
   and the imagination 10–11
   and literature 3–6, 10, 207–9
   political 10–11
Philosophy and Literature (Dutton and Hagberg) 5–6
Plato, on the arts and artists 6–7, 9–10
Plato and Europe (Potocka) 9
Playing with Punjab (Bambara) 155
Poetic Justice (Nussbaum) 10
poetry 8
political philosophy 10–11
Poniatowska, Elena
   appearing woman 190
   articulation of women's voices 170, 174–6, 177–9, 185, 188–9, 200–2, 216
   and the body 192–5
   colonial attitudes 192–4
   as a committed writer 195–8
   and continental thought 180–2
   criticism on 174–7, 189–92
   depiction of two-foldness 194–5
   dialogism of work 190
   écriture 181
   feminist epistemology 198–200
   feminist twist to story of Mexico 170–1
   imagined worlds of 175
   interior monologues 175, 177–9
   and knowing 198–200
   massacre at the Plaza de las Tres Culturas 169, 171
   and Mexico's oral tradition 191
   multiplicity of voices 188–9
   non-standard beliefs 172–4
   and otherness 182
   philosophical content 182–4
   political philosophy of 169–70
   portrayal of poor people 169–70
   and postcolonial thought 184–5
   range and scope of work 171
   and the regional variations of Mexico 176–7
   reportorial and fictional weave 196
   respect for the Goddess 217–18
   shifts in time and place 188–9
   and tragedy 214–15
   and the unseen side of reality 173–4

writing and the visual arts 180–1
  see also Dear Diego; Literature and Women in Latin America; Mexico; Voices from Tlateloloco
Portable Kristeva, The (Oliver) 86–7
Portrait of the Artist as a Young Man (Joyce) 12, 18
Portrait of the Bourgeoisie (Siqueiros) 180
Potocka, Jan 9
Putain Respectueuse, La (Sartre) 121–2

Q
Quiela* 189

R
Race, Gender and Desire (Butler-Evans) 159
Ramsey, Cam* 64
Ramsey, Mrs* 75
Ransom, Minnie* 136, 142
Rasta beliefs 145
Respectful Prostitute, The (Sartre) 121–2
Rhetoric and Philosophy (Cherwitz) 207
Rhetoric of Fiction, The (Booth) 12, 19
Rhoda* 86
Rivera, Diego 169
Rose, Phyllis 87
Roxman, Susanna 24

S
Sadler, Lynn Veach 36–7, 38
Salt Eaters, The (Bambara) 133–4, 136, 137–8, 139–41, 140–1, 142, 143–4, 146, 147, 152–3, 156–7, 159–61, 164–6
Sartre, Jean-Paul 106–7, 195
  compared to de Beauvoir 113, 121–3
  and the Other 123
Sedley, David 213
self and the other 97–100, 101–2, 106–7, 108, 110–11, 121–3, 127
  see also otherness
sex and sexuality 46–51, 71–2, 118–21
  see also bodies
She Came to Stay (de Beauvoir) 99–100, 101–2, 103–4, 105–6, 110–11, 114, 125–6, 127–8, 128
Shea, Maureen 177
Showalter, Elaine
  on Margaret Drabble 14–16, 25, 32–3, 40, 43
  on Virginia Woolf 66, 67–9
Siqueiros, David Alfaro 180
Sjoo, Monica 217–18
Skoller, Eleanor 23, 28–9
Smith, Patricia 154
social class, use of as literary strategy 216
Socio-political Vision of the Novels, The (Bradshaw) 91
soldadera 170, 190
Sommer, Doris 194, 196–7
Spitzer, Susan 43–4
Spivak, Gayatri 196
Stacey, Rosamund* 44
stasis 11
streams of consciousness 12, 65–7, 215
  see also interior voice
Strickland, Susan 201–2
Summer Bird-Cage, A (Drabble) 31
Sweet Violence (Eagleton) 214
symbolism of Margaret Drabble 36

T
Therapy of Desire, The (Nussbaum) 7, 9
This Sex Which is Not One 46
Thompson, Robert Farris 136, 142–3, 143–4, 151
Three Guineas (Woolf) 64
Tidd, Ursula 107
To the Lighthouse (Woolf) 4, 13, 59, 60, 62, 69–70, 75–6, 212
tragedy 214–15

U
unreliable narrators 18–19
utopias 11, 212–14

V
Vasconcelos, José 194
Velásquez 27
vernacular, use of as a literary strategy 216
Very Easy Death, A (de Beauvoir) 96, 97–8, 111
Vinrace, Rachel* 59–60, 60–1, 66–7, 67–8, 71, 83, 84, 86, 87, 90
Virgina Woolf: A Writer's Life (Gordon) 66
Virgina Woolf and the Fictions of Psychoanalysis (Abel) 77
Voices from Tlateloloco (Poniatowska) 169
Voyage Out, The (Woolf) 59, 60–1, 62, 66–7, 71–2, 78, 83, 86, 87, 91

W

Waterfall, The (Drabble) 24, 33, 37, 39, 41–3, 48–9
Waves, The (Woolf) 78, 86
Western thought and myth 9
What is Literature? (Sartre) 195
When and Where I Enter 156
Whitford, Margaret 84, 200
Wideman, John Edgar 133
Williams, Sherley Anne 158–9
Wincobank, Len* 36, 40
Wiredu, Kwasi 136–7, 162–3
Woman Destroyed, The (de Beauvoir) 119–23, 128
women
  afrocentric womanism 141–4, 151–3
  appearing woman 190
  articulation of voices of 170, 174–6, 177–9, 185, 188–9, 200–2, 216
  awareness of the women's movement 16
  black 134–5, 147, 154–6
  as central characters 217
  intellectual 38
  and literature and philosophy 14–18
  mestiza woman 191–2
  see also feminism
Woolf, Virginia
  abuse as a child 74
  altered states 73–4
  androgynous identity 67–8, 74
  compared to Margaret Drabble 70
  depiction of reality 60
  depiction of time 60–1
  desire to capture the moment 64–6
  and discussion of sexuality 71–2
  dissociative states 61–4, 82, 87, 88
  epiphanies of characters 13
  EuroChristian ontology 214
  feminism of 91–2, 93
  feminist criticism of 78–9, 79–82
  feminist view of 61, 77, 212
  focus on knowing 88–90
  and Lacanian theory 85–7
  mental difficulties 92
  and modernism 74, 90
  and mothering 80, 83
  philosophical aspects of 73–4, 213
  philosophical import of work 5, 67, 75–6
  and political causes 75
  and psychoanalytic theory 70–2, 79–82
  rationality 61–4
  refusal to make things easy 90–1
  repression and denial of sexuality 72
  scholarship on 77–8, 92
  skeleton beneath theme 91–2
  streams of consciousness 65–7, 215
  style 59
  and tragedy 214–15
  use of the visual 89–90
  use of time 4
  world of infancy 80
  see also Between the Acts; Mrs Dalloway; Three Guineas; To the Lighthouse; Voyage Out, The; Waves, The
Woolf's Feminism and Feminism's Woolf (Marcus) 75
Wright, Richard 147, 148
Writing of Elena Poniatowska: Engaging Dialogues (Jorgensen) 187–8, 189–90

X

Xaviere* 103–4, 107–8, 111, 117, 126

Z

Zeno of Citium 213

For Product Safety Concerns and Information please contact our EU
representative GPSR@taylorandfrancis.com
Taylor & Francis Verlag GmbH, Kaufingerstraße 24, 80331 München, Germany

www.ingramcontent.com/pod-product-compliance
Lightning Source LLC
Chambersburg PA
CBHW062216300426
44115CB00012BA/2089